New Dialectics and Political Economy

Also by Robert Albritton

A JAPANESE APPROACH TO POLITICAL ECONOMY (*with Thomas T. Sekine*)

A JAPANESE APPROACH TO STAGES OF CAPITALIST DEVELOPMENT

A JAPANESE RECONSTRUCTION OF MARXIST THEORY

DIALECTICS AND DECONSTRUCTION IN POLITICAL ECONOMY

PHASES OF CAPITALIST DEVELOPMENT (*with Makoto Itoh, Richard Westra and Alan Zuege*)

New Dialectics and
Political Economy

Edited by

Robert Albritton
Professor of Political Science
York University
Toronto, Canada

and

John Simoulidis
Department of Political Science
York University
Toronto, Canada

Selection, editorial matter and Chapter 4 © Robert Albritton 2003
Chapter 5 © Moishe Postone 2003
Chapters 1–3, 6–11 © Palgrave Macmillan Ltd 2003

First published 2003 by
PALGRAVE MACMILLAN
Houndmills, Basingstoke, Hampshire RG21 6XS and
175 Fifth Avenue, New York, N. Y. 10010
Companies and representatives throughout the world.

PALGRAVE MACMILLAN is the global academic imprint of the
Palgrave Macmillan division of St Martin's Press, LLC and of Palgrave
Macmillan Ltd. Macmillan® is a registered trademark in the United
States, United Kingdom and other countries. Palgrave is a registered
trademark in the European Union and other countries.

ISBN 0–333–99933–9

This book is printed on paper suitable for recycling and made from
fully managed and sustained forest sources.

A catalogue record for this book is available from the British Library.

A catalogue record for this book is available from the Library of Congress.

10 9 8 7 6 5 4 3 2 1
12 11 10 09 08 07 06 05 04 03

Printed and bound in Great Britain by
Antony Rowe Ltd, Chippenham and Eastbourne

Contents

Acknowledgements

The chapters in this volume were initially presented as papers at a workshop at York University, Toronto, Canada in March 2001. This workshop was made possible by the financial contributions of the Department of Political Science, the Academic Vice President, the Dean of Graduate Studies, the Dean of Arts, the Department of Sociology, the Social Science Division, the Social and Political Thought Program and The York University Graduate Students Association. John Simoulidis did an outstanding job of organizing the conference, and also did most of the editing of the manuscript. I would also like to thank Josh Dumont for helping with the editing. Most of all, I would like to thank the contributors to this important book on dialectics and political economy.

ROBERT ALBRITTON

Notes on the Contributors

Robert Albritton is Professor of Political Science at York University, Toronto, Canada. Recent publications include *A Japanese Approach to Stages of Capitalist Development* (London: Macmillan, 1991); *Dialectics and Deconstruction in Political Economy* (London: Macmillan, 1999); and 'The Unique Ontology of Capital', in L. Nowak and R. Panasiuk (eds), *Marx's Theories Today* (Amsterdam: Rodopi, 1998); and ed. with M. Itoh, R. Westra and A. Zuege, *Phases of Capitalist Development: Booms, Crises, and Globalizations* (London/New York: Palgrave, 2001).

Christopher J. Arthur taught philosophy for twenty-five years at the University of Sussex, England. Some of his recent publications include 'The Spectral Ontology of Capital', in A. Brown, S. Fleetwood and J. M. Roberts (eds), *Critical Realism and Marxism* (New York: Routledge, 2002); 'Capital-in-General and Marx's *Capital*' and 'Capital, Many Capitals and Competition', in G. Reuten and M. Campbell (eds), *The Culmination of Capital* (London/New York: Palgrave, 2002); 'From the Critique of Hegel to the Critique of Capital', in T. Burns and I. Fraser, eds., *The Hegel–Marx Connection* (New York: St. Martin's Press, 2000); and ed. with G. Reuten, *The Circulation of Capital: Essays on Volume Two of Marx's 'Capital'* (New York: St Martin's Press, 1998).

John R. Bell teaches in the School of Liberal Studies at Seneca College in Toronto. He is author of 'Dialectics and Economic Theory' in R. Albritton and T. Sekine (eds), *A Japanese Approach to Political Economy* (London: Macmillan, 1995); and with T. Sekine, 'The Disintegraton of Capitalism: A Phase of Ex-Capitalist Transition', in R. Albritton, M. Itoh, R. Westra, and A. Zuege (eds), *Phases of Capitalist Development: Booms, Crises and Globalizations* (London/New York: Palgrave, 2001).

Stefanos Kourkoulakos has studied philosophy of science and political economy at York University, Toronto. He is currently researching the argument structure of dialectical logic.

David McNally is Professor of Political Science at York University, Toronto, Canada. His publications include: *Political Economy and the Rise of Capitallism: A Reinterpretation* (Berkeley: University of California Press, 1988); *Against the Market: Political Economy, Market Socialism and the Marxist Critique* (New York: Verso, 1993); *Bodies of Meaning: Studies on Language, Labour and Liberation* (Albany: State University of New York Press, 2001); and *Another World is Posibble* (Winnipeg: Arbeiter Ring, 2002).

Patrick Murray is Professor of Philosophy at Creighton University, Omaha, Nebraska. His publications include *Marx's Theory of Scientific Knowledge* (Atlantic Highlands, New Jersey: Humanities Press, 1988); ed., *Reflections on Commercial Life* (New York: Routledge, 1997); and 'Marx's *Truly Social* Labour Theory of Value', in *Historical Materialism,* nos 6 and 7 (Summer 2000 and Winter 2000).

Bertell Ollman is Professor of Politics at New York University. His publications include: *Alienation: Marx's Conception of Man in Capitalist Society* (Cambridge: Cambridge University Press, 1971); *Social and Sexual Revolution* (Montreal: Black Rose Books, 1978); *Dialectical Investigations* (New York: Routledge, 1993); *How to Take an Exam ... And Remake the World* (Montreal: Black Rose Books, 2001).

Moishe Postone is Associate Professor of History at the University of Chicago. Recent publications include: *Time, Labour and Social Domination: A Reinterpretation of Marx's Critical Theory* (Cambridge: Cambridge University Press, 1993); ed. with E. Santner, *Catastrophe and Meaning: Debates on the Holocaust and the Twentieth Century* (Chicago: University of Chicago Press, in press); 'Contemporary Historical Transformations: Beyond Postindustrial and Neo-Marxist Theories', in *Current Perspectives in Social Theory*, vol. 19, 1999; 'Deconstruction as Social Critique: Derrida on Marx and the New World Order', *History and Theory*, vol. 37, no. 3, 1998; and 'Rethinking Marx in a Postmarxist World', in C. Camic (ed.), *Reclaiming the Sociological Classics* (Cambridge, Mass: Blackwell, 1988).

Geert Reuten is Associate Professor of Economics at the Department of Economics of the University of Amsterdam. His publications include, with M. Williams, *Value-Form and the State: The Tendencies of Accumulation and the Determination of Economic Policy in Capitalist Society* (London: Routledge, 1989); with C. J. Arthur (eds), *The Circulation of Capital: Essays on Volume II of Marx's 'Capital'* (New York: St Martin's Press, 1998); and with M. Campbell (eds), *The Culmination of Capital: Essays on Volume III of Marx's 'Capital'* (London/New York: Palgrave, 2002).

Thomas T. Sekine was Professor of Economics and Social and Political Thought at York University, Toronto, Canada from 1968 to 1994. He is currently teaching at the School of Commerce, Aichi-Gakuin University, Japan. Recent publications include *An Outline of the Dialectic of Capital*, 2 vols (London: Macmillan, 1997); and *A Japanese Approach to Political Economy: Unoist Variations* (London: Macmillan, 1995), co-edited with Robert Albritton.

Tony Smith is Professor of Philosophy and Political Science at Iowa State University. Recent publications include *The Logic of Marx's 'Capital'* (Albany: State University of New York Press, 1990); *Dialectical Social Theory and Its Critics* (Albany: State University of New York Press, 1993); and *Technology and Capital in the Age of Lean Production* (Albany: State University of New York Press, 2000).

Introduction: The Place of Dialectics in Marxian Political Economy

Robert Albritton

For many years the academic discipline of economics has been fixated on the mathematical modelling of abstract economic variables – an approach that makes a label like 'formalism' justified. While this approach has yielded some gains from the point of view of the existing economic order, its results tend to be limited to thinking about the economic dimension in isolation from other aspects of social life, and about the narrowly quantitative as distinct from the qualitative aspects of life. It is not surprising, then, to find a growing discontent with mainstream economic theory, particularly among today's youth, who face a lifetime of trying to cope with the degradation of a quality of life that has become like that in part through the fixation of previous generations on a limited and one-sided economic theory. It will certainly take a long time and extensive human collaboration to turn this situation around, but this book offers a theoretical step forward.

We seem to be rapidly approaching an historical crossroads where it will become necessary to rethink economics from the bottom up, and from the top down. In opposition to the formalistic approach to knowledge characteristic of mainstream economics, the contributions in this book explore a dialectical approach. Dialectics radically opens economic thinking to consider relations between the economic and non-economic, between the quantitative and qualitative, between the empirical and normative, between more abstract levels of theory and history, and between theories of political economy and theories of subjectivity. And dialectics itself is not a cut-and-dried methodology like the formalism of mainstream economics, but is a complex and multidimensional methodology open to a wide variety of interpretations and applications. Unlike the formalism of academic neoclassical economics, which compartmentalizes the economic, separating it from history and social life, dialectical approaches are more holistic and integrative.

In this book, the break with neoclassical economics is further advanced by developing dialectical approaches in connection with Marxian political economy. Not all Marxian political economists adopt a dialectical approach; yet there is a certain fittingness between dialectics and Marxian political economy, since they both aim to develop mediations connecting the economic with the non-economic, and abstract theory with historical analysis. In this volume, all the contributors consider Marx's *Capital* to be dialectical in some sense. The 'in some sense' should be emphasized because positions range from those who think that only the theory of pure capitalism can be rigorously dialectical, to the position that a dialectical mode of thinking can be applied to any object of knowledge.

If capital has a logic and that logic is dialectical in some sense, then the question of just how to relate the abstract theory of capital's logic to history becomes an extremely important issue. Most of the contributions in this volume address the issue of how to relate more abstract economic categories to history. And readers of this book will find that there are a variety of ways of doing this. Contributions that do not address this issue focus either on the question 'What is dialectical reason?' or 'In what sense is the theory of capital dialectical?' The range of contributions, then, extends from the most basic questions about the nature of dialectics to how dialectical economic thinking can inform socio-historical analysis. Those invited to contribute to this volume represent different positions on this range of questions.

David McNally opens the volume with a chapter that utilizes Hegel's distinction between 'false infinity' and 'true infinity' to elucidate a Marxian conception of freedom. The issue of freedom is seldom addressed by neoclassical economists, and when it is, as in Milton Friedman's *Capitalism and Freedom*, freedom means little more than consumer sovereignty, the right to accumulate riches, the right of workers to choose an employer and make a contract, and the right to exit or be left alone. Underlying such notions of freedom is a naïve conception of individuals as self-contained monads who control economic life by casting 'dollar ballots'. Such extremely one-sided and one-dimensional conceptions of freedom are wholly inadequate in a world of multidimensional dependencies and power relations.

McNally challenges this one-dimensionality by arguing that a free community is one in which 'individuals actively will the mediations that constitute them, they posit them as moments of *self-mediation*' (2). But capital in its repetitive, self-expanding motion abstracts from and extracts from concrete material life in a way that becomes indifferent to the qualitative particularity of that life. In its self-obsession with profit-making, it becomes a kind of 'self' opposed to the self-mediation of agents that come under its dominion. Or, in other words, capital becomes an end-in-itself that tends to reduce humans to being simply the means to its self-expansion. Its 'repetition compulsion' is a false infinity that achieves its infinitizing semblance by turning its back on the finite. But a true infinite must integrate the finite so that mediation can become self-mediation. It follows that only in a post-capitalist society can determination become a conscious self-mediating process.

In Chapter 2 Tony Smith takes on the one-dimensionality of mainstream economics in another way. He explores the possibilities of connecting a more abstract systematic dialectics of capital to historical analysis by considering ways in which dialectical thinking can elucidate our understanding of globalization. Smith makes an interesting distinction between 'meta-tendencies, tendencies, and trends'. The dialectic of capital theorizes the fundamental historically specific socio-economic forms of capital and their necessary structural tendencies, and these tendencies always operate to the extent that capital is present in history; yet there is, according to Smith, 'an ineluctable element of contingency, path dependency and human agency in the determination of the dominant trends of any concrete historical context. This gulf between (systematic) tendencies and (historical) trends cannot in principle ever be completely bridged' (27). Yet there are a variety of ways of achieving a close integration between Systematic and Historical dialectics. For example, Marx's theory of the falling rate of profit presents both a tendency and counter-tendencies. Smith argues that these opposing tendencies constitute a 'meta-tendency' that tends to alternate in history between periods of rising and falling profits. He goes on to argue for a similar meta-tendency that alternates between global economic forces subordinating states, and states asserting themselves in response to crises triggered by such forces. He concludes with the claim that the 'systematic necessity of the tendencies to uneven development, overaccumulation crises and financial crises' produce irrationalities that ultimately cannot be solved within the confines of capitalist social relations (39).

By focusing on the opposition between necessity and contingency, which is central to dialectical thinking, Reuten continues in Chapter 3 Smith's concern to relate abstract systematic dialectics to more concrete levels of analysis. His strategy is to integrate abstract systematic dialectics with a regime approach in order to be able to theorize 'fairly concrete constellations' within systematic dialectics. Reuten argues that systematic dialectics theorizes 'the essential working of its object of inquiry', and that in this case, the 'essence' refers to 'the interconnection of all the moments necessary for the reproduction of the object of inquiry' (43). The moments are necessary in the sense that without any one of them the object would fall apart. According to Reuten, there are 'three types of contingency: (i) Contingency of a moment's content – a particular (contradictory) moment is theorized as necessary, though its content is contingent ... . (ii) Major contingent externals ... . (iii) Minor contingent externals' (44). He goes on to examine the apparently historically contingent alteration of periods of price deflation with periods of price inflation. Using regime theory, he shows that, in the current regime, which is based on balancing the needs of finance capital and managerial capital, creeping inflation has become a necessity. Thus, in a particular regime, what was contingent can become necessary relative to that particular regime. Further, he shows that inflation is not simply a matter of state finance, but rather needs to be theorized as combining a kind of money and monetary system, a kind of banking system, and a kind of competition between capitals (in this case, finance and managerial). To conclude, Rueten claims that regime theory tends to place too much emphasis on historical contingency, and that with the aid of systematic dialectics, it can be strengthened by bringing forward tendencies that are necessary relative to capital's logic and the structural needs of the particular regime.

Mainstream economic theory either addresses the issue of subjectivity in the most simplistic fashion, or it ignores the issue all together. In Chapter 4 I dialogue with Lukács' analysis of the commodity form in order to begin developing better connections between political economy and the theory of subjectivity. It is my conviction that Lukács' conception of reification is crucial in understanding the commodity as a social form that has a strong impact on subject formation. I first interpret Lukács' positions on reification, totality, use-value, and subjectivity. I then return to these categories to extract critically what I believe to be useful in developing a theory of subjectivity relevant to a twenty-first century world, arguing that the main weaknesses in Lukács' account stem from his overstating the extent to which the total reification that is appropriate in the theoretical context of pure capitalism is directly applicable to actually existing capitalist societies. Despite the excessive essentialism in Lukács' theory, theorizing the commodity as the basic social form of capitalism can advance the theory of subjectivity enormously, which previously has largely lacked a political economy dimension.

Postone, in Chapter 5, also chooses to explore dialectics through a critical reappropriation of Lukács' famous essay 'Reification and the Consciousness of the Proletariat'. Postone believes that Lukács' theory can help to inform a 'renewed theoretical concern with capitalism' – one that 'breaks decisively with classical Marxist base–superstructure conceptions' (80), by grounding a critique of modern capitalist thought in the basic social forms of capitalist economic life. According to Postone, Lukács' 'critique extends beyond a concern with the market and private property', as '[i]t seeks to grasp critically and ground socially processes of rationalization and quantification, as well as an abstract mode of power and domination that cannot be understood adequately in terms of concrete personal or group domination' (81). Where Lukács' theory falls short is in its attachment to 'traditional Marxism', which, according to Postone, understands 'capitalism essentially in terms of class relations structured by a market economy and private ownership of the means of production'. Postone proposes to return to Marx's conceptualization of the 'commodity' in *Capital* in order to revise Lukács away from traditional Marxism. He achieves this by arguing that, in *Capital*, the historical subject is capital itself understood as an 'alienated structure of social mediation' and not the proletariat, as proposed by Lukács (89). By locating the historical subject in the proletariat, Lukács inadvertently turns capitalism into a problem of formalism in which form-giving value is divorced from use-value and the proletariat. This naturalizes use-value such that the proletariat becomes a trans-historical subject throwing off an historically specific superimposed formalism. If we bring Lukács back to Marx's *Capital*, then his cultural criticism can be used in a critique aimed at abolishing capital's dialectic, and the proletariat along with it. Socialism, then, would no longer be conceived as the self-realization of the proletariat, but instead as a movement that aims to transform alienated structures of domination into structures of true self-mediation.

John Bell begins Chapter 6 with the claim that '[a]n objective account of the operation of the capitalist economy is both necessary and possible because capitalism, unlike any other economic system systematically reifies or objectifies economic relations as impersonal, anonymous commodity relations' (101). It is these ontological features of capitalism that make it a suitable object to be theorized dialectically. According to Marx, 'As soon as capital has become capital as such, it creates its own presuppositions'. But this implies that we can theorize capital as a self-abstraction of historical capitalism that, by increasing its hold over its own presuppositions, can pursue profit in relative indifference to the world around it. If we allow the historical self-abstracting tendencies to perfect themselves in thought, we can theorize a purely capitalist society as a theory of the basic social forms connected to the inner economic categories that are necessary to capital's self-expansion. According to Bell, this is what Marx was attempting to do in *Capital*, though without full awareness. We can conceive of economic laws at this level of analysis precisely because we assume an ideal use-value space that allows value to unfold so as to subsume all use-value obstacles to its own self-expansion. Dialectical contradictions drive our thinking forward because they occur when a subject/object lacks adequate determination. The theory, then, is complete when the object being theorized becomes capable of self-determination without relying on any outside other. Such a theory avoids one-sided definitions of capital, because in this case capital as subject/object defines itself completely.

Sekine, in Chapter 7, builds on the analysis presented by Bell. According to Sekine, dialectics is only appropriate to an 'autobiographical subject', such as capital, that is capable of self-knowledge. Because capital pushes human economic motives to the limit, it becomes the 'god' of economic motives. This means that capital can take on many of the characteristics of Hegel's Absolute, which is also god-like. Capital, however, is less powerful than Hegel's Absolute and can only take hold of a use-value space to the extent that production can easily take the form of a commodity. In history, use-value spaces are always resistant to some extent, producing many 'externalities', but where capitalism has taken sufficient and successful hold of production, then the capitalist state must manage to internalize those externalities most threatening to capital's continuation. In the theory of pure capitalism, capital's commodity-economic logic pushes the state into the background, but, according to Sekine, at the levels of stage theory and historical analysis the state must be thoroughly integrated into the theory. And, while capital's logic is operative at all three levels, the use-value space becomes more fully specified as we move from the abstract to the concrete. What this means, among other things, is that different degrees or types of necessity are active at the three levels. In the context of pure capitalism, we theorize the necessary inner connections among the basic economic categories of capital. In the context of stage theory, we theorize the necessary policy and ideological supports of a stage-specific regime of accumulation (for example, liberal policies in connection with the mid-nineteenth-century regime of accumulation in England) and at the level of historical analysis we theorize the necessity of particular events, given certain preconditions (for example, the First World War).

Arthur argues in Chapter 8 for a different version of the dialectic of capital. He believes that a rigorous dialectic is only possible for the first part of capital that deals with circulation, because, in circulation, use-value can be bracketed. Once we enter the realm of production, however, we need human agents to discipline and supervise labour-power which, as living labour, can never simply be used without resistance. Indeed, labour-power can never be reduced to become an appendage of a machine. Capital itself may be considered 'dead labour', but this must be contrasted with the appropriation of living labour in the production process. Arthur argues, however, that: 'From the point of view of capital itself, this is a distinction without a difference, because it conflates the labour process and the valorization process in its concept of itself, as if living labour was nothing but a "speaking instrument" of its own action,' (139). Arthur considers the possibility that the labour theory of value needs to be supplemented with a nature theory of value, because '"nature naturing" is an important productive activity to set along-side "labour labouring"' (140). But at the same time there is an important difference, because labour can actively oppose capitalism, while nature may only frustrate capitalism unknowingly for material reasons. Thus Arthur is prepared to accept the labour theory of value. Arthur goes on to oppose Sekine's dialectic of capital, claiming that dialectic method 'must not only listen to capital but simultaneously interrogate it so as to make visible the repressed others, namely its dependence on, and exploitation of, Labour and Nature' (145). Arthur then concludes his essay by making some comparisons between his approach to the dialectic of capital and Sekine's approach.

Murray begins Chapter 9 by differentiating Marxian from mainstream economics, emphasizing the former's focus on historically specific social forms. The emphasis on social form is, in his view, central to both systematic and historical dialectics; yet these two levels of dialectical analysis are distinct. Both levels are concerned with necessity, though with historical dialectics, necessity takes place within contexts where there is considerable contingency. The dialectic of capital is distinct from Hegel's dialectic because it is not presuppositionless, and, contrary to Hegel, weaves material presuppositions into the systematic dialectical presentation. At the same time, Marx's dialectic is similar to Hegel's in moving from the abstract-in-thought to the concrete-in-thought. Initially, Murray sees five types or degrees of necessity within historical dialectics: (i) transformations from one mode of production to another; (ii) the actualization of social forms; (iii) the emergence of new forms; (iv) destablizing tendencies within a mode of production; and (v) struggles inside a mode of production, either for or against it (154–5). He also argues that historical dialectics cannot be separated from a moral theory of human perfectibility. The historical dialectic, then, studies the entrenchment and transformation of social forms of provisioning as human agents struggle towards a fuller, more creative and more humane life. Finally, while the historical dialectic is distinct from systematic dialectics, they are also implicated in each other, since systematic dialectics not only theorizes what capital is, but also 'where it is going'.

Bertell Ollman presents in Chapter 10 a view of dialectics at least partially at odds with views presented within the book up to this point. Ollman argues that systematic dialectics is not the only strategy of presentation that Marx utilizes in *Capital*, and that Marx employs multiple strategies precisely because his aims are multiple. Further, not only is it wrong to restrict dialectics to the mode of presentation in *Capital*, but also it is wrong in general to restrict it to a mode of presentation. Dialectics, in Ollman's view, has to do with thinking about change and interaction, and the approach Ollman outlines has six moments. Systematic dialectics, argues Ollman, cannot account adequately for historical change and it cannot account for the dialectical method used throughout Marx's writings and not just in *Capital*. He concludes his chapter with the claim that systematic dialectics could make a valuable contribution to Marxist theory, if it could open itself to thinking more broadly about dialectics instead of mainly being limited to what is presumed to be the central mode of presentation in *Capital*.

Stefanos Kourkoulakos focuses in Chapter 11 on deepening our understanding of the specificity of dialectical reasoning as a distinct and powerful mode of knowing. He claims that 'theoretically concrete and rigorous questions probing in depth into the distinctive elements and structures of dialectics are rarely posed' (186). In order to set the stage for his analysis, he first characterizes the standard Marxist approach to dialectics by formulating five interrelated propositions, which he proceeds to criticize. His basic argument is 'that dialectics can, and must, be consistently and sufficiently distinguished from formal logic and, in fact, constitutes a qualitatively radically distinct method of knowledge, one whose field of applicability is a very restricted, and optimal one' (189). Further, dialectics as classically formulated by Hegel, had an overriding basic purpose, and that was to defeat epistemological skepticism. Hegel achieves this purpose most effectively when he theorizes the logical structure of the Absolute, and while 'capital is not an Absolute subject, ... [it] is uniquely and sufficiently Absolute-like to be treated (in part, that is, only at a certain level of high abstraction) in similar fashion' (195). Thus, according to Kourkoulakos, 'Dialectics emerges as a special form of experimental reason, a *sui generis* method of logically constituting and ordering a self-contained, expressive totality' (196). Kourkoulakos, then, analyzes both the nature of necessity and of contradiction in dialectical reason, and concludes with the claim that 'Dialectics can be viewed as an essentially non-formal-logical means of thwarting imminent formal logical contradictions from arising', and 'the necessity of its claims in the process of argumentation/theorization is established with relative – yet remarkable immunity from epistemological skepticism' (200–201).

Part of rethinking economics involves questioning the postivist/formalist methodology to which it is wedded, and this volume represents a modest start in doing just this. We employ 'dialectics' to challenge mainstream economics and to offer new ways of thinking about capitalism. These new ways of doing economic theory open the possibility for more effectively addressing the kinds of burning issues that we face.

The two modern thinkers who did the most to advance our understanding of dialectics were Hegel and Marx; hence you will find them referred to often. Every contributor to this volume believes the Marx's *Capital* harbours dialectics in some sense and to some degree, but at the same time there are strong disagreements about what sense and degree, just as there are disagreements about the character and utility of dialectics in general. Because of these disagreements, it is impossible to claim that 'dialectics' has a single core meaning that all contributors agree upon. Yet, having said this, probably all contributors to this book would try to develop a theory of capitalism that would avoid the formalistic, ahistorical, dualistic, static and exclusionary character of so much mainstream economic theory. For it is these characteristics that make it so one-dimensional and one-sided.

The contributions to this book were first presented at a workshop held at York University in Spring 2001. The debates that took place were the kind of rich and fruitful encounters that are possible where there are important differences, but the differences occur within a common project to use dialectics to develop a more effective political economy. They represent some of the most creative work done to date on capitalism and dialectical thought, and among the contributors are some of the leading dialecticians in the world today.

Though they differ in approach, Christopher Arthur, Geert Reuten, Patrick Murray and Tony Smith are sometimes grouped into a school of thought referred to as 'The New Dialectics' or 'Systematic Dialectics', which is in fact much larger than these four thinkers. They are noted principally for using dialectical reasoning to rethink Marxian political economy. Similarly Thomas Sekine, Stefanos Kourkoulakos, John Bell and Robert Albritton can be grouped into the 'The Uno–Sekine School'. Based on the pathbreaking work of Japanese political economists Kozo Uno and his student Thomas Sekine, this school emphasizes the need to theorize capital's inner logic as a dialectical logic, a logic that lends itself to levels of analysis because it is never fully present in history. Bertell Ollman's early work on alienation was, and still is, enormously influential, as is his more recent work on dialectics. His views on the scope and core features of dialectics differ in important respects from both of the above-mentioned schools. Moishe Postone's book *Time, Labor, and Social Domination* is becoming increasingly well-known and influential around the world. Influenced primarily by the Frankfurt School of Critical Theory, he develops a new conception of dialectics in opposition to Theodor Adorno and Jürgen Habermas. He argues for a new dialectical reading of *Capital* that points towards a new conception of socialism that radically rethinks and reorganizes work and labour. While David McNally differs in important respects from Postone, they both use dialectics as a mode of thinking that points beyond capitalism towards a freer alternative.

1

BSL P16
B14 B31

Beyond the False Infinity of Capital: Dialectics and Self-Mediation in Marx's Theory of Freedom

David McNally (K. Marx)

> Is it correct to say that the 'bad infinity' that prevails in idleness appears in Hegel as the signature of bourgeois society?
>
> Walter Benjamin, *The Arcades Project*

While Marx's concept of justice has been the subject of extensive theoretical debate in recent years, the Marxian notion of freedom has not received comparable attention.[1] The renewal of interest in Hegel as a philosopher of freedom[2] offers, however, an occasion for revisiting Marx's thinking on this contested concept in modern political thought. And this context is fitting, since Marx's theory of freedom involves a critical reworking of key Hegelian ideas. This reworking is most apparent in Marx's early critique of Hegel's theory of the state,[3] but it remained central to his life's work, most notably his critique of political economy. While the critique of Hegel and the analysis of the problem of freedom in modern society are foregrounded only occasionally throughout that project, I hope to use the analysis of one largely neglected issue – the 'false infinity' of capital – to indicate the ways in which they continued to frame it in crucially important ways.[4]

That Marx's mature critique of political economy is bound up with his criticism of Hegel should come as little surprise since, as he wrote in 1844, 'Hegel adopts the standpoint of modern political economy'.[5] The critical analysis of modern political economy thus revisits the terrain of the critique of Hegel – and of his concept of freedom. In what follows I undertake, therefore, to reconstruct some crucial elements of Marx's theory of freedom by way of his critical theory of capitalism. To this end, I argue that the problem of freedom entailed, for Marx as for Hegel, the problem of infinity. In the course of delineating Marx's notion of capital as a form of 'false infinity', I attempt to show how it relates to issues such as economic and financial crises in capitalism, the rift in the metabolic relationship between humanity and nature, and structures of experience in bourgeois society. This analysis is meant to lay some vital groundwork for the reconstruction of Marx's concept of freedom.

1

Freedom and infinity in Hegel

For Hegel, a solitary individual cannot be free, just as a solitary individual consciousness cannot know itself. In the same way as the individual consciousness arrives at authentic self-knowledge only by superseding its immediate self-certainty and discovering the truth of itself as a *mediated self*, one constituted in and through universal social interrelations, so the individual will (the starting point of freedom) must overcome the immediate form of appearance of freedom as a purely negative separation of the individual will from all restriction and determination. Indeed, Hegel's first use of the concept of infinity in his *Philosophy of Right* comes by way of his description of the 'pure indeterminacy' of negative freedom. Resting as it does on 'flight from every content as from a restriction', negative liberty is 'the freedom of the void'; it involves the individual will withdrawing from (or seeking to destroy) all concrete determinations as external restrictions. This conception of freedom entails an 'abstract ego' which sets itself the impossible task of being 'the whole truth', a part which sets itself up as the whole, an isolated will which represents itself as 'the unrestricted infinity of absolute abstraction or universality'.[6] The negative freedom of the abstract ego is a form of 'false infinity' for Hegel since, as we shall see, it sets itself up in opposition to all determination and finitude, to the world of finite entities outside the self.

Hegel's political theory retraces at the level of will much of the route traversed by self-consciousness in the *Phenomenology of Spirit*. The dialectic of self and other which generates self-understanding in the *Phenomenology* moves from an immediate sense of self-certainty through stages of external opposition between a self-contained consciousness and the mediations (objects of experience, other individuals, social institutions, the state and so on) that appear to stand over and against it as limits, constraints and external determinations. Only through loss of immediate self-certainty and an arduous voyage of self-discovery in this sphere of otherness can self-consciousness comprehend its being as actualized only in and through its being-for-others (its self-recognition in the complex of mediations that in fact constitute it). And a parallel process occurs in the movement of individual will towards authentic freedom. In the course of developing the institutional forms appropriate to freedom, human agents must come to recognize the laws and institutions of the modern state as necessary moments of their own freedom. In so doing, they overcome the opposition between subjective freedom (the individualized ego) and objective freedom (the ethical life of the state), between particular and universal. In a truly ethical and free human community, individuals actively will the mediations that constitute them, they posit them as moments of *self-mediation*. Only when it discovers its authentic freedom in the ethical life of the state, only when it thus returns to itself through the determinations of social and political life, is the will genuinely free: 'the will is not a will until it is this self-mediating activity, this return into itself'.[7] And it is only at this stage that we encounter true infinity in the sphere of political life.

The will that has integrated its determinations into its own self-activity 'is truly infinite,' writes Hegel, 'because its object is itself and so is not in its eyes an "other" or barrier; on the contrary, in its object this will has simply turned backward into itself'.[8] As this movement from false to true infinity is so crucial to Hegel – and, as we shall see, figures so importantly in Marx's critical theory of capital – let us explicate these concepts more fully.

Hegel's most extended treatment of infinity occurs in his *Science of Logic*. The notion of infinity emerges in his discussion of determinate being. Hegel is concerned there to mark the way in which the determinateness of any entity logically entails understanding what it is not. Non-being is thus a necessary moment of determinate being; negation is necessary to determination. The determination of a given object of thought thus posits a 'something else' outside the 'something' being defined. That 'something else' must then be integrated into its definition. Yet, as soon as we have done that, the object encounters a new barrier, another 'something else' that defines it negatively. The process of knowledge thus seems to imply that the definition of any entity requires an endless procedure of positing it in relation to each and every object that it is not. The truth of the object would seem to forever elude all acts of defining it; truth appears to reside in the realm of absolute (infinite) knowledge that finite knowing can never reach. This process of trying to conceptualize an object by means of positing and overcoming one barrier after another partakes of what Hegel defines as bad, false, or spurious (*schlechte*) infinity. False infinity involves an unending process, one that can never arrive at its destination, precisely because this destination is logically impossible – because the infinite posited as the not-finite can never be encountered through the labour of knowing the finite. It is perhaps worth remarking in this context that the post-structuralist preoccupation with infinite difference, with a language system in which meaning is always only differential, represents a species of Hegel's bad infinity.[9]

So long as infinity is treated as an abstraction from all finitude, as the negation of each and every finite entity, then no logical movement within the world of the finite will ever approach it. Every negation of a finite object simply posits the infinite as other than that object. No matter how many times we perform the same act of abstract negation, we find that the infinite still stands apart as the not-finite. The result is a bifurcation in which 'there are two worlds, one infinite and one finite', and no way of bridging their separation. Moreover, since the world of the infinite is one of two worlds, it is in fact finite, a limited part of a set.[10] Despite a never-ending repetition of the same logical operation, therefore, the infinite remains 'a perpetual ought'. We are trapped, consequently, within a (false) 'progress to infinity' which consists in 'the perpetual repetition of one and the same content, one and the same tedious alternation of this finite and infinite', that is, of a finite and a pseudo-infinite.[11] As Hegel informs us in the *Philosophy of Right*, bad or false infinity is thus represented by the straight line that goes on for ever.[12]

True infinity, on the other hand, is represented by the circle, by a movement that returns into itself. True infinity involves the overcoming of the gulf between the finite and the infinite; it entails finding the infinite within the finite, and vice versa. From the standpoint of affirmative (not endlessly negative) infinity, we see that 'both finite and infinite are this *movement* in which each returns to itself through its negation; they *are* only as *mediation* within themselves', that is, as self-mediating.[13]

And here we return to Hegel's concept of freedom. As we have seen, concrete freedom for Hegel requires the movement from immediacy, through loss of self in external mediations, to self-mediation. The attainment of self-mediation, the overcoming of the antagonism between individual and social, particular and universal, is the socio-political project of human freedom. The human will, writes Hegel, is not truly a will 'until it is this self-mediating activity, this return into itself'. Only when will is self-actualizing in and through its social determinations (mediations) have we arrived at 'the concrete concept of freedom'.[14] And this occurs, as he tells us in the *Phenomenology*, when history loses its external, thing-like character and becomes 'a *conscious*, self-*mediating* process'.[15] Freedom requires the recuperation of socio-historical agency, the discovery that the 'absolute' is human history comprehended and, hence, freely made. And this involves the movement from false to true infinity.

As we have seen, genuine infinity (the universality towards which freedom and reason aspire) lives only in and through the finite. It is only when finite, embodied, historical beings discover the infinite within their world-building projects (spirit) that they transcend the mere externality of the infinite – as in religious depictions of a God utterly outside the time of human history. A parallel process occurs on the political level in human communities that have not attained reason and freedom, in which societal mediations have an alien 'positivity' over and against individuals. In such contexts, individual subjects never reach a point of self-recognition in their mediations; the infinite (truth, freedom) remains something external, and the individual moves endlessly from one unreconciled relationship between self and other, particular and universal to another. In contrast to the will that 'is truly infinite' because 'its object is itself and so is not in its eyes an "other" or barrier', the objective elements of socio-political life – most crucially, the state – appear in the form of barriers, alien others that limit and obstruct the individual will. Moreover, they appear as an endless series of barriers, a series that, like the straight line, extends itself for ever.

Bad infinity entails, therefore, a sort of repetition-compulsion. Human agents endlessly lose themselves in a world of otherness in which experience rehearses essentially the same process and results: the encounter with, negation of, and new encounter with 'external' objects that are experienced as barriers. There are no qualitative transformations that break this continuum and provide grounds for self-development and self-return; there is no self-mediating activity. Just this dynamic of false infinity, I now hope to show, is at the heart of Marx's critical account of capital.

The false infinity of capital

The problem of infinity emerges clearly at the outset of Part 2 of *Capital*, volume 1, 'The General Formula for Capital'. That formula, of course, is M-C-M', where M stands for money, C for commodities, and M' for a quantity of money greater than the initial amount (that is, where M' > M). By its very nature, then, the formula M-C-M' involves quantitative expansion. Whereas the formula C-M-C involves a qualitative change (commodity *x* is sold for money so as to purchase commodity *y*), the general formula for capital involves the same quality – money – as its point of departure and termination; the only change is of a quantitative nature, since 'one sum of money is distinguishable from another only by its amount'.[16] Rather than a means to an end (as in the circuit C-M-C, where money serves as the means of exchanging one qualitatively unique good for another), the general formula for capital posits money as an end in itself. Moreover, it is of the nature of capital that this circuit must be constantly renewed – the augmented money capital that appears as the point of termination (M') of an initial circuit must re-enter the circuit as a new point of departure. After all, if it is withdrawn it is no longer capital; instead it will have become a means for the purchase of commodities and entered the circuit C-M-C. 'The movement of capital is therefore limitless,' Marx writes.[17]

In elaborating upon the difference between these two circuits of wealth, Marx provides a lengthy footnote citing Aristotle's distinction between household management (*oikonomia*) and the art of acquisition (*chrematistics*). Whereas household economy, the art of 'natural wealth', treats wealth as the means to human ends and is thus inherently limited, chremastistics 'is concerned only with getting a sum of money'; its goal is not goods but their universal equivalent. As a result, 'the art of acquisition is unlimited', there is 'no limit to the end it seeks'.[18] Marx uses similar terminology in his discussion of the distinction between C-M-C and M-C-M'. Having said that the objective of capital is to approach 'absolute wealth', Marx refers to the aim of the capitalist as 'the unceasing movement of profit making'.[19]

Indeed, Marx contends that, as a form of capital, money encounters an internal contradiction between its 'quantitative limitation' at any one point in time and the 'qualitative lack of limitation' that defines money in principle.[20] Put in slightly different terms, every finite form of capital as a sum of money stands as a barrier to capital's drive towards infinity, its telos as 'absolute wealth'. Inherent in capital, therefore, is an unending process of self-negation; capital drives beyond its previous limit only to find itself still separated from its goal: infinite wealth. This is what Marx means when he writes of capital in the *Grundrisse* that 'measuredness contradicts its character, which must be oriented towards the measureless'.[21] As money (the beginning and end point of its general formula), capital thus embodies a contradiction: every concrete form it takes as a specific sum of money contradicts its 'general concept' – absolute wealth. As a result, it moves endlessly through 'the constant drive to go beyond its quantitative limit: an endless process'.[22]

The parallels here with Hegel's notion of false infinity are striking. Capital's unceasing drive to overcome the limits of each of its determinate forms of appearance, to create a 'specific surplus value because it cannot create an infinite one all at once',[23] locks it into an unending quest for the impossible – a drive to achieve infinity by augmenting its finite form. There are obvious resonances here with Hegel's reference to the 'perpetual repetition of one and the same content' (in this case, money). The truth of capital – absolute, infinite wealth – is posited as an end outside of, beyond and subsisting in a purely negative relationship to its finite forms of appearance, as the non-finite. It is instructive, then, that later in the *Grundrisse*, Marx specifically cites Hegel's treatment of the problem of finitude and infinity in this regard. 'As representative of the general form of wealth – money – capital is the endless and limitless drive to go beyond its limiting barrier,' declares Marx. 'Every boundary [*Grenze*] is and has to be a barrier [*Schranke*] for it'.[24] And at exactly this point in the text he inserts a footnote to Hegel's *Logic* which cites two relevant passages on the problem of the finite and the infinite.

Capital is locked into a dynamic of false infinity precisely because every concrete form in which it appears constitutes a denial of its bad teleology, its unceasing quest for an infinite that exceeds all finitude, all measure, all embodiment. Moreover, as I hope to show, this is one way of describing crucial features of the contradiction between use-value and value which is at the heart of Marx's account of the contradictory character of capitalism.

Aspects of false infinity: economic, financial and environmental crises and the revenge of the finite

That the contradiction between use-value and value is also a form of false infinity has rarely been recognized in the literature. The point is, however, anticipated in Sekine's apposite statement that 'The so-called "contradiction between value and use-values" ... means that the abstract-general (infinite) principle of capital represented by "value" and the concrete-specific (finite) reality of human economic life represented by "use-values" do not mix naturally'.[25] As I have suggested, this inability to 'mix naturally' conforms to the pattern of Hegel's false infinity. Moreover, this false infinity manifests itself in moving contradictions which entail crises, or what I am describing here as aspects of bad infinity.

One of the advantages of reconstructing the contradiction between use-value and value in relation to the false infinity of capital is that it allows us to grasp the multidimensionality of this contradiction. Capitalism, as should have been obvious from Marx's analysis in *Capital*, does not have a single crisis tendency. To be sure, breakdowns in the self-reproduction of capital are inherent in the contradictory unity that is the commodity. But this contradiction is multi-levelled; it is produced and reproduced at multiple points in the circuit of capital. Capital's crises are literally overdetermined insofar as they involve the interaction of many phenomenal forms of its fundamental contradiction. Speaking in terms of false infinity, we might say that capital's ability to overcome one of its barriers simply places it in opposition to yet another barrier of its own making.

As we have seen, bad infinity involves a part trying to make itself the whole. False infinity involves an ostensible infinite that flees from 'every content as from a restriction', an infinite based on violent abstraction from all determination, or what Hegel calls 'the unrestricted infinity of absolute abstraction'. Yet, the finite always has its revenge; it continually re-emerges in opposition to this spurious infinity, exposing it as just one in opposition to another (that is, as finite). In the case of capital, finitude is signified by use-values. Capital's contradictions thus centrally entail its inability truly to surmount its determination by use-values. Put differently, at the heart of capital's self-contradictory character is its inability to be truly self-positing (infinite), since it does not capitalistically produce its own vital presuppositions – notably living labour and the natural environment. With these points in mind, let us now unfold some of the implications of the notion of the false infinity of capital in terms of the crucial Marxian distinction between use-value and value.

i) The bad infinity of abstract labour and the barrier of working class resistance

From the standpoint of the general formula for capital, the time spent in the sphere of use-values – buying machinery and raw materials, purchasing labour, supervising production, eliminating waste, shipping goods, and so on – is for capital a diversion from its transformation back into money (M'). Yet, as Marx's analysis shows, valorization, the self-expansion of capital, requires its entry into the sphere of production and its consumption of means of production and labour-power (hence the formula for production capital, $M - C \ [MP + LP] \ldots P \ldots C' - M'$, where MP signifies means of production, *LP* indicates labour-power, and *P* signifies the process of production of new use-values for capital). Capital's infinitizing movement (its unending drive to produce surplus value and expand) thus requires that it embed itself in the finite forms of means of production and concrete labour. Capital thus confronts an inherent conundrum: its drive to infinity, to make itself an absolute abstraction, requires its immersion in the sphere of finitude; value can expand only by a journey through the sphere of use-values. Capital's 'solution' to this conundrum is to strive endlessly to negate all the limits imposed upon it by actual use-values, to try to overcome its own fixity (finite determination) by reducing the time spent in the sphere of production (where it is 'locked' into the use-value forms of raw materials, plant and equipment, and concrete labour). If it were possible – which it is not – capital would take leave entirely of the sphere of production of use-values in order to assume the 'pure' form of money breeding money; it would utterly annihilate space in favour of time.

From the standpoint of dialectical social theory, the crucial use-value limit imposed upon capital is that represented by labour-power. Labour in the sphere of production is *concrete*, it involves the life-activity of finite, unique embodied individuals with specific needs and desires who undertake concrete physical-technical processes of production utilizing raw materials, equipment and facilities to produce discrete use-values. Yet capital is in principle indifferent to the concrete labour that went into producing specific commodities. Its preoccupation is with the intensification of concrete labour, its translation into abstract labour; capital struggles against the concrete particularities of labour in order to force its correspondence to (or surpassing of) the standards of socially necessary labour-time in order to reap or exceed the general rate of profit, reproduce itself in an adequately expanded form, and continue its movement towards (bad) infinity.

It is here that the critical analysis of capital discloses class struggle as an inherent feature of the capital relation. After all, the inherent tendency of capital is to completely transform concrete labour into abstract labour, utterly homogeneous, interchangeable quantities of the same disembodied stuff. It should be obvious that Marx's use of the term 'abstract' is far from accidental. As Melvin Rader has pointed out, for Hegel and Marx, 'the verb "to abstract" means to separate. Hegel, for example, says that to amputate an arm is to abstract it from the human body'.[26] Capital's abstracting operation *vis-à-vis* concrete labour should be understood in these terms. Capital literally drives to separate labour from the human body (like the arms to which Hegel refers), to abstract it completely from living labourers in order to turn it over entirely to the imperatives of capital. Capital's inner movement is to appropriate all the energies and powers of living labourers, to overcome the limits of the human body, to stretch and intensify labour to the point that it overcomes its own physical and socio-cultural limits, its human embodiment. Concrete, embodied, sentient, desiring, labouring beings constitute barriers to capital which, in its quest for infinity, it tries to drive beyond.

The living labourer, however, is bound to resist the abstracting dynamic of capital because labour-power 'does not exist apart from him', because what capital seeks to entirely appropriate to itself is 'the worker's specific productive activity ... his vitality itself'.[27] Moreover, the worker has entered the exchange with capital with an entirely different *telos* than has capital. Whereas capital treats this exchange as a means to its self-augmentation and thus treats labour as 'a force belonging to capital itself', for the worker the exchange is about procuring the means of life. From the side of the worker, the exchange with capital obeys the Aristotelian logic of natural wealth (C-M-C): the workers' goals are to exchange labour-power for money (wages) in order to produce the means of life. The circuit of wage-labour, as Lebowitz calls it, thus obeys a finite teleology, one embedded within the needs and desires of concrete living labourers. It follows that the exchange between capital and labour involves the intersection of two different circuits with conflicting goals and logics.[28] The result is class struggle on the side of labour, working class resistance to the bad infinity of capital. And this resistance constitutes the most important barrier precisely because workers can form a conscious counter-project to capital.

ii) Infinity, living labour and the barrier of fixed capital

Capital, of course, tries to drive relentlessly beyond the barriers constituted by working class resistance in the sphere of production. While this can, and often does, take the form of direct battles to control and discipline labour, capital's most important weapon in this regard is the reorganization and intensification of work brought about by the introduction of new technologies which reduce workers' control over the pace and processes of production. Capital attempts to undermine workers' resistance and intensify labour by having the pace and structure of work determined by the technical demands of machines themselves. The automated factory system is the appropriate industrial form for capital precisely because the system of machinery creates the technical possibility of a production process that never stops, that goes on forever. Yet this technical possibility of unending production, this bad infinity of capital, comes up repeatedly against the limits posed by living labourers. With machine-based industry, writes Marx, capital 'would go on producing forever, if it did not come up against certain natural limits in the shape of the weak bodies and the strong wills of its human assistants'.[29] Capital drives beyond each and every form of working class resistance, however, by regularly revolutionizing the means of production in order to further subordinate living to dead labour.

Yet, revolutionizing the means of production in order to overcome the barrier posed by workers' resistance only posits yet another barrier to capital – this one constituted by the determinate forms of fixed capital, the complex use-value structures involved. In trying to mobilize mechanization to surmount the barriers posed by human labour-power, capital overcomes one use-value limit (represented by labour) only by tying itself more and more to other use-values which are relatively fixed and inflexible: specific kinds of factories, machines and equipment – what Marx called *fixed capital* – which require substantial inputs of labour and have a fairly long life cycle. Capital's drive to free itself from the constraints imposed by workers' resistance thus has the paradoxical effect of locking it into ever-larger and more complex structures of fixed capital. And these complexes of fixed capital in turn pose further barriers to the bad infinity of capital.

Put simply, the problem for capital is that, as a result of the constant tendency to cheapen commodities (an inherent part of constant revolutionizing of the means of production), the actual market value of these elements of fixed capital declines. Yet individual capitals are not in a position to immediately shed the fixed structure of use-values they have built to overcome previous barriers. Their drive to make labour-power more elastic (to stretch it more readily towards infinity) has been abetted by means of cost inelasticities associated with complex use-values; once again, finite determinations stand in the way of capital's infinitizing drive. These elements of fixed capital are meant to last for many years; indeed, capital can only recoup its costs over a production cycle of perhaps ten years or more. However, as the constant revolutionizing of the means of production brings new machines on stream which are equally or more efficient and cheaper – think of computers at the moment – the older machines cannot transfer as much value to each commodity; they have effectively been devalued. After all, the prices charged by those working with older means of production must conform to the average costs of production (which are falling as a consequence of innovations coming on line). Consequently, market prices will not fully compensate less efficient producers for the original costs of their generally older means of production. In this way, capital's own drive to revolutionize instruments of production poses problems for the reproduction of the values locked up in earlier means of production. The downward pressure on values and prices (which are tending to fall towards the level appropriate to the newest, cheapest and most efficient means of production) translates into lower profits for those producers who have relatively higher costs (especially for fixed capital, which has already been purchased at previous prices); in some circumstances this translates into a crisis of reproduction for individual capitals, a crisis with considerable scope for generalization. Marx put much of this quite succinctly in the manuscripts published as *Theories of Surplus Value*:

> since the circulation process of capital is not completed in one day but extends over a fairly long period until the capital returns to its original form, since ... great upheavals and changes take place in the market in

the course of this period, since great changes take place in the productivity of labour and therefore also in the real value of commodities, it is quite clear, that between the starting point, the prerequisite capital, and the time of its return at the end of one of these periods, great catastrophes must occur and elements of crisis must have gathered and develop.[30]

Put in different terms, this contradiction involves a clash between two different orders of temporality: the 'instant time' of value as an absolute subject, and the 'determinate time' of the finite forms of capital. This contradiction consists, therefore, 'in the fact that the capitalist mode of production tends towards an absolute development of the productive forces irrespective of value and the surplus value this contains ... while on the other hand its purpose is to maintain the existing capital value and valorize it to the utmost extent'.[31]

As a number of commentators have noted,[32] recognition of this tendency requires a much more dynamic and complex notion of profitability crises than traditional or 'fundamentalist' accounts of an ostensible long-run tendency for the rate of profit to fall. Recast in the dynamic terms of capital's false infinity, profitability crises cannot be depicted in terms of a long-run secular tendency for the organic composition of capital to rise (a view that works with a notion of homogeneous, linear time) but, rather, must be understood as the regular positing and overcoming (by means of crises and restructurings) of a barrier defined by the contradiction between revolutions in the value composition of capital and the fixity (finite determinations) of the use-values required for the production of relative surplus value.

iii) The false infinity of fictitious capital

One of the key mechanisms capital employs for superseding this contradiction is the credit system. The enormous investments required to re-engineer production at various intervals (say, every ten years or so) often cannot be self-financed. Moreover, as I have just described, great technological revolutions in systems of production often impose major costs well before the depletion of the life-cycle of older systems. Industrial capitals go to the credit markets, therefore, to borrow investment funds with a promise to pay them back (with interest) out of future surplus value. Indeed, this is the foundation of the credit system which 'has its roots in the specific mode of realization, mode of turnover, mode of reproduction of fixed capital'.[33] As capitalism develops, whole new markets are created which trade in 'fictitious capitals', effectively IOUs on future income. Corporate stocks, bonds and notes are joined by various forms of government paper, consumer loans and the like. A whole financial superstructure evolves on ever more speculative foundations: investors are trading not in actual goods, but in papers and electronic entries that promise to deliver funds out of incomes that do not yet exist.

It appears here as if capital has found its pure form: money begetting money without passing through the mediation of labour and concrete use-values. The mere purchase and sale of paper or electronic tokens of value seems to generate value augmentation, M-M' without the mediations of commodities, labour-power, or elements of the natural world. Capital seems to have achieved a purely virtual form; and this produces the speculative manias that accompany all credit-driven booms. The credit system now 'appears as the principal lever of overproduction and excessive speculation in commerce'; and in the course of a speculative mania, 'the reproduction process, which is elastic by nature, is now forced to its most extreme limit'.[34] Financial speculation in fictitious capitals produces a capitalist dream-world in which capital infinitely produces itself out of itself. This is the substructure of the 'irrational exuberance' that characterizes speculative manias. Without any entry into the sphere of use-values, capital assumes the form of 'money breeding money', an 'automatic fetish' – indeed, the 'pure fetish form' – in which capital seems to take leave of the world of the finite and enter its own infinite beyond.[35] In recent years, this pure fetishism has emerged in a grab-bag of theories of a 'new economy', a digital or information economy finally emancipated from the material processes of the past. In fact, this fetish form of capital, so familiar in vulgar economics, has become a staple of postmodern theorists of the information economy.[36]

Of course, speculative financial capital can no more escape the dynamic of bad infinity than can any other form. Every financial crisis and stock market crash represents a revenge of the finite, as interest-bearing money discovers its intimate ties to the finite world of use-values. After all, fixed capital and fictitious capital are two interconnected extremes within the contradictory unity of capital as a whole. Just as the formation of fixed capital depends on fictitious capital, so fictitious capital relies on the viability of fixed capital. Should industrial capitalists be unable to realize the value of their investments, fictitious capital will be plunged into crisis (since it will not receive repayment with interest). And this becomes dramatically clear whenever there is a serious decline in rates of return on productive capital. Whenever industrial capital encounters difficulties in turning concrete labour and its products into money (the representative of abstract labour), there emerges a crisis in the credit system, as paper and electronic assets are exposed as little more than the fictitious capitals they are. But having forced capital accumulation to its most extreme limit, having erected a 'colossal system of swindling and gambling' with respect to paper and electronic assets, speculative financial capital 'accelerates the violent outbreaks of the contradiction'.[37] As a result, the most dramatic manifestations of the crisis often appear in the credit markets: 'at first glance, therefore, the entire crisis presents itself as simply a credit and monetary crisis'.[38] And such crises are yet merely one more manifestation of the false infinity of capital, its inability to detach itself from the finite determinations of the world of use-values.

iv) Capital's false infinity and the destruction of the natural environment

Capital's drive to emancipate itself from all use-value determination involves it in a widening circle of contradictions. At their root, these come back to the contradiction at the heart of the commodity between value and use-value. The infinitizing drive of capital proceeds as if the limits of the finite elements of production could be surpassed unendingly. As a result, the drive for capitalist wealth contradicts the very foundations of all wealth – nature and living labour. Rather than finding a true infinity in its finite conditions of possibility, capital systematically negates them as hostile barriers. Furthermore, since capital's self-expansion requires these presuppositions, they are regularly reposited and negated as forms of alterity, as capital's hostile 'others' which must be entirely overcome if capital is to attain infinity. The inevitable result is the degradation of the labourer and the destruction of the natural environment: 'Capitalist production, therefore, only develops the techniques and the degree of combination of the social process of production by simultaneously undermining the original sources of all wealth – the soil and the worker'.[39]

Marx's emphasis on the natural presuppositions of production – in this case, the soil – is often overlooked. This has at least something to do with an erroneous conflation of his claim that the value of commodities is determined strictly by labour with a 'Promethean' disregard for the natural elements of all production. Yet Marx was insistent that his theory did not neglect nature as a source of use-values. 'The earth,' he wrote, 'is active as an agent of production in the production of use-value, a material product, say wheat. But it has nothing to do with producing the *value of the wheat*.'[40] He made the same point in the *Critique of the Gotha Programme*.[41] The indifference to nature ascribed to Marx is thus really a function of his delineation of *capital*'s indifference to nature in the determination of values. Yet precisely this indifference was central to his claims for the irrationality of capitalism as a system.[42]

The young Marx argued that a similar indifference to nature is evident in Hegel's philosophical system – perhaps another indication of the homology of capital and Hegel's Spirit.[43] In his 1844 critique of Hegel, for example, Marx argued that the emptiness of Hegel's *Science of Logic* ultimately drives Hegel back to nature in order to remedy Spirit's lack of content. Similarly, in his critique of Hegel's doctrine of the state a year earlier, he suggested that Hegel's attempt to fill his speculative political philosophy with social content that would reconcile the contradictions of bourgeois society drove him towards an absurdly biological defence of hereditary monarchy. Having speculatively excavated the modern state of its real (antagonistic) social substance, Hegel turned to nature to give it its necessary content. Yet this absurdity obeyed a logic inherent in Hegel's system, an inevitable return of the repressed: 'Nature takes its revenge on Hegel for the contempt he has shown her.'[44]

Throughout *Capital*, Marx similarly draws attention to the irrational consequences of capital's bad infinity in relation to the finitude of nature. But in this case, capital's indifference to the natural conditions of production leads to fundamental disturbances in the metabolic relationship between humanity and nature. Taking capitalist agriculture as a case in point, he argues that the pursuit of 'monetary profit' is destructive of the 'permanent conditions of life':

> The way that the cultivation of particular crops depends on fluctuations in market prices and the constant changes in cultivation with those price fluctuations – the entire spirit of capitalist production which is oriented towards the most immediate monetary profit – stands in contradiction to agriculture, which has to concern itself with the whole gamut of permanent conditions of life required by the chain of human generations.'[45]

In fact, after documenting the ways in which capitalist production produces terrific upward and downward fluctuations in the prices of raw materials (and the irrational instabilities this creates for both industry and agriculture), Marx concludes: 'The moral of the tale ... is that the capitalist system runs counter to a rational agriculture.'[46] This irrationality is related to the over-specialization inherent in the radical separation of town and country in capitalist society. This separation does enormous damage to both urban life and the soil, poisoning the environment of the former and depleting the natural productivity of the latter.[47] In so disturbing 'the metabolic interaction between man and the earth', capitalist production 'hinders the operation of the eternal natural condition for the lasting fertility of the soil'.[48] Capital is thus systematically hostile to the 'eternal natural' conditions of human life and the production of use-values, squandering the very preconditions of human life. Recurring environmental disasters are inscribed, consequently, within the very logic of capital's false infinity.

Self-mediation and true infinity in Marx's theory of freedom

Let us now draw this discussion back to our starting point: the problem of freedom. For Marx, the theory of concrete freedom can be developed only in the way we have proceeded – that is, by means of the immanent critique of capital and its theoretical exponents, Hegel and the classical political economists. It is true, of course, that Marx's theory pivots on an ontology of freedom. But this ontology requires historical specification if it is to serve as a theory designed to guide a radical practice, and that historical specification must proceed by way of immanent critique.

Marx's ontology of freedom is rooted in the form of human labour as a conscious transformation of the human social environment. Marx's famous account of the teleological structure of human labour[49] is also an account of freedom – of the capacity of human beings to make themselves and their environment, to shape consciously their mediations with each other and with nature. Unlike any other species, then, humans have the capacity to transcend the mere facticity of the external world and their own species-nature by mediating consciously their metabolic relationship with (external and internal) nature. Freedom – the capacity for autonomy (Kant), for self-making and self-mediation (Hegel) – is a structural feature of the teleology of human labour.

Criticizing Adam Smith in the *Grundrisse* for treating labour in general as a curse, for having conflated it with alienated wage labour, Marx argues that 'Smith has no inkling whatever that this overcoming of obstacles is in itself a liberating activity', and that the aims of labour can be a means of 'self-realization, objectification of the subject, hence real freedom'.[50] Indeed, the inner structure of labour as 'liberating activity', as 'real freedom', is precisely what Marx commends when he praises Hegel's *Phenomenology of Spirit* for having divined the 'dialectic of negativity' through which the human being is grasped as 'the result of his own labour'.[51] For Marx, in other words, the essential basis of freedom is humanity's capacity for self-production. And as with Hegel, this freedom can be exercised for Marx only within a human community. Like language and labour, freedom cannot be the attribute of a solitary individual: 'only in the community ... is personal freedom possible'.[52] In fact, labour is meaningful – that is, it generates a field of meanings – precisely because it represents the objectification of human purposes in a socio-material field.

Yet the ontological capacity for freedom is something quite different from its actual socio-historical expression. In fact, while praising Hegel for his dialectic of negativity, Marx also commends his critical account of human estrangement.[53] And if freedom is an essential human capacity, then estrangement must entail a deficit of freedom. Furthermore, once we supplant Hegel's idealist account of human estrangement with a real socio-historical account, one that grasps alienated labour as its essential structure, then we can see the ways in which freedom is lost in capitalist society. Thus, however much human ontology is an ontology of freedom, a critical social theory must come to terms with whether the actual relations of social life are consistent with the actualization of freedom. The theory of concrete freedom thus opens on to a socio-historical analysis of the structures of human practical activity.

And this returns us to Hegel's account of freedom and true infinity. For concrete freedom, freedom which is actualized in social life, can only be accomplished when the mediations that constitute the individual are moments of *self-mediation*. Where Marx departs from Hegel, however – and this departure signals a theoretical and political revolution – is in his insistence that concrete freedom, genuinely self-mediating activity, begins with (and returns to) the most foundational of practical activities – labour as *praxis*. This requires, as I shall demonstrate, that human social labour take on the form of conscious self-mediation.

Here I must record my dissent from Moishe Postone's claim that capitalism is a society of 'self-mediating' labour.[54] While I have set out my disagreements on this count at greater length elsewhere,[55] a brief review of the issues at stake should help to illuminate the interrelationships among concrete freedom, self-mediation and true infinity.

As I have argued above, commodity-based economic life is systematically antithetical to self-mediation. Because commodity-economic logic involves a systematic dislocation between human practical activity (concrete labour) and the mediated forms it creates (commodities and money), there is no return to self here, no establishment of structures of meaning based upon a concrete unity of the being-for-self of the commodity as a product of specific acts of labour and its social meaning or value (its being-for-others). It also follows that capitalist society involves a dislocation in the structure of meaning – the intentions that form the basis of concrete labour are negated and distorted into the self-propelling world of capital and its (alien) meanings. This is why mediation between particular and universal involves the intervention of an abstracted 'third party' (money), an alienated mediator that forcibly holds together what is dis-integrated, a 'holding together' that is fraught with tensions and contradictions. As the young Marx put it with respect to the failed mediations in Hegel's theory of the state (the estates, legislature and so on), what we have in the case of money is a 'middle term' that is 'a wooden sword, the concealed antithesis between the particular and the universal'. Money, like Hegel's mediating institutions, represents a pseudo-mediation: 'far from accomplishing a mediation, it is the embodiment of a contradiction'.[56]

And such pseudo-mediations lock us into structures of bad infinity; rather than reconciling universal (infinite) and particular (finite), they alternate between the two, reproducing their antagonistic relationship. In the case of the capitalist economy, the finite particular (concrete labour) is left behind – lost and forgotten – in the search for infinite exchangeability and abstract universality (a universal being-for-others that stands over against its determinate being as a product of concrete acts of labour). This abstract universality is conferred by money, which represents the thoroughgoing reification of social life – the crystallization of the products of human activity into real abstractions that, rather than functioning as moments of self-mediating activity, dominate it as alien powers. Money as the universal middle term freezes the relations between particular and universal into the repetitive structure of what Hegel calls the standpoint of 'reflection'.

In his *Logic*, Hegel criticizes the standpoint of reflection for trying to locate an essence lurking behind (and independent of) phenomenal appearances, a sphere of universality detached from particulars. Because the relationships among mere entities (beings) cannot provide a basis for universal truths, the doctrine of Being (and the standpoint of immediate entities) reverses itself into the doctrine of Essence. Yet, reflection succeeds merely in counterposing abstract universals (or essences) against concrete phenomena. Hegel criticizes this standpoint for connecting the two aspects of a dialectical relationship mechanically. In the doctrine of Essence, two sides of a relationship are treated as independent entities external to one another – one inessential; the other essential. The concrete, phenomenal form of a thing is thus treated as inessential in relation to an Essence that lies outside itself: 'Essence is held to be something unaffected by, and subsisting in independence of, its definite phenomenal embodiment.'[57]

Something similar happens with commodities and money, in Marx's view. Commodities are incapable of self-mediation because they embody an irreconcilable antagonism. On the one hand, they are concrete useful things (use-values) produced by specific acts of concrete labour. But on the other hand, they are produced as commodities, as goods utterly bereft of specificity, and capable, therefore, of exchange with all others. In entering into exchange, commodities undergo a metamorphosis; they leave behind their concrete form as specific goods capable of satisfying unique wants in order to become repositories of a single, abstract, commensurable (and hence interchangeable) substance – value. They move, in other words, from concrete particulars to abstract universals. But, rather than self-mediation, this movement involves simple alternation. Commodities are severed from their origins and forced through an abstracting process in which they become pure quanta of human labour in the abstract, labour abstracted from every element of its concrete, sensuous being. Yet, this movement from particularity (use-value) to universality (value) lacks genuine mediation. Rather than being related dialectically, these two sides of the commodity stand in opposition to one another. The antithesis between commodities and money merely expresses this absence of self-mediation.

Because the value of commodities – their social meaning (being for others) – is something radically separate from their being as use-values produced by unique and specific acts of labour, capitalism involves a systematic dislocation in the structure of meaning. Commodities do not refer back (or return) to the labour that produced them; instead they refer to the infinite abstraction (and abstract universality) of value with which they can never form a unity. Just as the standpoint of reflection finds an essence sep-

arate from phenomena, so the capitalist economy involves a structural dislocation between concrete being (use-value/concrete labour) and essence
(value).[58] Unable to achieve anything more than an abstract universality
severed from concrete particularity, concrete labouring activity in capitalist
society cannot attain self-mediation. It can only enter the alternating cycle
of bad infinity in which it sacrifices its finite particularity on the altar of
abstract universality (false infinity).

For people in bourgeois society, therefore, 'their mutual interconnection
here appears as something alien to them, autonomous, as a thing'. In the
commodified society governed by access to money (as repository of value),
'the individual carries his social power, as well as his bond with society, in
his pocket'[59] – that is, as a thing that offers (abstract) universality. Money is
the necessary form of appearance of the alienated relations of commodified
society, the pseudo-mediator that reproduces the contradiction between
particular and universal. Commodities (and the concrete labour that produced them) require an other that reflects their (abstract, universal) value
back to them. Value appears as an essence over and against the mere beings
– commodities and labourers – of the capitalist economy (Hegel's standpoint of reflection). The internal differentiation within the commodity –
between use-value and value, concrete labour and abstract labour – can
only be expressed through an 'external opposition' – by having money
stand over and against commodities as their essence.[60]

This point is crucial. Self-mediation involves concrete universality and
true infinity – the living unity of particular and universal, finite and
infinite, which is the token of human freedom. An abstract universal
denuded of all determination and particularity represents a pseudo-solution
to the antagonism of particular (use-value, concrete labour) and universal
(value, abstract labour). Just as Hegel's doctrine of the state involves middle
terms that embody the contradiction between private will and general will
rather than overcome it, so money merely reproduces the antagonism
between use-value and value, concrete and abstract labour (indeed, this is
the symmetry between Hegel's philosophy and classical political economy
remarked upon by the young Marx). Money and the state represent, therefore, abstract universals that reproduce the very contradictions – the very
alternating logic of false infinity – they are meant ostensibly to resolve.

Just as a member of bourgeois society alternates endlessly between the
roles of *bourgeois* (particular) and *citoyen* (universal) which cannot be recon-
ciled, so concrete labourers are compelled to subject themselves to the
economic logic of the commodity form if they are to reproduce themselves.
Yet this involves an abstracting logic, a loss of particularity and concreteness, as human activities and their products enter a system of reification.
That this dynamic can never come to rest, that it continues *ad infinitum* –
that, in Hegel's words, the relationship 'sets up with endless iteration the
alternation between these two terms' – marks capitalism as a system of false

infinity, one lacking genuine self-mediation; that is, the return to self (self-recognition) of labourers in the sphere of their products. In order to live, workers re-enact repeatedly the exchange with capital, only to find that they must also sacrifice repeatedly integral parts of the life they seek to fulfill. The universal form – money – does not become the ground for the self-expression of concrete labour; instead, it is an external (abstract) universal that negates concrete labour. Rather than a structure of self-mediating labour, then, capitalism is a structure of systematic abstraction, a structure of false infinity in which living labour is forgotten and effaced systematically. Moreover, this relationship produces a runaway process of unregulated accumulation, and the aspects of bad infinity I have itemized above.

Marx's revolutionary vision (derived by immanent critique) of a society of freedom involves, by contrast, a notion of true infinity. When Marx sets out his vision of a potential society of 'social individuals' operating in a context where 'the free development of individualities' is the aim of production,[61] he projects a structure of self-mediation in which individuals simultaneously produce themselves as free agents and the general social relationships in which all participate as members of a society of concrete freedom. In such circumstances, individuals posit their activity 'as immediately general or social activity',[62] not as private, pre-social activity which must be sacrificed (subjected to an alien form) to acquire universality. And, in conditions of concrete freedom, this can only mean that they consciously will those conditions conducive to the freedom of all, that they participate in a form of social association 'in which the free development of each is the condition for the free development of all',[63] or, in Hegel's terms, in which 'freedom wills freedom'.[64] And from all that has gone before, it should be obvious that this might be possible only where the activity of concrete individuals is not subjected to the logic of commodification and reification – and, therefore, that notions of a socialism based on market regulation are internally contradictory.[65]

It is worth noting here that the reconciliation of finite and infinite that characterizes true infinity need not entail an Aristotelian notion of fixed limits. While this older view 'appears very lofty when contrasted to the modern world', writes Marx, since the human being appears as the aim of production, not a means to external ends, it is nonetheless a particularistic, and not a universal form. Only when production takes as its goal 'the development of all human powers' as 'the end in itself' does it overcome the static particularity of the ancient view and move towards universality – a universality that is twofold, characterized by its embrace of the species (all humankind) and its embrace of the developmental dynamic of human powers, as opposed to the limited forms of previous modes of life. Marx adopts, therefore, the standpoint of freely associated producers in 'an absolute movement of becoming', one that creates the space for individuals to pursue open-ended projects of self-development.[66]

It is important to point out, however, that this absolute movement of becoming can attain true infinity only if it validates the infinity (universality) of its finite, constitutive elements. It should now be clear that, with respect to labour, this refers to the free development of the associated producers as concrete individuals with specific needs and desires. Perhaps less obvious, however, is what it means for humanity's metabolic relation with nature. Genuine freedom requires the rational regulation of that metabolism. And this means, Marx insists, an abiding respect for the inherent properties and processes of the natural environment. Communal production in the context of rational foresight means both a 'rational agriculture' and the preservation of the natural environment for future generations: 'Even an entire society, a nation, or all simultaneously existing societies taken together, are not the owners of the earth. They are simply its possessors, its beneficiaries, and have to bequeath it in an improved state to succeeding generations.'[67]

A society of freedom, in other words, is one in which the world-building projects of humans obey not an external logic, but an immanent one – a society in which human practical activity is 'self-mediating' – and history, as Hegel puts it in this *Phenomenology*, becomes a 'conscious self-mediating process'. And this can only mean one in which nature loses its external character as obstacle or barrier, and is recognized and regulated as our 'inorganic body',[68] whose finite, determinate characteristics are not to be negated abstractly but rather integrated actively into the 'absolute movement of becoming' that signifies true infinity and genuine freedom.[69]

Notes and References

1. The literature on Marx and justice is so extensive that no attempt will be made here to catalogue it. For some of the most important contributions see Cohen, M., Nagel, T. and Scanlon, T. (eds), *Marx, Justice and History* (Princeton, NJ: Princeton University Press, 1980); Nielsen, K. and Patton, S. C. (eds), *Marx and Morality* (supplementary volume of *Canadian Journal of Philosophy*, 1981); Cohen, G. A., 'Freedom, Justice and Capitalism', *New Left Review*, vol. 126, March/April, pp. 3–16 (1981); Elster, Jon, *Making Sense of Marx* (Cambridge University Press, 1985); Lukes, Steven, *Marxism and Morality* (Oxford University Press, 1985); Geras, Norman, 'The Controversy about Marx and Justice', in N. Geras, *Literature of Revolution: Essays on Marxism* (London: Verso, 1986). Among those works that actually address Marx's concept of freedom, Dunayevskaya, Raya, *Marxism and Freedom*, 3rd edn (London: Pluto Press, 1971) barely touches the philosophical issues raised in this chapter; Brenkert, George G., *Marx's Ethics of Freedom* (London: Routledge & K. Paul 1983) is more a discussion of Marx's ethics than of his concept of freedom, and Brien, Kevin M., *Marx, Reason and the Art of Freedom* (Philadelphia, Pa: Temple University Press, 1987) almost totally fails to approach this issue through Marx's relationship to Hegel. Gould, Carol, *Marx's Social Ontology* (Cambridge, Massc: MIT Press, 1978), does open up some of the key issues involved.

2. For example, see Franco, Paul, *Hegel's Philosophy of Freedom* (New Haven, CT: Yale University Press, 1999).
3. Marx, Karl, *Early Writings*, trans. R. Livingstone and G. Benton (Harmondsworth: Penguin, 1992).
4. Two important exceptions to this neglect of the false infinity of capital are Arthur, C. J., 'A Compulsive-Neurotic Subject' in Hampsher-Monk, I., and Stayner, J., (eds), PSA Conference, Glasgrow, *Studies in Marxism*, vol. 6, 1998, *Contemporary Political Studies*, vol. 2, (1996); and Browning, Gary K., *Hegel and the History of Political Philosophy* (New York: St. Martin's Press, 1999), ch. 7. I would like to thank Chris Arthur for providing me with a more recent (and thus far unpublished) version of his paper.
5. Marx, *Early Writings*, p. 386.
6. Hegel, G. W. F., *Philosophy of Right*, trans. Knox, T. M. (Oxford: Clarendon Press, 1954), pp 22, 21, 23.
7. Hegel, *Philosophy of Right*, p. 24.
8. Hegel, *Philosophy of Right*, p. 30.
9. McNally, David, *Bodies of Meaning: Studies on Language, Labour and Liberation* (Albany, NY: State University of New York Press, 2001), ch. 2.
10. Hegel, G. W. F., *Science of Logic*, trans. A. V. Miller (Atlantic Highlands, NJ: Humanities Press International, 1969), pp. 139–40, 144.
11. Hegel, *Science of Logic*, p. 142.
12. Ibid., p. 232.
13. Hegel, *Science of Logic*, p. 147.
14. Hegel, *Philosophy of Right*, pp. 24, 228.
15. Hegel, G. W. F., *Phenomenology of Spirit*, trans. A. V. Miller (Oxford: Oxford University Press, 1977), p. 492.
16. Marx, K., *Capital*, vol. I, trans. B. Fowkes (Harmondsworth: Penguin, 1976), p. 251.
17. Marx, *Capital*, vol. I, p. 253.
18. Aristotle, *The Politics*, trans. T. A. Sinclair (Harmondsworth: Penguin, 1962), 1257 b10–b40.
19. Marx, *Capital*, vol. I, pp. 252, 254.
20. Marx, *Capital*, p. 231.
21. Marx, K., *Grundrisse*, trans. M. Nicolaus (Harmondsworth: Penguin, 1973), p. 271.
22. Marx, K., *Grundrisse*, p. 270. A more extended and highly illuminating discussion of this question is provided by C. Arthur, 'The Infinity of Capital'.
23. Marx, *Grundrisse*, p. 334.
24. Marx, *Grundrisse*, p. 334.
25. Sekine, T., *An Outline of the Dialectic of Capital*, vol. 1 (London: Macmillan, 1997), p. 9.
26. Rader, M., *Marx's Interpretation of History* (New York: Oxford University Press, 1979), p. 150.
27. Marx, *Grundrisse*, p. 267.
28. Lebowitz, M., *Beyond Capital: Marx's Political Economy of the Working Class* (New York: St. Martin's Press, 1992).
29. Marx, *Capital*, vol. I, p. 526.
30. Marx, K., *Theories of Surplus Value*, Pt. 2 (Moscow: Progress Publishers, 1968), p. 495.
31. Marx, K., *Capital*, vol. III, trans. D. Fernbach (Harmondsworth: Penguin, 1981), pp. 357–8.

32. See Harvey, D., *The Limits to Capital* (Chicago, Ill.: University of Chicago Press, 1982); and Weeks, J., *Capital and Exploitation* (Princeton, NJ: Princeton University Press, 1981).
33. Marx, *Capital*, vol. I, p. 732.
34. Marx, *Capital*, vol. II, p. 572.
35. Marx, *Capital*, vol. III, pp. 516, 517.
36. McNally, D., 'Marxism in the Age of Information', *New Politics*, vol. 6, Winter (1998), pp. 99–106; and McNally, *Bodies of Meaning*, ch. 2.
37. Marx, K., *Capital*, vol. III, p. 572.
38. Marx, K., *Capital*, vol. III, p. 621.
39. Marx, *Capital*, vol. I, p. 638.
40. Marx, *Capital*, vol. III, p. 955 [italics in original]. This raises some thorny issues related to the Marxian theory of rent, which are outside the bounds of this chapter.
41. Marx, K. *Critique of the Gotha Programme* (New York: International Publishers, 1966), p. 3.
42. Foster, J. B., *Marx's Ecology* (New York: Monthly Review Press, 2000), makes some quite important arguments in this regard, albeit on a basis that is lacking some of the key philosophical ingredients derived from Marx's critique of Hegel.
43. See Arthur, C., 'From the Critique of Hegel to the Critique of Capital' in T. Burns and I. Fraser (eds), *The Hegel–Marx Connection* (New York: St Martin's Press, 2000); and Murray, P., *Marx's Theory of Scientific Knowledge* (Atlantic Highlands, NJ: Humanities Press, 1988), pp. 213–30.
44. Marx, *Early Writings*, p. 174.
45. Marx, *Capital*, vol. III, p. 745, n. 27.
46. Marx, *Capital*, vol. III, p. 216.
47. Foster, *Marx's Ecology*, pp. 163–6.
48. Marx, *Capital*, vol. I, p. 637.
49. Marx, *Capital*, vol. I, pp. 283–4.
50. Marx, *Grundrisse*, p. 611.
51. Marx, *Early Writings*, p. 386.
52. Marx, K. and Engels, F., *The German Ideology*, trans. R. Pascal (New York: International Publishers, 1963), p. 74.
53. Marx, *Early Writings*, p. 385.
54. Postone, M., *Time, Labor and Social Domination: A Reinterpretation of Marx's Critical Theory* (Cambridge: Cambridge University Press, 1996), pp. 172, 183, 237.
55. McNally, D., 'The Dual Form of Labour in Capitalist Society and the Struggle over Meaning: Comments on Postone', *Historical Materialism*, forthcoming.
56. Marx, *Early Writings*, pp. 151–2.
57. Hegel, G. W. F., *The Logic of Hegel: From the Encyclopedia of the Philosophical Sciences*, 2nd edn, trans. W. Wallace (London: Oxford University Press, 1892), p. 112.
58. This is the same formal structure that the early Lukács identified as at the heart of the novel: the impossible quest for individual meaning in a world of reification, see Lukács, G., *Theory of the Novel*, trans. A. Bostock (London: Merlin, 1971).
59. Marx, *Grundrisse*, p. 157.
60. Marx, *Capital*, vol. I, p. 199.
61. Marx, *Grundrisse*, pp. 705, 706.
62. Marx, *Grundrisse*, p. 832.

63. Marx, K., *The Revolutions of 1848* (Harmondsworth: Penguin, 1973), p. 87.
64. Hegel, *Philosophy of Right*, pp 27, 260, 267.
65. See McNally, D., *Against the Market: Political Economy, Market Socialism and the Marxist Critique* (London: Verso, 1993); and Ollman, B., 'Market Mystification in Capitalist and Market Socialist Societies', in B. Ollman (ed.), *Market Socialism: The Debate Among Socialists* (New York: Routledge, 1998).
66. Marx, *Grundrisse*, pp. 487, 488.
67. Marx, *Capital*, vol. III, p. 911.
68. Marx, *Grundrisse*, pp. 488, 490.
69. This recognition of the finite integrity of nature, in other words, is a moment of self-recognition. Overcoming the false infinity of capital means, among other things, transcending the dangerously one-sided and idealist notion of Spirit as super-natural by reintegrating it with our finite, natural, embodied character as historical bodies. See McNally, *Bodies of Meaning*, pp. 7–9.

2

Systematic and Historical Dialectics: Towards a Marxian Theory of Globalization

Tony Smith

In the Marxian theory of capital, the term 'dialectics' refers primarily to three endeavours: the systematic reconstruction of the essential determinations of capital (systematic dialectics); the reconstruction of the main lines of capitalist development (a species of historical dialectics); and the dialectics of theory and practice.[1] In the first section of this Chapter I shall discuss some essential features of systematic dialectics in *Capital*, and explore how they are related to historical developments in capitalism. I shall then attempt to show the relevance of systematic dialectics to the comprehension of the historical dialectic of our present era, the so-called 'age of globalization'. This will require extending the systematic dialectic past the point where Marx left off in *Capital*. The chapter concludes with a brief remark on the relevance of the expanded systematic account of capital to the question of praxis today.

Systematic dialectics in *Capital*: tendencies, trends and a meta-tendency

The categories derived in the course of the systematic progression in *Capital* define the essential social forms that make capitalism distinct from other modes of production. These categories are thus historically specific. But the theoretical ordering of these categories is *not* historical. Early categories need not have appeared earlier in history; while later ones need not map more recent developments.[2]

What, then, determines the systematic order? The starting point is a given totality, the capitalist mode of production. Each categorial level is an attempt to comprehend this totality, beginning with the simplest and most abstract manner of categorizing it. Early stages in the dialectical ordering necessarily fail to define this whole. This provides a theoretical warrant for moving to another categorial level, defined by a more complex and concrete way of comprehending the same totality. The methodology of systematic dialectical social theories thus involves both a 'push' and a 'pull' movement. The shortcomings of a particular categorial level – that is, the inability on that level of abstraction to account adequately for the self-reproduction of the given totality – 'push' the theory forward to the next stage. The theoretical imperative not to conclude the systematic ordering until the given totality has been comprehended fully in thought 'pulls' the theory to its end point.[3]

The simplest and most abstract manner of depicting capitalism as a totality is as a society of generalized commodity exchange. Within the commodity form, labour is undertaken privately and must subsequently prove its social necessity through the successful sale of produced commodities. Under the commodity form, any particular concrete act of labour may prove to be socially wasted; only socially necessary labour produces a commodity with 'value'. And so the socially necessary labour that produces value is conceptually distinct from concrete exertions in time, and may thus be termed 'abstract labour'. Neither abstract labour, nor the value produced by it, can be measured with a stopwatch or any other concrete form of measurement. And yet a socially objective measure of value is a necessary precondition for generalized commodity exchange. Money, a 'real abstraction', is this socially objective measure of value. In this manner, Marx establishes the systematic necessity linking the commodity form and the money form.[4]

Once money has been introduced explicitly, any attempt to comprehend generalized commodity production as a system designed to meet human needs must be abandoned. The valorization imperative – money must beget money! – is the dominant principle of this system, and the satisfaction of human needs occurs only in so far as it is compatible with this dictate. In other words, the next most concrete and complex manner of comprehending the capitalist mode of production is as a system in which the sum total of money accumulated at the conclusion of a given period exceeds that invested at the beginning of that period. There is thus a systematic necessity connecting the money form and the capital form, M-C-M'. 'Value' now takes on the form of an objective social power, standing above and beyond individual commodities and society as a whole, subjecting every nook and cranny of the social world to its rule.

Any adequate theory of capital must explain the mystery of capital. How exactly does money, an inert thing, beget money? Marx begins his answer by noting explicitly what had previously been merely implicit: in a society of generalized commodity exchange, labour power is itself a commodity. Marx assumes that wages are sufficient to purchase the commodities required for the reproduction of wage labourers. Once labour-power has been purchased, however, wage labourers are forced to produce an amount of economic value exceeding what they receive back in the form of wages. The capital form is explained by surplus labour, a surplus labour that takes on the historically specific form of surplus value. Capital, as Marx vehemently insists, is not a thing, but a social relationship, the social relation of exploitation. The generalized circulation of commodities, and the alien power of the value form, are both reproduced systematically on the level of total social capital through the class exploitation of wage labour by capital.[5]

Volume II of *Capital* explores the way in which this thesis remains in force after we have introduced various forms of circulation necessary for the systematic reproduction of the capital form. And *Capital* Volume III explores how this thesis continues to hold after the introduction of various systematically necessary forms of intra-capital competition (competition between sectors of industrial capital with different turnover times and compositions of capital; competition within sectors of industrial capital between firms with different levels of productivity; and competition over the distribution of surplus value between industrial capital, on the one side, and merchant capital, financial capital, and landlords, on the other). These determinations enable us to comprehend capital in ever more concrete and complex ways. But they do not establish an independent source of surplus value apart from wage labour. They instead explain how surplus value produced in a given period by wage labourers is redistributed through the various circuits in a manner allowing the systematic reproduction of the capitalist mode of production.

As has already been noted, the categories in this systematic progression refer to historically specific social forms. Systematic and historical considerations are related in *Capital* in another way as well: Marxian systematic theory is *revisable*. Historical developments in capitalism may reveal that something previously taken as necessary to the logic of capital does not in fact have this status. And historical developments may lead us to discover systematic necessity in areas previously overlooked. At this point, however, the gap between the systematic logic of capital and historical developments in capitalism appears to be immense. Marx's systematic dialectic consists of a progression of social forms defining the 'inner nature' of capital, that is, social forms in place in any given period of capitalism. In themselves, these social forms tell us what capital is, but not what it might become.

Capital, however, provides not just a theory of social forms, but also a theory of the necessary structural tendencies inherent in these forms. These tendencies underlie the transition from any given period in the history of capital to the next. In *Capital*, Volume I, for example, the social form defined by the capital/wage labour relationship is the main theme. On this level, Marx derives a tendency for technological and organizational innovations at the point of production that increase the rate of surplus value. In Volume II, Marx shows that the drive to introduce innovations reducing circulation time is no less inherent in the capital form than the drive to introduce innovations in the production process proper. A systematic tendency towards innovations reducing constant capital costs is derived at the beginning of Volume III. And one of the most important implications of the later parts of this third volume is that the drive for innovation in the commercial, financial and agricultural sectors is no less intense than in the industrial sector.[6]

These sorts of tendencies are in place always and everywhere that the capital form is in place. On the other hand, these tendencies refer to historical processes extending over time. They further our comprehension not just of what capital is, but also of what it necessarily tends to become. In this manner they provide a bridge between systematic dialectics and historical dialectics. But they hardly remove the gulf between the two. There is no a priori principle dictating how the various tendencies derived on different levels of the systematic ordering relate to each other in concrete historical circumstances. In other words, there is no way to argue from the various *tendencies* that are necessarily given with the social forms defining capital to the dominant *trends* in place in any particular historical context.[7]

In specific cases, one set of tendencies may modify another, while itself operating in a relatively straightforward fashion. In other cases, matters may be reversed. In yet different cases each set of tendencies may modify the workings of the others to a considerable extent, or one set of tendencies may even put another out of play completely in certain circumstances, while at other times and places it is itself put out of play. Further, we cannot assume that the tendencies arising in early stages in the systematic dialectic necessarily have more weight in a given historical conjuncture than those derived in subsequent levels, nor can we assume that the reverse holds.[8] For all the systematic necessity of the various tendencies, there is thus an ineluctable element of contingency, path dependency and human agency in the determination of the dominant trends of any concrete historical context. This gulf between (systematic) tendencies and (historical) trends cannot in principle ever be completely bridged.

Nonetheless, it is possible to narrow the gap between the systematic and the historical dimensions of Marx's theory of capital somewhat further. Besides the tendencies derived with systematic necessity from the social forms defining capital, it is sometimes possible to derive a 'meta-tendency' with a comparable claim to systematic necessity, that is, an overarching tendency conjoining two first-order tendencies. The classic example of such a meta-tendency is found in the discussion of the rate of profit in *Capital* Volume III, where tendencies for the rate of profit to fall are derived with systematic necessity from the social forms defining capitalism alongside counter-tendencies pointing in the opposite direction with no less force. In any given concrete set of circumstances either set of tendencies may modify, dominate or be dominated by the other in countless contingent ways. It does not follow from this, however, that Marx's systematic theory has nothing further to offer to the comprehension of historical developments regarding profit rates. A 'meta-tendency' uniting the two sets of tendencies can also be derived with systematic necessity: the joint operation of the tendencies and counter-tendencies itself tends to form a cyclical pattern.

Suppose the set of tendencies leading to a falling rate of profit comes to dominate in a specific period or region for some set of contingent reasons. Once it is in place, it is necessarily the case that at some point the other set of (counter-) tendencies will tend to become of increasing importance. The inverse pattern holds as well; historical periods in which tendencies to higher rates of profit dominate tend to alternate with epochs in which the tendencies to a falling rate of profit come to the fore. All things considered, the longer the set of tendencies to a falling (rising) rate of profit form the dominant trend, the greater the probability that the set of tendencies leading to a rising (falling) rate of profit will come to dominate.

It is surely not the case that the simultaneous operation of any two sets of tendencies always generates a 'meta-tendency' of this sort. But a generalization can be proposed: whenever two sets of tendencies with equal claims to systematic necessity are derived such that the continued dominance of one set necessarily tends to increase the probability of a shift to the dominance of the other set, a pattern of alternation necessarily tends to emerge. *This meta-tendency, derived within the systematic dialectic of capital, provides a general heuristic framework for comprehending the historical dialectic of capital.*

Once again, not all sets of tendencies derived with systematic necessity from the capital form have a set of counter-tendencies opposing them in this manner. For our purposes, the most important ones lacking 'symmetrical' counter-tendencies are those underlying the ever-increasing scale of capital accumulation, the tendencies to the concentration and centralization of capital. These determinations account for the strong element of linearity superimposed on the alternating patterns of capitalist development. The return to the beginning part of a cycle never brings us precisely back to the point of departure. Each new commencement of a profit cycle tends to begin at a higher point of accumulation than the previous one.[9]

In section 3 I shall attempt to apply these methodological considerations to the globalization debate. First, however, a brief statement of the relevant portion of this debate must be provided.

The globalization debate

Are contemporary processes of globalization transforming fundamentally the relationship between states and global markets? On one pole of the debate are those who believe that globalization expands the exit options available to financial and industrial capital greatly, and thus places states in an 'electronic straitjacket'.[10] International flows of finance capital in currency markets, bond markets and equity markets tend to shift away from countries that maintain high levels of government deficit spending or steep corporate and income taxes. Globalization also heightens significantly the ability of industrial capital to engage in capital flight, through either foreign direct investment or subcontracting arrangements.

The presence of such exit options does not in itself logically rule out any particular state policy. But defenders of what we may term 'the hyper-globalization thesis' assert that these options necessarily tend to make many forms of state activity much less feasible. In an age of global capital flows it becomes less and less feasible for the state to engage in deficit financing in order to stimulate demand and secure full employment, or to use taxes to lessen inequality significantly and maintain traditional welfare state protections. Neoliberals argue, in effect, that the historical dialectic of capitalism has entered a new stage, characterized by a qualitative shift of power from states to global markets. They applaud these developments on the grounds that they remove distortions brought about by state economic intervention.[11]

At the other end of the spectrum we find those who deny that globalization has essentially eroded state capacities. These theorists insist that the most significant fact about globalization is that it has been, and will continue to be, a state project, pursued by central banks, departments of the treasury, and other sections of the state apparatus. These state agencies, representing the interests of finance capital and multinational producers and distributors, have shifted the balance of power between capital and wage labour through deregulation, privatization and the liberalization of markets. The concept of 'globalization' has been an important ideological weapon in this political project, deployed to persuade the public that technological and economic developments eliminate alternatives to neoliberalism. But the term does *not* describe accurately some new stage in capitalist development in which the state is all but powerless in the face of global markets. 'Globalization' is, in brief, 'globaloney'. If the political will were present to pursue an alternative progressive agenda of full employment and lesser inequality, this agenda could be effectively implemented.

An adequate Marxian perspective on the historical dialectic of globalization must be informed by Marx's systematic theory. The globalization debate, however, involves determinations not developed in *Capital*. At one point, at least, Marx planned to conclude the systematic dialectic of capital with volumes on the state, foreign trade and the world market.[12] He later abandoned this idea, and it would be ludicrous to attempt to complete the project here. Nonetheless, some central themes of a Marxian account of these social forms must be introduced as we proceed.

Towards a Marxian perspective on globalization

I argued above that three crucial notions connect a systematic ordering of social forms with historical dialectics: (i) the derivation of the tendencies necessarily given with these social forms; (ii) the meta-tendency of alternation; and (iii) the tendency for this alternation to be played out on an ever-increasing scale of accumulation. The remainder of this chapter will be devoted to an application of these three notions to the dialectics of globalization.

(1) The simultaneous operation of tendencies

One of the biggest advantages of systematic dialectics is that it provides a methodology able to accommodate one-sided and apparently inconsistent perspectives, each of which possesses an element of the whole story. The mere fact that Marx insisted that further volumes devoted to the state, foreign exchange and the world market were necessary to complete his systematic project implies a very important claim: there is *both* a necessary tendency for capital to operate within a territory administered by a state *and* a necessary tendency for trade, foreign direct investment and flows of finance capital to extend beyond territorial limits. Both sets of tendencies are in place always and everywhere that the capital form is in place. This implies a rejection of extreme formulations of both the 'hyperglobalization' thesis and the 'globaloney' thesis.

In the global economy, the state is at one and the same time increasingly significant and increasingly insignificant. It is increasingly significant in that the tasks of the state whose necessity can be derived in a systematic dialectic are, if anything, more pressing in the age of globalization. It is increasingly insignificant in that the law of value, operating on the systematic level of the world market, now operates with ever more force *vis-à-vis* the states and national economies subsumed under this law. Any adequate historical account must grant equal force to both dynamics. Both points are worth developing further.

A Marxian theory of the state must explore the role of the state in furthering capital accumulation. This role includes: (i) enforcement of property rights; (ii) regulation of money; (iii) crisis management; (iv) provision of infrastructure, R&D, training, and other 'public goods'; and (v) maintenance of access to necessary raw materials, markets and so on. Globalization hardly erodes these essential state functions.

Enforcement of property rights

All the main forms of economic globalization – foreign direct investment (FDI), international trade, and flows of financial capital – require the enforcement of property rights. This remains the responsibility of states. FDI will occur only if states extend the same sorts of protections guaranteed under their system of jurisprudence to the holders of foreign investments. Regarding trade, in a world of rapid technological innovation the scope of intellectual property rights acknowledged and enforced by states becomes a matter of increasing importance. In the realm of finance capital, the state retains the capacity of decreeing which contracts are enforceable and which are not, a power that can affect which financial transactions occur in the global economy, and which do not.[13] The globalization of economic activity, and the specific paths taken in the course of globalization, are thus to a considerable extent a function of the power of states to define and enforce rights to property and exchange.

Regulation of money

Money has always been the Achilles heel of the neoliberal dream of a self-sufficient free market.[14] The reproduction of capitalist markets requires state activity regarding money. On the level of the global economy the same point holds. Even neoliberals hold that the satisfactory reproduction of the global economy over time requires appropriate monetary decisions by states, especially their central banks.

Crisis management

Of course, defining what counts as an 'appropriate' monetary decision in a given context is a matter of great dispute. What is hardly in dispute, however, is that when crises break out in the global economy, governments must assume special responsibility to 'restore investor confidence'. In the continued absence of an international monetary agency with the power to create credit money, the responsibility for increasing liquidity in the global economy rests ultimately with national governments. Some states, at least, also retain a capacity to intervene to prevent losses to particular players from threatening global markets as a whole, as Alan Greenspan's organization of the bailout of Long Term Capital Management suggests. Further, investors continue to call on the state to 'socialize' the costs of global downswings by displacing them on to working men and women, the unemployed, the elderly and so on. One mechanism for socializing these costs is through the state taking over private debts, as both the Japanese and Korean states have recently done.

Provision of infrastructure

The extent to which particular regions enjoy success in the global economy today is to a considerable extent a function of their governments. Governments help to create the conditions for regional success through support for education and training, funding for infrastructure and research, the formation of formal and informal networks of elites, government/business partnerships for specific projects of importance to regional growth and so on.[15]

Maintenance of access to raw materials and markets

In the global economy access to foreign supplies of needed raw materials, foreign labour power and technologies, foreign markets for exported goods and services, foreign sources of capital and so on, regularly requires state negotiation. Continued access may also regularly require military intervention by the state, or at least an effective threat of military action.[16] Here too there is not the least sign that the globalization of economic activity is leading to the historical obsolescence of the state.

If the state were as irrelevant as many neoliberals suggest, we would expect those who own and control capital to become increasingly indifferent to its workings. But nothing of the sort is occurring. The extent to which holders of economic power employ legal, quasi-legal, and outright illegal methods to influence state policy is, if anything, increasing. The conclusion appears clear. Certain types of state activity, and even certain types of state, may be disadvantaged in the epoch of globalization, but the systematic necessity of the state form is not put out of play in the present historical period.

But neither does the present stage of history undermine the claim that the law of value necessarily operates in the world market over and above individual states. This is, I believe, the culminating claim of a Marxian systematic dialectic of social forms. To my knowledge, the clearest account of why Marx placed the categories 'foreign trade' and 'the world market' at the culmination of his theory is found in the following passage:

> If surplus labour or surplus-value were represented only in the national surplus product, then the increase of value for the sake of value and therefore the extraction of surplus labour would be restricted by the limited, narrow circle of use-values in which the value of the [national] labour would be represented. But it is foreign trade which develops its [the surplus product's] real nature as value by developing the labour embodied in it as social labour which manifests itself in an unlimited range of different use-values, and this in fact gives meaning to abstract wealth ... [I]t is only foreign trade, the development of the market to a world market, which causes money to develop into world money and *abstract labour* into social labour. Abstract wealth, value, money, hence *abstract labour*, develop in the measure that concrete labour becomes a totality of different modes of labour embracing the world market. Capitalist production rests on the *value* or the transformation of the labour embodied in the product into social labour. But this is only [possible] on the basis of foreign trade and of the world market. This is at once the pre-condition and the result of capitalist production.[17]

With foreign trade and the world market, the initial determinations of Marx's systematic ordering ('abstract wealth, value, money, hence *abstract labour*') are finally grounded adequately. The circle completes itself, the presuppositions are posited, the initially implicit becomes fully explicit. The final necessary conditions of the possibility of the systematic reproduction of capital as a totality are derived.

This implies that there is a necessary structural tendency for circuits of capital to extend beyond any given geographical restriction. The above passage speaks mainly of cross-border trade in commodities. But other tendencies can be derived as well. In Volume I of *Capital*, Marx discussed tendencies for the concentration and centralization of capital. This implies a tendency for units of capital to expand to the point where their geographical range of operation exceeds any given territorial limit set by the state form. Cross-border trade is only one example of transcending this limit. Foreign direct investment, cross-border mergers and acquisitions, and the establishment of cross-border production chains are other tendencies of industrial capital necessarily given with the social form, 'world market'. Similarly, flows of finance capital necessarily tend to exceed the territorial limits set by the state form, whether these flows occur within the circuits of currency markets, equity markets, or bond markets.[18]

The elements of systematic necessity associated with the social forms of the state and the world market thus remain in place in the present historical stage of capitalism. This is surely relevant to our assessment of the historical dialectic of globalization. Capital requires the state, and so there is a good reason to reject theories neglecting the continuing importance of the state form. It is also the case, however, that the world market necessarily tends to subsume particular states under it. And so there is a good systematic reason to reject perspectives ignoring how state capacities are restricted or eroded by the world market in the course of capitalist development. There is both a systematic tendency for the state to assert itself over the market, and a systematic tendency for the world market to assert itself over the state. Both tendencies are given simultaneously always and everywhere that the capital form is in place. The 'hyperglobalizers', who speak of the fundamental erosion of state capacities, and those who affirm the unchecked power of the state, equally defend one-sided, and hence mistaken, viewpoints.

Unfortunately, this line of thought does not get us all that far. Most neoliberals grant the systematic necessity of the state form; very few speak of 'the death of the state'. They hold, nonetheless that in the present historical context global markets are eroding state power in a fundamental and irreversible fashion. Similarly, most defenders of the 'globaloney' thesis grant the systematic necessity of the world market, while insisting that progressive policies at the level of the state can still be implemented effectively in the contemporary era. Most adherents of each perspective, in other words, fully acknowledge the tendencies emphasized by the other, while insisting that today they are (or can be) trumped by the set of tendencies they themselves emphasize.

Systematic dialectics cannot rule out either of these historical possibilities. There are many ways in which different sets of tendencies may operate simultaneously, and it is surely possible that, in a given historical context, one set of tendencies trumps another. At this point it may appear that systematic dialectic has nothing more to contribute to debates regarding the historical dialectic of globalization. Its resources, however, are not yet exhausted.

The meta-tendency of alternation

In Marx's discussion of rates of profit, he did not merely point out that there are two sets of tendencies pointing in opposite directions, each with an equally valid claim to systematic necessity. He also went on to derive the systematic necessity for a meta-tendency, a cyclical pattern in which periods dominated by tendencies to a falling rate of profit tend to alternate with periods in which counter-tendencies hold sway. In this manner he derived a framework for comprehending the historical dialectic of capital from systematic considerations. Might a similar move be made regarding the state and the world market?

Whenever two sets of tendencies with equal claims to systematic necessity are derived such that the continued dominance of one set necessarily tends to increase the probability of a shift to the dominance of the other, a pattern of alternation necessarily tends to emerge. This appears to be the case here. On the one hand, the more effective the state is at fulfilling the functions necessary to capital accumulation, the more units of capital will tend to grow, and the more they grow, the more they tend to participate in circuits of cross-border capital flows. The extension and intensification of flows in global circuits of capital eventually undermine the very state projects whose success led to that extension and intensification. Any particular set of state capacities is thus inevitably restricted in scope, fragile in nature and reversible in practice, however successful it might be in a given era. On the other hand, the more the tendencies built into the social form of the world market hold sway, the more social disruptions are imposed on national economies, including disruptions in the capital accumulation process. Past a certain point, these disruptions necessarily tend to generate a search for state policies that effectively lessen them, thereby establishing the preconditions for further capital accumulation.

There is thus a close parallel here to the relationship between the tendencies and counter-tendencies of profit rates. Here too the necessary result of the domination of a given set of tendencies in a particular context is to increase the odds of a shift to a state of affairs in which the opposing set of tendencies comes to dominate. If this line of thought is accepted, then we can once again derive a general heuristic framework for the study of the dialectics of capitalist development from the systematic dialectic of social forms: periods in which the state asserts its sovereignty in relatively effective ways tend to alternate regularly with periods in which state sovereignty is more effectively subordinated to the imperatives of the world market.

Far more argumentation would be needed to derive the systematic necessity of this meta-tendency satisfactorily. That, alas, must wait for another day. Here I shall simply mention some possible illustrations of this working hypothesis in the hope of making it somewhat more plausible.

Giovanni Arrighi's masterful study of the rise and decline of hegemonic powers in the world economy over the course of capitalist history provides a first example.[19] While each case involves numerous historically specific and contingent matters, a general pattern can nevertheless be perceived. The rapid economic expansion of an incipient hegemonic power tends to begin with expenditures far exceeding what could be justified in narrow calculations of profit and loss. State prestige and military strategy ('territorial logic') provide a spur to investment in infrastructure, research and development, and so on, far beyond what could be justified in terms of a narrow 'capital logic'. Hegemonic regions in the history of capitalism thus win and retain their hegemonic status through the effective exercise of state capacities. The decline of these powers reveals a common pattern as well. When profit opportunities in the given regions eventually begin to decline, capital increasingly flows elsewhere in search of surplus profits, undermining the hegemonic position of the state.[20]

The same general pattern can be used as a framework for interpreting key threads of development in the twentieth century. At the beginning of the century, the tendencies associated with the world market dominated empirical trends. By some measures, 'globalization' even reached levels surpassing those applying at the time of writing.[21] This period concluded with the financial crises and depression of the 1920s and 1930s. A long period then commenced in which the tendencies associated with the assertion of state sovereignty dominated empirical trends, beginning with state-engineered competitive devaluations, protectionism and rearmament. Out of the rubble of world war, the Keynesian state emerged in the industrialized West, with its social programmes, regulated currencies and closed capital accounts. The emergence of 'the developmental state' in Japan (and later the 'four tigers' and 'four dragons'of East Asia) paralleled this development.[22] But the very success of the Keynesian states of the West and the developmental states of Asia contained the seeds of their demise. Both state forms successfully nurtured multinational industrial and financial corporations that became increasingly effective at evading state regulation. In Marxian terms, both nurtured units of capital that extended their participation in global circuits of industrial and financial capital in the hope of appropriating surplus value produced beyond national borders. Leading firms in both the industrial and financial sectors increasingly pressured states to agree to greater and greater levels of 'freedom' for capital. The last decades of the twentieth century can thus be interpreted as a return to a period in which the tendencies associated with the world market dominate historical trends. And, once again, the dominance of global markets has led to severe and recurrent financial crises. In the near future the severity and regularity of these crises may generate another historical reversal and renewed assertions of state sovereignty. Of course, there are no guarantees this will occur; history remains a domain of contingency, path dependency and social agency. But state responses to financial crises in Asia suggest that there is a strong tendency in this direction.[23] The same sorts of responses can be expected if (when) financial crises of comparable magnitude break out in the USA or Europe.

A similar pattern of alternation appears to hold in poorer regions of the global economy as well. Many regions of the so-called South began the twentieth century subordinate to economic imperatives imposed by colonizing states. Decolonization involved assertions of state independence and a commitment to state-led industrialization. This industrialization, however, tended to rely on extensive borrowing from industrialized countries in order to purchase expensive capital inputs (as well as to fund the luxury consumption and foreign accounts of local elites). Eventually these debts forced structural adjustment programmes on these countries, which furthered the integration of their economies into the world market at the cost of considerable erosion of state capacities. Even neoliberal academics and policy-makers now concede that this erosion of state capacities has gone too far, and that more effective state institutions must somehow be forged.[24]

State and world market; world market and state. The historical dialectic of capital is a spirit-numbing con game in which nationalists and globalists take turns promising a humane and just form of capitalism, and waiting for the promises of the other to prove illusory – as they invariably do.

In the capitalist mode of production it is necessarily the case that any meta-tendency of alternation tends to be played out over a linear process of ever-increasing accumulation. The discussion thus far of the historical dialectic of globalization has abstracted from this. How might it be incorporated?

The significance of increasing scale

How is the historical dynamic of globalization played out on an ever-increasing scale of capital accumulation? A systematically informed Marxian account of this dynamic must be based on tendencies whose systematic necessity can be derived on the level of the world market. These include the tendencies to uneven development, overaccumulation crises and financial crises.

Marxian theorists agree widely that there are mechanisms in the world market that necessarily tend to enable capitals at the 'centre' of the global system to reproduce and expand their advantages over regions at the 'periphery'. A quick summary of some of the mechanisms underlying uneven development must suffice here.[25] Investment funds by definition are found disproportionately in wealthy regions of the global economy. These funds tend to flow predominantly to regions with extensive consumer markets, high levels of labour and management skills, adequate infrastructure, access to state-of-the-art research and development, and so on. This implies that capital investment generally tends to flow from wealthy regions to other wealthy regions, where all these factors are generally present to the greatest extent. As a result, the 20 per cent of the world's population located in the wealthy countries of the North consumes 86 per cent of global output.[26]

The funding of research and development (R&D) is of special importance. Successful process and product innovations allow the appropriation of surplus profits.[27] Units of capital with access to advanced R&D thus tend to win surplus profits in the course of exchange. This establishes the possibility of a virtuous circle; surplus profits can be ploughed back into further R&D, providing the preconditions for future surplus profits. For units of capital without access to advanced R&D, however, the circle is vicious. Lower levels of profits tend to lead to lower levels of R&D, severely limiting opportunities to appropriate surplus profits in the future. The virtuous circle tends to be found in wealthy regions of the global economy, while the vicious circle pervades poorer regions.[28] In this manner, the drive to appropriate surplus profits through technological innovation, the most fundamental feature of intercapital competition, systematically reproduces uneven development in the global economy over time.[29]

Many other determinations of the world market reinforce the tendency to uneven development, including the remission of profits resulting from foreign direct investment in poorer regions, capital flight undertaken by local elites desiring to escape currency risks and/or protect the fruits of corruption, the ability of units of capital in wealthy regions to play off subcontractors in poorer regions against each other, the ability of firms to manipulate the 'prices' of commodities 'exchanged' in intra-firm transactions, the tendency for poorer regions to fall into 'the debt trap', and so on. Rather than explore these themes here, however, I shall simply note that as the scale of concentration and centralization of capital has proceeded, the scale of uneven development has worsened, as the following ratios of per capita income in the richest and the poorest regions of the global economy reveal:

> 1820: 3 to 1
> 1913: 9 to 1
> 1950: 11 to 1
> 1973: 12 to 1
> 1992: 16 to 1.[30]

A systematic tendency for overaccumulation crises in the world market can also be derived from the drive to appropriate surplus profits through innovation. The logic of inter-capital competition tends to lead necessarily to the introduction of new, more productive plants into an industry, since these new entrants are in a position to win surplus profits. But established plants do not withdraw automatically when this occurs.[31] Given that their fixed capital costs are already 'sunk', their owners and managers may be happy receiving the average rate of profit on their circulating capital. They also may have relationships with suppliers and customers that are impossible (or prohibitively expensive) to duplicate elsewhere in any relevant time-frame. Or their management and labour force may have industry-specific skills. Or they may have access to state subsidies for training, infrastructure or R&D that they would not be able to obtain in other sectors. Their failure to withdraw results in a tendency to an overaccumulation of capital, manifested in excess capacity and declining rates of profit. In more traditional Marxist terms, insufficient surplus value is produced to valorize the investments that have been made in fixed capital, leading to a fall in profit rates for an extended historical period.[32] Marx himself discussed this tendency on the relatively abstract theoretical level attained at the beginning of *Capital* Volume III. But it holds on the concrete level of the world market as well. Robert Brenner has provided considered empirical evidence that the lower rates of profit and growth that afflicted the world economy beginning in the late 1960s was primarily a result of excess capacity in the leading sectors of the global economy.[33]

When overaccumulation crises break out, previous investments in fixed capital must be devalued. At this point, the entire system becomes convulsed in endeavours to shift the costs of devaluation elsewhere. Each unit, network and region of capital attempts to shift the costs of devaluation onto other units, networks, and regions.[34] And capital as a whole attempts to shift as much of the cost as possible onto labour by increasing unemployment, lowering wages, and worsening work conditions. As the concentration and centralization of capital proceeds, the overaccumulation and devaluation of capital necessarily tends to occur on an ever more massive scale. Global turbulence and generalized economic insecurity increasingly become the normal state of affairs.

Financial capital plays a central role in setting off overaccumulation crises. Temporarily idle profits, depreciation funds and precautionary reserves are pooled in the finance sector and allocated to firms and sectors with high rates of growth because of surplus profits.[35] With credit money the extension of credit to these plants and sectors can be a multiple of the pooled reserve funds. In this manner, financial capital 'appears as the principal lever of overproduction and excessive speculation in commerce'.[36]

Once an overaccumulation crisis begins, the rate of investment in sectors suffering overcapacity problems slows significantly. A large pool of investment capital forms, seeking new firms and sectors with a potential for high future rates of growth.[37] If the flows of investment capital to these new sectors are high enough, capital market inflation results.[38] The expectations of future earnings – rational or otherwise – eventually becomes a relatively secondary matter, as financial assets are purchased in the hope of profits from the subsequent sale of these assets.[39] Throughout the course of this speculative bubble, however, financial assets ultimately remain claims on the future production of surplus value. When it becomes overwhelmingly clear that the prices of these assets do not correspond to likely future profits, the speculative bubble collapses and a financial crisis ensues.

The intertwining of the tendencies to overaccumulation crises and financial crises implies that the impact of concentration and centralization on the former extends to the latter as well. The devaluation of credit and fictitious capital necessarily tends to occur on an ever more massive scale. Units, networks and regions of capital attempt to shift the costs of devaluation elsewhere on to other units, networks and regions. Most of all, capital attempts to shift as much of the cost as possible on to labour. Global turbulence and generalized economic insecurity increasingly pervade the world market.

Conclusion

The practical conclusion that follows from the systematic necessity of the tendencies to uneven development, overaccumulation crises and financial crises should be clear. Neither the capitalist state nor the capitalist world market can resolve the fundamental irrationality and social antagonisms at the heart of capitalist social relations. Further deregulation of global capital flows will not reverse this state of affairs, nor will resurgence of nationalism, or a 'new international financial architecture'. Nor will attempts to institute social democracy on a global scale. Only a revolutionary rupture from the capital form can accomplish this world historical task. This is, I believe, the main conclusion of a systematically informed Marxian account of the historical dialectic of globalization.

Notes and References

1. This list is not comprehensive. For other examples of dialectical inquiries within a Marxian framework see Ollman, B., *Dialectical Investigations* (New York: Cambridge University Press, 1993); and Ollman, B. and Smith, T. (eds), *Dialectics: The New Frontier*, special issue, *Science and Society*, vol. 62, no. 3 (1998).
2. Marx, K., *Grundrisse* (New York: Vintage, 1973), p. 107; Smith, T., *The Logic of Marx's 'Capital'* (Albany, NY: State University of New York, 1990), pp. 21–2; Arthur, C., 'Against the Logical-Historical Method: Dialectical Derivation versus Linear Logic', in F. Moseley and M. Campbell (eds), *New Investigations of Marx's Method* (Atlantic Highlands, NJ: Humanities Press, 1997).
3. Marx, *Grundrisse*, pp. 100–1.
4. See Murray, P., 'The Necessity of Money: How Hegel Helped Marx Surpass Ricardo's Theory of Value', and Campbell, M., 'Marx's Concept of Economic Relations and the Method of '*Capital*', both in F. Moseley (ed.), *Marx's Method in 'Capital': A Reexamination* (Atlantic Highlands: Humanities Press, 1993).

5. See Mattick, P., 'Some Aspects of the Value–Price Problem', *International Journal of Political Economy*, vol. 21 no. 4 (1991–2).
6. See Smith, T., 'A Critical Comparison of the Neoclassical and Marxian Theories of Technical Change', *Historical Materialism*, vol. 1 (1997).
7. See Sayer, A., *Method in Social Science: A Realist Approach* (London: Hutchinson, 1984) and Reuten, G., 'The Notion of Tendency in Marx's 1894 Law of Profit', in Moseley and Campbell, *New Investigations of Marx's Method*.
8. Smith, T., 'Brenner and Crisis Theory: Issues in Systematic and Historical Dialectics', *Historical Materialism*, vol. 5 (2000).
9. 'Cycle' should be taken in the broadest sense of the term, including 'long waves' of expansion and slowdown as well as shorter economic cycles.
10. Friedman, T., *The Lexus and the Olive Tree* (New York: Anchor, 2000).
11. Wriston, W., *The Twilight of Sovereignty* (New York: Scribners, 1992).
12. Marx, *Grundrisse*, pp. 227, 264.
13. Strange, S., *Mad Money: When Markets Outgrow Governments* (Ann Arbor, Mick.: University of Michigan Press, 1998), p. 190.
14. Reuten, G. and Williams, M., *Value-Form and the State* (New York: Routledge, 1989), p. 243.
15. Kantor, R. M., *World Class: Thriving Locally in the Global Economy* (New York: Touchstone, 1995).
16. Chomsky, N., *World Orders Old and New* (New York: Columbia University Press, 1996).
17. Marx, K., *Theories of Surplus Value*, vol. III (Moscow: Progress, 1971), p. 253.
18. Of course, not all of these systematic tendencies determine the dominant concrete trends in all periods of capitalist history. Some of them could not be manifested until a sufficiently high level of concentration and centralization of capital had been attained. For documentation of recent trends, see Held, D., McGrew, A., Goldblatt, D. and Perraton, J., *Global Transformations: Politics, Economics, and Culture* (Stanford, Calif.: Stanford University Press, 1999).
19. Arrighi, G., *The Long Twentieth Century* (New York: Verso, 1994).
20. '[T]he villainies of the Venetian system of robbery formed one of the secret foundations of Holland's wealth in capital, for Venice in her years of decadence lent large sums of money to Holland. There is a similar relationship between Holland and England. By the beginning of the eighteenth century, Holland's manufactures had been far outstripped. It had ceased to be the nation preponderant in commerce and industry. One of its main lines of business, therefore, from 1701 to 1776, was the lending out of enormous amounts of capital, especially to its great rival England. The same thing is going on today between England and the United States. A great deal of capital, which appears today in the United States without any birth-certificate, was yesterday, in England, the capitalized blood of children', Marx, K., *Capital*, vol. I (New York: Penguin, 1976) p. 920.
21. Hirst, P. and Thompson, G., *Globalization in Question: The International Economy and the Possibilities of Governance* (Cambridge: Polity, 1996).
22. Wade, R., *Governing the Market: Economic Theory and the Role of Government in East Asian Industrialization* (Princeton, NJ: Princeton University Press, 1990).
23. State-led Keynesian fiscal expansion has enjoyed a general resurgence in Asia, often accompanied by increased state controls of short-term capital inflows (Malaysia, Hong Kong, Taiwan, with the explicit encouragement of Japan), state purchases of equity and restrictions on stock market trading (Hong Kong,

Taiwan), industrial planning to reduce excess capacity (Korea), nationalization of bad debts (Korea, Japan), and so on. See Wade, R. and Veneroso, F., 'The Gathering World Slump and the Battle Over Capital Controls', *New Left Review*, vol. 231 (1998).

24. World Bank, *Good Governance and Development* (Washington, DC: World Bank, 1992).

25. See Moody, K., *Workers in a Lean World* (New York: Verso, 1997), ch. 3; Toussaint, E., *Your Money or Your Life! The Tyranny of Global Finance* (London: Pluto, 1999); and Went, R., *Globalization: Neoliberal Challenge, Radical Responses* (London: Pluto, 2000) for fuller discussions.

26. Elliott, L. and Brittain, V., 'The Rich and Poor are Growing Further Apart', *Guardian Weekly*, Sept. 20 (1998), p. 19.

27. Smith, T., 'Surplus Profits from Innovation: A Missing Level in Volume III?', in M. Campbell and G. Reuten (eds), *The Culmination of 'Capital': Essays on Volume Three of Marx's Capital* (London/New York: Palgrave Macmillan, 2001).

28. At present, 95% of research and development is located in the so-called 'first world', and 97% of all patents are held by individuals and institutions based there. Friedman, T., *The Lexus and the Olive Tree*, p. 319.

29. Marx, *Capital*, vol. III (New York: Penguin, 1981), pp. 344–5.

30. Moody, K., *Workers in a Lean World*, p. 54.

31. Reuten, G., 'Accumulation of Capital and the Foundation of the Tendency of the Rate of Profit to Fall', *Cambridge Journal of Economics*, vol. 15 (1991); Brenner, R., 'The Economics of Global Turbulence', *New Left Review*, vol. 229 (1998).

32. Smith, 'Brenner and Crisis Theory'.

33. Brenner, 'The Economics of Global Turbulence'.

34. Smith, T., *Technology and Capital in the Age of Lean Production* (Albany, NY: State University of New York, 2000), ch. 5.

35. Marx, *Capital*, vol. III, p. 567.

36. Marx, *Capital*, vol. III, p. 572.

37. de Brunhoff, S., *The State, Capital, and Economic Theory* (London: Pluto, 1978), p. 47.

38. Toporowski, J., 'Monetary Policy and Capital Market Inflation in Europe', Paper presented at the Fifth Workshop on Alternative Economic Policy in Europe, Brussels (1999), p. 2.

39. Marx, *Capital*, vol. III, pp. 615–16, 742.

3

On 'Becoming Necessary' in an Organic Systematic Dialectic: The Case of Creeping Inflation

*Geert Reuten**

E31   P14
B51 G32

This chapter provides a reflection on the notions of 'necessity' and 'contingency' within the method of systematic dialectics. The main methodological idea is that something that 'was' contingent, may become necessary, thus emphasizing systematic dialectics as an organic method. The development of the general price level will serve as an illustrating case for this thesis. The main idea is that 'creeping inflation' is necessary to capital – which seems paradoxical in view of the fact that in the 1920s we witnessed in leading capitalist countries a prolonged period of deflation; and in the 1970s a period of galloping inflation (that is, not 'creeping' inflation).[1]

Stated otherwise, this chapter is a methodological investigation about the theorization, within systematic dialectics, of fairly concrete constellations. Subsidiary to that, and the two main ideas of the chapter just indicated, the methodological notion of regime (though not in the strict regulationist meaning of the term) as a possible way of theorizing contingencies, runs throughout the chapter. What I am trying to find out is how systematic dialectics and a regime approach might be connected – if at all.

I begin in the first section with a brief outline of the method of systematic dialectics, focusing on the difference between necessary moments versus contingencies. I then move on to outlining the content of the problematic of the chapter in a cursory historical way: twentieth-century periods of inflation/deflation and of various standards of money in a later section, questioning next to what extent such periods might be theorized as regimes or stages of capitalism. Note that many of the problems I discuss

* An early draft of this chapter was discussed at the March 2001 Workshop on Dialectics and Political Economy at York University, Toronto. I thank Robert Albritton for inviting me, and him and the other participants for their stimulating commentary. I am particularly grateful to Tony Smith for a 'second round' critique. I also thank Nicola Taylor, as well as my colleges of the Amsterdam Research Group in Methodology and History of Economics, especially Mark Blaug and Robert Went, for very useful comments.

here are not unique to systematic dialectics – in some way, they would have to be dealt with in any methodological approach.

The methodological problem: systematic dialectics and the theorization of contingency

In this section I provide a very brief indication of the method of systematic dialectics, restricting it to some aspects that are important for the purposes of this contribution. Other systematic dialecticians will not disagree with the importance of the aspect of the method stressed below – necessity versus contingency – though some may disagree with moving that aspect of the method to centre stage (as I tend to do in my research).[2]

The method of systematic dialectics aims to 'show' the essential working of its object of inquiry – the whole in essence.[3] It starts from abstract-general and simple categories, developing those gradually to concrete-particular and complex ones. Thus the 'show' is marked by conceptual levels of abstraction/concretion (rather than by the one level of definitions, as in orthodox linear logic). These provide the order and pace supporting the aim of setting out the object of inquiry's 'moments' (that is, its entities, institutions and processes);[4] more precisely, the object's essence, which is the interconnection of all the moments necessary for the reproduction of the object of inquiry. Thus 'mere contingencies' (externals), discussed below, do not belong to the essence.

The emphasis on reproduction reveals that we are dealing with an organic whole, therefore 'knowledge of it must take the form of a system of related categories rather than a series of discrete investigations'.[5] The emphasis on 'necessary' reveals that we are out to lay bare first of all the continuous moments rather than the merely contingent expressions. That is, we are out to distinguish contingencies – aspects and expressions that could come and go without affecting the reproduction of the system – from all the necessary moments, the lack or distortion of which would make the system, the object, fall apart.[6]

Along with the requirement of (i) setting out the interconnection of the necessary moments of the whole, we have (ii) the related requirement of transcending (*aufhebung*) any contradiction that emerges at some level of abstraction. Since contradiction can have no real unmediated existence, it is also this insufficiency of an earlier level that drives the presentation to further concretion, eventually arriving at the level at which abstract contradictions find a concrete modus of, perhaps conflicting, existence in everyday life.

If a systematic dialectical presentation is successful we have satisfied both requirements. The problem is, however, that the character of the object of inquiry may be such that these two requirements do not coincide. That is, we may not reach the concrete modus of a transcended contradiction at the level of necessary moments. To my knowledge, this is generally the case for the capitalist mode of production. Thus we arrive in the end at transcendences/'solutions' that are merely contingent solutions, the unbridgeable conflicts of which may give rise to new contingent solutions replacing the former, and so on.[7]

Generally, we have three types of contingency:[8]

(i)   *Contingency of a moment's content*; where a particular (contradictory) moment is theorized as necessary, though its content is contingent. For example: credit money as accommodating the accumulation of capital is necessary, and this requires necessarily a central bank; however, central banking may contingently be accomplished either by collaboration between private banks, or by a policy institution;

(ii) *Major contingent externals*. These are in no way necessary to the reproduction of the system (thus contingent); nevertheless, their phenomenal importance may require that we shed light on them in light of the systematic – sometimes also because they are, mistakenly, associated with the system. For example, wars or racial discrimination; and

(iii) *Minor contingent externals ('the endless sea of contingency')*. For example, the colour of the suit of a central bank director. These contingencies have no systemic associations, but may nevertheless have some importance to life (the banker's wife hates black suits – we may dream up stories how this might affect the meeting of the board and so on; minor contingent externals may even reach the front pages).

Leaving aside the 'type three' contingency, a major question arises. Is it helpful to theorize contingencies in some particular, orderly way, other than in light of a systemic whole, as in regimes or stages, for example? Do we have criteria for theorizing them, other than the empirical finding that some constellations – especially those that amalgamate 'type one' contingencies – happen to be rather stable for some period of time? Note that in Reuten and Williams (1989) (see Note 2), inflation – the main subject-case of the rest of this chapter – was theorized as a 'type two' contingency in the context of cycles.[9] I shall argue in a later section (implicitly) that it should be theorized as a *necessary* transcendent moment of the contradictory unity of two major factions of capital: finance and managerial capital.

The problem of content: two major (apparent) contingencies

Periods of price deflation and inflation

Compare the following six, stylized, twentieth-century periods for leading capitalist countries:[10]

(i)   around WW I: galloping inflation
(ii) 1920–35:   deflation[11]

(iii)	around WW II:	galloping inflation
(iv)	1948–73:	creeping inflation
(v)	1973–79:	galloping inflation
(vi)	1979–2000:	creeping inflation

Considering these figures it would seem that (galloping/creeping) inflation or deflation are contingent phenomena. To the extent that deflation or inflation are of key importance to the development of the capitalist economy (as I shall argue in the final section), it might seem obvious to try to theorize the phenomenon of inflation – together with other important issues – by way of regimes or stages of accumulation of capital. However, paradoxically in face of the figures above, I shall argue – towards the end of this chapter – that creeping inflation is necessary to capitalism, or rather that it has (organically) become, and therefore is, a necessity. (Afterwards that still leaves open the possibility of describing historically earlier periods as stages leading up to the current. I say 'leading up', since – as indicated later on – no reverse is possible.)

If creeping inflation has indeed become a necessity, this highlights a major contradiction of capitalism since at least the mid-1930s, namely that continuous productivity increase is key to the system (what Marx called its 'progressive mission'), yet does not result in a general price decrease, but rather in a general price increase.[12] (Note that, as indicated below, in the nineteenth century, capitalist productivity increases did translate – roughly – into price decreases.)

Standards of money

A second apparent economic contingency of the twentieth century was the prevailing monetary standard. Throughout the nineteenth century, capitalist money was always based on a commodity: gold, silver or both. Although at the beginning of the twentieth century fiat money (credit money) had become dominant for national purposes, the clearing of international payments was due in gold. Over the century this changed, first into the 1944 Bretton Woods dollar–gold standard (in which international payment in gold might still be required), and then, from 1973 onwards, into a system of both nationally and internationally pure fiat money. Both the international exchange rates and the national exchange rates (the latter summing up to the general price level) are determined by forces of market supply and demand – though 'assisted' by the interest rate policies of central banks (including 'open market operations' and 'gentlemen's agreements' with private banks); assisted also, if possible, by the central bank's direct interventions in buying and selling foreign currency. It seems not too far fetched to link changes in the standard of money to the in-/deflationary periods of the previous subsection. However, that might not seem to make things more or less contingent.

Under the gold standard, the general price level had always been contingent on the mining of additional stocks of gold/silver. So a lag of labour productivity in gold-digging behind that of other products would see a fall in the general price level – in turn stimulating gold production. However, should gold become absolutely scarce (depletion), then inevitably the general price level would fall. Whereas absolute scarcity of gold might generally explain a decreasing price level, that link was not consistently the case, not even prior to the 1944 Bretton Woods accord. Monetary policies affected what happened. It is hard to ascribe any necessity to them, apart from the fact that to the extent economies were 'open' in trade, price deflation with trade competitors evoked price deflation 'at home'.

Such spiralling was what the Bretton Woods accord with its, generally, fixed exchange rates tried to prevent. Nevertheless, it mimicked the 'classical' balance of the gold-payments mechanism: 'cheap' countries would through their exports build up currency reserves which, feeding into their national economy, would again increase their prices (in quantity theory of money arguments), so restoring the balance of payments. Although this explains why between 1944 and the early 1970s (when the Bretton Woods system collapsed) international price levels moved roughly in line with each other, it does not explain why there was creeping inflation rather than an international general price decrease in accordance with productivity increase. At first sight, once again, this seems a contingency, though amenable perhaps to theorization in terms of stages/regimes.[13]

Monetary standards and prices

Before elaborating further we shall extend the time horizon. Table 3.1 shows rough indicators of the standard of money (both international and domestic) and of the development of the price level; for the leading capitalist countries from 1820, beginning with France and Britain for 1820–1870; extending to Germany and the USA for 1870–48; and afterwards the USA, Japan and the current EU countries. Note that in these stage types of accounts much hangs on the dating of the periodization. For the nineteenth century I follow Maddison's (1995) periodization.[14] For the twentieth century, Maddison has 1913–50, 1950–73, 1973–92 (since his concern is not prices but growth); I take as additional bench marks the two world wars as well as the 1979 shift in stance of US monetary policy.[15] The year 1973 also marks the end of the Bretton Woods system.

Regimes and stages

The description in the previous section might seem to point towards theorizing regimes of accumulation or stages of capitalism – which, of course, should encompass more than just these two factors, as well as their inter-

Table 3.1 Money standard and general price level: leading capitalist countries, 1820–2000

Period	(1) Money standard		(2) Prices	
	International	Domestic		
1820–70	Bimetallic (gold, silver)	Mono- or bimetallic	Deflation	1820–50 deflation
				1850–70 creeping inflation
1870–1910	Gold	Gold proportion (or fiduciary limit)	Deflation	1870–95 deflation
				1895–1910 creeping inflation
Around WWI	Floating gold (and controlled)	Fiat money	Galloping inflation	
1920–35	Floating gold (and controlled)	Gold proportion	Deflation	
Around WWII			Galloping inflation	
1948–73	Gold-$ (controlled)	Gold-$ proportion	Creeping inflation	
1973–79	Floating fiat money: money of account	Regulated fiat money	Galloping inflation	
1979–2000	Floating fiat money: money of account	Regulated fiat money	Creeping inflation	

Note:
Countries: 1820–70: France and Great Britain; 1870–1920: idem plus Germany and USA; 1920–48: idem plus Japan; 1948–2000 USA, Japan and EU-15. For 1820–1948/1973 wholesale prices; from 1948/1973 GDP deflator.
Sources: Eichengreen, B., *Globalizing Capital*, chs 1–3; Vilar, P., *Oro y Moneda en la Historia 1450–1920*, trans. J. White (*A History of Gold and Money 1450–1920*) (London: NLB, 1969), p. 333 (based on Cassel and Warren & Pearson, 1935); Foreman-Peck, J., *A History of the World Economy: International Economic Relations Since 1850* (Brighton: Wheatsheaf/Harvester, 1983), pp. 72, 162; Maynard, G., *Economic Development and the Price Level* (London/New York: Macmillan/St. Martin's Press, 1963), p. 118 (based on Kuznets, 1952), and p. 214 (based on Ohkawa, 1957); Mitchell, B. R., 'Statistical Appendix', in C. M. Cipolla, (ed.), *The Fontana Economic History of Europe – Contemporary Economics 2* (Glasgow: Collins/Fontana, 1976); EC, *European Economy*, no. 79 (2000).

connection.[16] Although this is not inevitably inherent to the regimes and stages approaches, my problem with many of them is, first, that the current 'concrete' is precluded from feeding the general theory (thus the general theory seems fixed); and second (and related), an unclear connection of the intermediate and the general-abstract theory.[17]

If we link a regime framework to the method of systematic dialectics, the regime would describe – against the background of general-abstract determinations:[18] (i) the particular and contingent resolution of contradictions (the type one contingencies of p. 44); (ii) other elements (type 2); such that, (iii) the resolutions are coherent and more or less persistent (for the time span of the regime). It is, of course, inherent to the approach that, in principle, both the resolutions and the other elements are reversible or changeable (they can in principle be annulled). A regime comes to an end (its crisis) when resolutions are no longer coherent: one or more of the resolutions 'develop' so that the lot runs into incoherence.[19] Therewith the system-inherent contradictions are reposited as unresolved.

The crucial issue from the point of view of the problematic of this chapter is the reversibility of solutions (for example, from Taylorism to Toyotism to Taylorism or something else; from intensive to extensive to intensive accumulation – there seems to be no other possibility; or from inflation to deflation to inflation, or to a constant price level if that is at all possible). Of course, if a moment is or has become irreversible, can the system get back to a gold standard, or perhaps move to a new non-physical standard? Then it would seem that it is no longer a regime issue, but becomes a general determination. I shall argue in the next section that this is the case for both creeping inflation and fiat money (full credit money).[20]

This in itself does not do away with the possible usefulness of the concepts of regime or stage. It qualifies it. It also qualifies, as I shall indicate briefly in the last section, the process of constructing the method of systematic dialectics.

The potential conflict between finance capital and managerial capital, and the modus of creeping inflation

Corporate finance: twentieth century

At the time of writing, the founding capital for the majority of business companies is gathered from external finance. This is a twentieth-century matter and this point is crucial to the further argument in this chapter. The corporate financing of industry on a general scale began towards the end of the nineteenth century. Before that time, corporate financing was restricted either to very risky projects, such as long-distance trade, or to large projects such as canals and railways. In Britain, for example, key industries such as textiles did not adopt the corporate form prior to 1885.[21] Thus there was hardly any separation of capital into finance capital and what I shall call 'managerial capital'.[22] Furthermore, most lending to industry by banks was restricted both to (on average) some 20 per cent of total assets, and to short-term financing.[23]

Capital to start most enterprises, wrote C. P. Kindleberger, came from an individual and his family and friends; fixed capital needs were small, buildings were often rented, and inputs were bought on credit. Growth came from retained profits.[24] Thus it can be argued that, with the development of capitalism, with the necessary concentration and centralization of capital, the corporation comes into being – and thus the separation between finance capital and managerial capital.[25]

The oppositions between finance capital and managerial capital

While the opposition between labour and 'capital in general' is fundamental to the capitalist mode of production, its concrete course is also determined by opposition within capital. First, the opposition of 'like' capitals; that is, the competition of capitals within and between branches of production, each going through the same types of metamorphosis of $M - C \dots P \dots C' - M'$ (the subject of Marx's *Capital* up to Part 4 of vol. III). Second, the opposition between capitals specializing in a stage of the circuit of capital.[26] For developed capitalism, the opposition between finance capital and managerial capital is most important here.[27]

This provides the theoretical background to what I shall say about the systematic dialectical method in the next section. However, I cannot set out the case in full detail within the confines of this chapter.

Restricting comment to the main lines, the focal point for the conflict between the two factions of finance capital (FC) and managerial capital (MC) is the general price level.[28] In general, FC favours the constellation of deflation, seemingly, and MC the constellation of inflation – at least moderate deflation and inflation (later I shall expand briefly on galloping inflation). One or the other constellation affects the relative power positions of FC and MC concerning the division of surplus value between the two factions. Price deflation puts FC in a dominant power position since it can refuse ('strike', 'wait') to lend out capital because, with deflation, it reaps purchasing power in any case. With price inflation we have the reverse power position: FC is forced to lend, since any 'waiting' corrodes capital's purchasing power. These bargaining positions affect the level of the real interest rate.[29] Since dividends on share capital are linked to the interest rate, the reasoning applies to both forms of FC: interest-bearing capital and share capital.[30]

Managerial capital is the vested interest of higher management in the company – at the locus of production, the direct locus of the capital–labour relation. This is a vested interest in terms of both the fetishization of the capital form and direct pecuniary remunerations related to the profit of enterprise (salary, bonuses, options). It is not merely 'management' drawing part of the company's income, it is indeed managerial capital, represented formally by the company's reserves as built up from 'withheld' profits and any revaluation of capital (the latter in times of inflation).

Note that even when managerial capital is 'large', a pure fiat money constellation requires, of necessity, that accumulation of capital is in part accommodated by credit, unless the system is allowed to run into price deflation. (At constant prices, credit money must grow parallel to the rate of accumulation.)[31]

Note also, concerning inflation and revaluation of capital, that with continuous inflation, inflationary gains on fixed capital (revaluation) and the higher depreciation allowances along with it, are continuously ahead of the repurchase of fixed means of production at higher prices.[32]

Table 3.1 might suggest that, historically, deflation is connected to the domestic gold standard (circulation of currency based on gold or a proportion of gold stock). Be that as it may, the important question is why the 'political' standards of Bretton Woods and after generated inflation rather than deflation. ('Political' is in inverted commas not because they were not political, but because the gold standard was equally political.) Again, why does productivity fail increasingly to translate into general price decrease, or general price deflation?[33]

Cope with continuous deflation?

Can the developed capitalist system cope with continuous deflation? Apart from all the reasons dealt with in Keynes' *General Theory*[34] – most importantly the postponement of investment, since tomorrow's purchases will be cheaper than today's – deflation extending beyond a couple of years would lead to the abolition of managerial capital (but not of the managers). The point is that, with continuous deflation, we have continuous devaluation of capital (the counterpart of the example in note 32) – that is above any 'normal' devaluation of capital related to productivity increase. In the end, this would outrun the company reserves, unless, of course, increased retained profits compensate for the deflationary devaluation. The latter seems unlikely, since deflation generally boosts the level of the real interest rate (the initial thesis) and, parallel to it, the 'dividend rate'.[35]

An abolition of managerial capital has two consequences. First, management will turn into high paid labour of supervision rather than being the managers of the capital–labour relation at the point of production.[36] Thus finance capital (now in fact capital, since the conceptual and practical separation is annulled) is faced with a management of which it may not be confident. Second, given the abolition, finance capital as a whole no longer secures bargaining gains from deflation (though there remains a difference between the intra-FC factions of share capital and interest-bearing capital); on the other hand, it has to bear the 'normal' devaluation of capital related to productivity increase;[37] hence the general negative effects of deflation (cf. Keynes) prevail.

Thus, in effect, FC may have an interest in 'merely' moderate deflation, and not in continuous 'severe' deflation. (This is why I said earlier that FC 'seemingly' favours deflation.) Be that as it may, the system will not fall back into generalized price deflation because of: (i) oligopolistic powers of managerial capital and thus oligopolistic pricing (as analysed by Aglietta in the context of planned early depreciation of capital);[38] and (ii) the accommodation of oligopolistic pricing – hence inflation – by central banks.

The thesis that the system cannot cope with continuous deflation does not by itself exclude a temporary drop of the price level (inasmuch as the systemic necessity of upholding property rights does not exclude robbery). The Japanese situation at the time of writing is a case in point. Once you get into a deflationary situation, monetary policy becomes lame. A near-zero discount rate of interest (Japan) should stimulate managerial capital to act, but it is faced with the incessant devaluation of capital. Nevertheless, surely the case is anomalous to the statement that the system will not fall back into generalized price deflation because of oligopolistic pricing and an accommodating monetary policy.[39]

Cope with continuous galloping inflation?

However, the system equally cannot cope with continuous galloping inflation. As indicated, (galloping) inflation erodes finance capital. With the eventual withdrawal of the non-banking part of FC from business investment (investing alternatively in real estate, art and so on – the net effect of which is an increase in bank reserves), managerial capital must rely on the banking part of FC alone. Banks consequently bear the full risk, for which they will of course require a risk premium. Moreover, rather than long-term loans, banks provide short-term credits, which are inflation-proof as the interest rate adapts. Nevertheless, this builds a vulnerability into the banking system.[40] Facing this, the system will not fall back to galloping inflation (apart from extra-systemic situations such as wars) because of the monetary policies of central banks and their direct and indirect ties with the rest of the banking system.[41]

Creeping inflation

The only possibility between generalized deflation and galloping inflation is creeping inflation. From the arguments given above we may infer that creeping inflation is necessary to the developed capitalist system.[42] Some lower boundary of creeping inflation is what the monetary authorities euphemistically call 'price stability' (an inflation of around 2 per cent). It is also the point where the interests of the oligopolistic powers of managerial capital and finance capital intersect. Thus it is the 'bliss' point at which finance capital and managerial capital can unite harmoniously in opposition to labour. (Note that a policy target of, on average, zero inflation risks to turning into a deflationary spiral once the price level drops below zero.)

Michel Aglietta rightly concentrated his analysis of inflation on 'creeping' inflation.[43] The question is whether it is a matter of a particular monetary regime, or a matter indispensable to the system. In both cases it hinges on the combination of a kind of money, a particular operation of the banking system, and a particular kind of competition between capitals. (The French regulationists saw quite early that this is crucial. In much of the rest of the Marxian tradition, inflation has largely been theorized – for too long and erroneously in my view – as merely a matter of state finance.)[44]

Notes on the systematic dialectic of an organic system

My discussion of inflation in the face of the conflict between finance capital and managerial capital has perhaps been too brief to convince every reader completely that creeping inflation is necessary to the reproduction of the capitalist system. In what follows I shall nevertheless assume that the case is convincing, since my methodological argument below extends beyond this particular case.

Generally, one can make two kinds of system-level mistakes within a method of systematic dialectics.[45] The first, well known, is to take an entity or process as being necessary because it has been 'enduring': 'the enduring ergo necessary fallacy' (of course, necessity has to be argued for systemically, and this hopefully prevents the mistake, but nevertheless this is still a potential mistake to be guarded against.)[46] The second, introduced in this chapter, is to take an entity or process as being contingent because it has changed/varied over time or been absent for a time: 'the varying ergo contingent fallacy'. Not falling into the first fallacy is already difficult enough. The second poses an even more demanding problem for the systematic dialectical theorization of, in our case, capitalism. What is 'systemic' about systematic dialectics seems not a once and forever issue.

Do these difficulties suggest a good argument for adopting the theoretical framework of regimes or stages for analyzing 'contingent' constellations in the light of the 'enduring necessities'? No, such a framework does not solve these problems: we still have to decide which are the 'general system' characteristics. To avoid this problem such approaches have to stretch an 'intermediary' theory into a 'general' structure of its own, albeit against the background of a number of supra-general characteristics such as wage labour and money.[47] I do not want to say that this may not be fruitful. Nevertheless, when the (real) constellation as captured by the theory of regime/stage falls apart – for example, the Fordist regime – it is an inherent aspect of such an approach to have to start theorizing it all anew.[48] (So be it; from the regime perspective one is almost forced to cast change in terms of system 'crisis', evidently requiring new theorizing.)

Although the starting point of systematic dialectics is very different – it rather works from the other side of theorizing to the limits of necessity – the problems of the regimes/stages approach offer a blow-up of the systematic dialectical problem. From the systematic dialectical perspective, the regime approach generally risks theorizing too much as historically contingent (the 'intermediary' theory); it historicizes too much.

Within its own framework, however, systematic dialectics is in danger of a similar risk, though on a reduced scale. This is what I have tried to show in the light of the case of creeping inflation: we may be inclined to theorize inflation as contingent because this is how the issue presents itself historically.[49] The upshot of this chapter is that a one-time contingent entity or process may become necessary.

Therefore we have to introduce history, time and development into the systematic dialectic. One implication is that a systematic dialectical presentation cannot claim to extend beyond the epoch in which it is formulated. Alternatively, one might say that as long as the object is in a state of becoming, so also is its theory (cf. Hegel's owl of Minerva).

With our case in mind, it might be tempting to say that, at least prior to 1973, capitalism was not 'full grown'. However, especially since we are dealing with a contradictory entity, we shall never have sufficient grounds for saying that it is fully grown now. Rather, since we are dealing with a social system and not with the ontogenesis of the offspring of a species, we are dealing with an organic whole to which the terms 'mature' or 'fully grown' are not applicable. Therefore 'history', or better expressed, the 'course of the system' affects its being. Nevertheless there are manifold moments that apply to the leading capitalist nations of 1820 or 1870 as much as to the present day.[50]

However, in the case of capitalism it is not so (as far as I am aware) that 'previous' systemic necessities disappear. They seem irreversible, so we have a historical organic addition of necessities. Hence the system becomes ever more restrictive.[51] If this is sound, then we have a systematic plus a so-called contingent history,[52] which reacts back on the systematic. What once was contingent, may not be contingent later – we have an organically growing necessity.

All this should not be read to imply that we must get rid of the notion of regimes or stages; rather, I have been trying to set out a possible marriage between systematic dialectics and regime theory. Systematic dialectics will always end up with a set of contingent contradictions; sometimes these may fit into a 'constellation' or balance of forces that grant them a more-or-less persistent character. Besides, one may in retrospect describe earlier periods as stages leading up to the current. I say 'leading up to' since no reversal is possible.

Summary

I have set out that within a systematic dialectical method, contingencies may become necessities. Necessities are entities, forces, institutions and processes required for the reproduction of the system; in this case the capitalist system. Contingencies may become necessities to the extent that the object of the dialectical presentation is an organic system. (It seems, however, that there is no analogous process whereby necessities become contingent, thus the system seems to become ever more restrictive.)

The case I have discussed is the notion of inflation, in particular, creeping inflation. The growing concentration and centralization of capital – itself a necessary expression of the cyclical accumulation of capital – necessarily requires the 'externalization of capital' into finance capital and managerial capital. Though separate entities, they are an 'opposition-in-unity' *vis-à-vis* labour. Their existence – especially their existence in relative harmony – requires, of necessity, creeping inflation, rather than deflation or galloping inflation.

Notes and References

1. This is how the matter is presented. In fact, research on the case in the context of a wider project made me reconsider the method.
2. Extended accounts of the method of Systematic Dialectics, with somewhat varying emphasis by different authors, are, for example, Reuten, G. and Williams, M., *Value-Form and the State: The Tendencies of Accumulation and the Determination of Economic Policy in Capitalist Society* (London/New York: Routledge, 1989), pp. 11–36; Smith, T., *The Logic of Marx's 'Capital': Replies to Hegelian Criticisms* (Albany, NY: State University of New York Press, 1990, pp. 3–18); Smith, T., 'Marx's *Capital* and Hegelian Dialectical Logic', in F. Moseley (ed.), *Marx's Method in 'Capital': A Reexamination* (Atlantic Highlands, NJ: Humanities Press, 1993); Arthur, C. J., 'Systematic Dialectic', *Science & Society*, vol. 62, no. 3 (1998); Reuten, G., 'The Interconnection of Systematic Dialectics and Historical Materialism', *Historical Materialism*, vol. 7 (2001).
3. It would be misleading to think of 'essence' as a kernel thing. Rather, in a Hegelian vein, 'essence' is a complex of entities and processes required for the reproduction of the object of inquiry.
4. 'A *moment* is an element considered in itself, which can be conceptually isolated, and analyzed as such, but which can have no isolated existence' (Reuten and Williams, *Value-Form and the State*, p. 22).
5. Quoted from Arthur, C. J., 'Introduction', in C. J. Arthur (ed.), *Marx's 'Capital': A Student Edition* (London: Lawrence & Wishart ,1992), p. x; cf. Marx, *Grundrisse*, Introduction (New York; Vintage, 1973).
6. Just to present the reader with a picture: the capitalist mode of production (CMP) would fall apart without the moment of technical change or without the moment of a credit system. Nevertheless, *within* the CMP technical change or the credit system could, contingently to the CMP – thus without it falling apart – take several historically specific guises. This differentiation between necessary and contingent moments/aspects/expressions is not to say that contingencies are unimportant in everyday life. They may be very important. The capitalist system can do without wars, but wars have a crucial effect on life. The concepts of necessity and contingency thus relate to a particular object of inquiry.
7. For a simple picture, think of macroeconomic policy stances and of institutional rearrangements between a finance ministry and a central bank. We would not see those changes if, for example, Friedman-type monetary policy were simply

necessary to the existence (survival) of the capitalist system.

8. See also Reuten and Williams, *Value-Form and the State*, pp. 30–2.
9. Reuten and Williams, *Value-Form and the State*, ch. 5.
10. France, Germany, Great Britain, Japan, USA. WWI = First World War; WWII = Second World War; details about countries and periodisation are provided later on. 'Creeping inflation' is roughly identified with a price level change of 0–5% and 'galloping inflation' by one of >5%. (For the purposes of this chapter I neglect hyperinflation). A rate of inflation below 5% per year was indicated by Samuelson in 1948, and Samuelson and Solow in 1960, as moderate: 'such a mild steady inflation need not cause too much concern' (Samuelson, quoted by Leeson, R. in 'The Eclipse of the Goal of Zero Inflation', *History of Political Economy*, vol. 29 no. 3 (1997) p. 455).
11. These are averages. It is notorious that Germany had a hyperinflation at the beginning of the period (1920–4); France also had a number of inflationary years (esp. 1923–6). Each of these countries had an average deflation.
12. I say 'since the mid-1930s', though in that period there have been some deflationary years, for example, in most West-European countries for two or three years between 1952 and 1955, one or two years between 1958–9, and again one or two years between 1967–8.
13. In a fabulously documented 'The Eclipse of the Goal of Zero Inflation', Robert Leeson sets out how, in the context of Keynesian policy goals and in the face of the Phillips relation, the climate amongst economists turned around 1950 from a zero inflation allegiance in to one of creeping inflation. I do not want to suggest that this is an explanation for creeping inflation.
14. Maddison, A., *Monitoring the World Economy 1820–1992* (Paris: OECD, 1995).
15. See, for example, Eichengreen, B., *Globalizing Capital: A History of the International Monetary System* (Princeton, NJ: Princeton University Press, 1996) pp. 145–6.
16. For an overview of current theories, see Albritton, R., Itoh, M., Westra, R. and Zuege, A. (eds), *Phases of Capitalist Development: Booms, Crises and Globalizations* (London/New York: Palgrave Macmillan, 2001). See also the survey and synthesis of the stages theories of regulation, long wave and social structure of accumulation in Went, R., *The Enigma of Globalisation* (London: Routledge, 2002) chs 4–6.
17. The second problem (of connection) may not apply to the Uno–Sekine stages approach; however, its 'pure theory' does not theorize necessities but rather an 'ideal type' which – the first problem – cannot be affected by the (current) 'concrete'. In this sense, the Uno–Sekine approach to dialectics is different from the version of systematic dialectics that I propose.
18. In the sense of general-abstract *system* determinations (I do not mean trans-historical general determinations).
19. In order to prevent a tautological bite, we would require some severe restrictions on the concept of coherence.
20. I use the term 'irreversibility' in both a wider and a stronger sense than 'path dependency' or 'trajectory'. Once, for perhaps accidental reasons, the gold standard is adopted (as was the case in Britain at the end of the eighteenth century), the system is placed on a 'trajectory' that is *difficult* to reverse (cf. Eichengreen, B., *Globalizing Capital*, p. 6). If some element has the characteristics of 'path dependency' within a regime, yet it can be done away with in another regime, then it is *not* irreversible. An irreversibility thesis makes a theory of course

vulnerable. If we look for non-falsifiable theories it would be 'safer' to say that, apparently, e.g. creeping inflation is an element of one or perhaps several regimes.

21. Kindleberger, C. P., *A Financial History of Western Europe* (London/Boston/Sydney: George Allen & Unwin, 1987 [1984]), ch. 11. Although Kindleberger (pp. 206–7) is not super clear on this, there was up to the end of the nineteenth century perhaps more corporate financing of industry in France than in Britain.

22. For various conceptual reasons I prefer this term to the term 'industrial capital' used by Marx in *Capital*, vol. III.

23. Kindleberger (*Financial History*, pp. 92–4) indicates the figure of 20% for Smith's Bank in Britain; he also mentions a number of exceptions to short-term lending.

24. Kindleberger, *Financial History*, pp. 91, 192.

25. Marx's generalizations about the joint stock company in Part 5 of *Capital*, vol. III are rather visionary in the face of the actual development at the time it was written (that is, 1864–5).

26. The former opposition is at the level of 'capital in general', the second at the level of the 'externalization of capital', as Arthur has called it (Arthur, C. J., 'Capital in General and Marx's *Capital*', in M. Campbell and G. Reuten (eds), *The Culmination of Capital: Essays on Volume III of Marx's 'Capital'* (London/New York: Palgrave/Macmillan, 2001).

27. A discussion of these categories of finance capital and managerial capital as a development of Marx's categories in Parts 4 and 5 of *Capital*, vol. III can be found in Reuten, G., 'The Rate of Profit Cycle and the Opposition Between Managerial and Finance Capital: A Discussion of *Capital III* Parts Three to Five', in Campbell, and Reuten, *The Culmination of Capital*. Note that the category of managerial *Capital* is a development from Marx's concept of industrial capital.

28. More details are in my paper mentioned is the previous note; complements of it are in Reuten, G., 'Destructive Creativity', in R. Bellofiore (ed.), *Marxian Economics – A Reappraisal*, vol. 2 (London: Macmillan, 1998).

29. These constellations are a relative, not an absolute indicator of the interest rate. If the level of the interest rate leaves no 'profit of enterprise', M–C will generally 'wait', borrowing even in times of inflation. ('Generally', since market strategic considerations may require temporary losses at the margin.)

30. The link between dividend and interest can be argued for on both theoretical and empirical grounds.

31. This is elaborated in Reuten and Williams, *Value-Form and the State*, ch. 2 §5 and §10.

32. An example may illustrate this. Suppose: (a) at the beginning of year 1 a machine is bought for $2000; (b) it is financed completely with credit (partial external finance modifies the example to that extent); (c) it is depreciated in two years; and (d) there is a continuous rate of inflation of 10%. Simplifying, the depreciation allowances at the end of year 1 are $1100 and at end of year 2 $1210 – together $2310. When the credit is cancelled the revaluation gain is $310. At the beginning of year 3, renewal for $2310 may again be financed externally (cf. Reuten and Williams, *Value-Form and the State*, p. 153).

33. This, I believe, was also the key point of Aglietta's path-breaking work *Régulation et Crises du Capitalisme* (Calmann-Lévy, 1976); my question has a different focus, and the answer will be different. For the purposes of this paper I step over the precise difference between general price decrease and price deflation (and

increase and inflation) rightly emphasized by both Aglietta and De Vroey. See Aglietta, M., *Régulation et Crises du Capitalisme*, trans. D. Fernbach (*A Theory of Capitalist Regulation: The US Experience*) (London: NLB, 1979); De Vroey, M. 'Inflation: A Non-monetarist Monetary Interpretation', *Cambridge Journal of Economics* (1984).

34. Keynes, J. M., *The General Theory of Employment Interest and Money* (London: Macmillan, 1936).

35. Keynes, the great theoretician of deflation, writing in hindsight of the first prolonged period of high corporate finance together with deflation, saw the key elements of the problem and advocated a political adaptation of the system directed at the 'euthanasia of the rentier' (that is, finance capital) together with the 'socialization of investment' so as to save 'private enterprise' (that is, 'managerial capital' in my terminology).

36. Marx, in *Capital*, vol. III, was somewhat over-optimistic about the working out of this (see my 'The Rate of Profit Cycle').

37. In my 'The Rate of Profit Cycle' (note 27), this point has been worked out in more detail, especially in the context of Marx's theory of the rate of profit cycle (TRPC) – usually called the TRPF.

38. Aglietta, M., *A Theory of Capitalist Regulation*.

39. Generally, a monetary policy moderating inflation is much easier than a monetary policy countering deflation (cf. Keynes' *General Theory*). In this respect, target rates of inflation of some 2% in the upper boom phase of the cycle are rather dangerous to the reproduction of the system, since the downturn may then easily run into a deflation against which monetary policy is lame.

40. On these issues, see Reuten and Williams, *Value-Form and the State*, ch. 5, pp. 147–57.

41. The strongest evidence for this is: (i) the reaction of the US Fed in 1979 to the then growing rate of inflation – followed by central banks of the rest of the OECD countries – doubling lending rates within two or three years; and (ii) the constitution of the European Central Bank, which has the target of moderate inflation written into its charter. (In an earlier publication, I argued that this target, despite being upheld in boom periods, in fact implies a general deflationary bias over the cycle ('De harmonie van het kapitaal', in Reuten, G., Vendrik K. and Went, R. (eds), *De Prijs van de EURO* (Amsterdam: Van Gennep, 1998). I now think that was wrong. However, with a 2% inflation target reached in the boom period, a deflation during recession is a serious risk.)

42. Of course it is rather dangerous to make stark statements (in this case, the necessity of creeping inflation) about a current era. Hegel was quite right that absolute statements about an epoch can only be made at its dusk. However, if we want to grasp the current epoch, it is preferable to cast statements about it (in a Popperian vein) in a vulnerable, falsifiable, way.

43. Aglietta, *A Theory of Capitalist Regulation*.

44. See, however, Mandel, E., *Der Spätkapitalismus* (Suhrkamp, 1972) trans. J. De Bres (*Late Capitalism*) (London: New Left Books, 1975) ch. 13, where he distances himself from the state finance view of inflation.

45. 'System' mistakes. Of course there are all kinds of other mistakes one can make, such as ill argumentation.

46. In the context of the discussion in this chapter, an important example has been to take 'commodity money' and a commodity standard as necessary. This mistake has been discussed extensively from within the Systematic Dialectical method

by Michael Williams, especially concerning Marxian theories (Williams, M., 'Money and Labour-Power: Marx after Hegel or Smith plus Sraffa', *Cambridge Journal of Economics* (1998); and 'Why Marx Neither Has Nor Needs a "Commodity Theory of Money"', *Review of Political Economy* (2000)). Note that, for Martha Campbell, Marx's commodity money *starting* point in *Capital*, vol. I is a methodical device which nevertheless allows him to end up with credit money in *Capital*, vol. III. However, this does not affect Williams' systemic argument. Within systematic dialectics, it would be odd to introduce a contingency early in the presentation. Apart from that, it is doubtful if Marx took a *commodity* (any) standard of money as being contingent. See Campbell, 'Money in the Circulation of Capital' in C. J. Arthur and G., Reuten (eds), *The Circulation of Capital: Essays on Volume Two of Marx's 'Capital'* (London/New York: Macmillan/St. Martins Press, 1998); and 'The Credit System', in Campbell and Reuten, *The Culmination of Capital*.

47. In reference to the regulation approach, a similar point has been made by Mavroudeas, but without acknowledging the problems that a general theory has to solve, and to which the regimes and stages approaches offer a solution even if not a fully satisfactory one; thus, while Mavroudeas has a number of good critical points, I distance myself from his antagonism *vis-à-vis* stages approaches. See Mavroudeas, S., 'Regulation Theory: The Road from Creative Marxism to Postmodern Disintegration', *Science & Society*, vol. 63 no. 3 (1999).

48. The extent of the 'all anew' is different for different approaches. In other words, the extent of the general theory suggests to what extent the problem has been evaded.

49. This is also what we did in Reuten and Williams, *Value-Form and the State*, ch. 5 (for the mistakes I take responsibility). The phrase 'presents itself' should not be read as implying theoryless observation.

50. In sum: the key moments of wage labour and the monetary value-form, hence capitalist production, hence the subordination of human productive activity to the criterium of money, were, of course, realized prior to 1870. The combination of corporate finance, generally introduced at the end of the nineteenth century (required because of the concentration and centralization of capital), and the restriction to capital accumulation imposed by a metallic standard, first initiated the move to domestic credit money (culminating in the 1944 Bretton Woods accord) and then to international credit money (the demise of Bretton Woods in 1973). The 1970s further politicized central banking in response to the conflict between finance capital and managerial capital, culminating in the 1979 change in the policy stance of the US Fed. Thus 1979 is a further benchmark. Another benchmark is the 1991 charter of the European Central Bank (ECB), with its main duty of realizing a 2 per cent creeping inflation, together with a cutting loose of its political policy from any democratic accountability. Thus the key element of money is neither a free market entity nor a free citizens' entity. Nevertheless, these apparently abstract 'system forces' find a fleshy counterpart. Their personification, much like the feudal monarch, is the central banker, tied to financial 'tenants' much like the feudal vassals who kept the monarch in power. Both are cases of distant exploitation in the general's general interest. (It requires a little imagination to see that the ECB charter is the model for a future global central bank, personified by the central banker.) However, the vassals were again kept in power by their serfs. This parallel also applies.

51. I am considering systemic necessity – that is, necessity for the reproduction of the system. A short period of deflation, say five years, is 'possible'. Beyond that, deflation is not a determinate possibility, since it would disrupt the reproduction of the system.
52. This first part, systematic history, was analyzed in Reuten and Williams, *Value-Form and the State*.

4

Superseding Lukács: A Contribution to the Theory of Subjectivity

Robert Albritton

B51
P14

Lukács' long, difficult and incredibly rich essay, 'Reification and the Consciousness of the Proletariat', is one of the most influential essays of the twentieth century.[1] Some of the more important influences stemming from this essay are: the recognition of a close connection between Hegel and Marx, the importance of dialectical thought in challenging dualistic, formalistic and isolating modes of thought, the importance of social location for developing certain forms of consciousness or knowledge, the importance of attempting to develop mediations between theory and practice aimed at overthrowing capitalism, and an extended discussion of some of the reifying forces of capitalism including their impact on capitalist ideology. It is Lukács' particular emphasis on the concept of reification that is perhaps most original to him (even considering the influence of Max Weber and Georg Simmel), and, in my view, is his greatest theoretical achievement. I say this for two reasons. First, a careful study of capital's inner logic as presented by Marx in *Capital* and, as developed further by Japanese political economists Kozo Uno and Thomas Sekine, demonstrates that reification is an absolutely central characteristic of capital.[2] Second, a theory of capital's peculiar reifying force can contribute a great deal to thinking about the impact of capital on the formation of subjects both collective and singular, and about the possibilities of action in concert to bring about democratic socialism.

This second point leads me towards stating the purpose of this essay. In my view, a recent unhealthy trend in social thought has been a growing division between theories of subjectivity and theories of political economy. Theories of subjectivity have often been based on psycho-sexual development in the family à la Freud and Jacques Lacan, or on various forms of cultural theory involving normative disciplining, discursive inscribing, or performative creation à la Michel Foucault and Judith Butler. In both cases, the resulting theories of subjectivity, though not without important contributions, tend to be culturalist with hardly a trace of the possible impact of capitalism on subject formation. On the other hand, much political economy is often one-sidedly abstract, global and structural, while ignoring the mediations that might connect political-economic social forces with more contextual and complex webs of subject formation. This gap between political economy and cultural theory, or between theories that are more oriented to objective macrostructural forces and those oriented towards the psyche or contextual constructions of subjectivity has been noted and lamented by a variety of theorists.[3] Indeed, I believe there are signs that intellectual energy increasingly is being redirected towards bridging this gap. It is a bridging, however, that is hugely difficult, particularly given that the currently hegemonic empiricist and postmodern epistemological trends tend to undermine bridging efforts. Perhaps such efforts will be given the biggest boost if there is a renewal of internationally significant left-wing movements, since this will tend to weaken the divisiveness and relativism that feeds, and is fed by, postmodern emphases on difference.

So why go back to dialoguing with Lukács as a theoretical strategy to begin to build bridges between political economy and cultural theory? After all, many would see his theories as being hopelessly essentialist, totalizing and class reductionist. First, Lukács attempted to draw out and develop the conception of reification embedded in Marx's *Capital*, and in my view 'reification' is potentially the most important single concept for achieving greater integration between political economy and cultural theory. Second, given the powerful influence of Lukács' essay, it is important to return to the original to become very clear about the shortcomings of his conception of reification, so that in reappropriating it, we avoid the traps into which he fell. Third, there is some tendency for postmodernists to dismiss thinkers such as Lukács, who are labelled as 'essentialist,' while I believe that much can be salvaged from his work despite its essentialist excesses.

Lukács' reification

According to Lukács, the overriding characteristic of capitalist society is reification, and he derives this conception primarily from Marx's discussion of the fetishism of commodities in *Capital*. What reification means, according to Lukács, is that while capitalism is ultimately a set of social institutions generated relationally by human beings, it takes on a life of its own such that the motion of things, namely commodities and money, come to play a dominant role in social life. Under capitalist social relations, persons are connected by commodities and money so that these 'things' come to embody social forms and form social relations among themselves (the market) which, in turn, govern economic life. Furthermore, this commodification of social life is dynamic and expansive, such that there is some tendency for social relations to become homogenized as they are subsumed increasingly to the quantitative calculations of the commodity form. In other words, capitalism has a self-abstracting character in the sense that it forces reality, at least to some extent, to correspond more and more to the motion of its abstract economic categories. Similarly, it can be said to have an inherent dynamic that is self-reifying and self-objectifying. Lukács claims that the key to 'a clear insight into the ideological problems of capitalism and its downfall'[4] lies 'in the solution to the riddle of commodity-structure',[5] and the solution to the riddle can best be grasped by exploring reification in all its dimensions.

In order to be clear about reification, Lukács claims that 'it would be necessary ... for the commodity structure to penetrate society in all its aspects and to remould it in its own image'.[6] Or, as he puts it on the next page: 'The commodity can only be understood in its undistorted essence when it becomes the universal category of society as a whole.'[7] In other words, we must assume total commodification and reification in order to be crystal clear on the structure of the commodity form, just as Marx makes these assumptions in clarifying the law of value in *Capital*. But making such assumptions is the basis for what Uno[8] and Sekine[9] have called the 'theory of a purely capitalist society'. As I shall argue in more depth later, Lukács falls into an absolutely fundamental theoretical trap when he fails to distinguish between the total reification of pure capitalism and the partial reification of actually existing capitalism. It is this trap more than any other that leads him into dangerously excessive degrees of essentialism.

I want to focus on four dimensions of Lukács' theory of reification: first, the concept of reification itself in its most fundamental meaning; second, Lukács' use of the concept 'totality'; third, his reflections on Marx's concept 'use-value'; and fourth and finally, the beginnings of a theory of subjectivity. Lukács has many colourful descriptions of reification from which I have picked the following for a start:

> man in capitalist society confronts a reality 'made' by himself (as a class) which appears to him to be a natural phenomenon alien to himself; he is wholly at the mercy of its 'laws', his activity is confined to the exploitation of the inexorable fulfilment of certain individual laws for his own (egoistic) interests. But even while 'acting' he remains, in the nature of the case, the object and not the subject of events.[10]

To the extent that this quotation is true, it must have pretty radical implications for any theory of subjectivity under capitalism. From the point of view of the inexorability of economic forces, opposition to them appears to be irrational. In other words, reification forces us to give up responsibility for our economic life and instead to confine our actions to individual efforts to maximize utilities in accord with the iron laws of capitalism. Furthermore, according to Lukács, under such total reification, while we can still act, our action always tends to be a sort of reaction or, if you like, the action of an objectified subject. Indeed, Lukács thinks that the reifying force of capitalism is so strong that we shall tend to be the objects and not subjects of events unless we can act in a powerfully collective manner to overthrow reification. If we even partially accept what Lukács is arguing here, it would seem that one of the first steps in connecting theories of capital with theories of subjectivity is to explore the ways in which reification undermines and channels our agency, and central to such a project for Lukács would be to solve 'the riddle of the commodity structure'.[11]

In what ways, to what extent, and with what consequences does commodification sink into various areas of our life, from religion to economics, and from sports to politics? How are our desires and identities shaped and directed by commodification, whether male or female, straight or gay, rich or poor, black or white, third world or imperialist world, rural or urban? Surely commodification cuts across all these practices and identities to some extent, and to that extent may generate various bases of solidarity. Political economy's capability of theorizing such homogenizing forces is increasingly important in a world where the emphases on difference have cultivated a divisiveness that neoliberalism feasts upon.

According to Lukács' quotation, the movements of capitalist society, though in fact stemming from human action, seem about as unalterable as the movements of the earth's tectonic plates that cause earthquakes. This seeming naturalness of capital's motions makes them very difficult to criticize in ways that will penetrate the minds and hearts of its subjects. This difficulty is compounded by capital's atomizing tendencies, tendencies which lean towards reproducing individuals as egoistic subjects focused primarily on advancing themselves in the economic game in opposition to all other individuals who do the same. To the extent that this state of affairs is realized, acting subjects are converted into the objects of economic events over which they have little or no control. In short, all economic action tends to become reaction, and economic action not in tune with capital's laws of motion is thwarted. Finally, while it clearly is possible to resist capitalism and radically transform it, its nature-like automaticity is real for Lukács. It will continue to expand itself according to its inner logic unless it is resisted.

The second dimension of reification I should like to consider is its connections with Lukács' concept 'totality'. According to Lukács, lacking any control over the whole, capitalists make up for this by attempting to exercise despotism over the part that they do own and control. Thus, while the anarchy of the whole that produces periodic crises cannot be controlled, at least to the extent that capitalists have despotic control over their part, they might better withstand the dangerous storms of crises. If workers are atomized and reduced to being nothing more than appendages of machines, then they will not be able to effectively resist in times of crises.

The capitalist class, then, tends to think in terms of tight rational control over partial systems, while the whole is beyond its grasp and to some extent beyond its reason.

Moreover, just as factories are closed systems of partial laws according to Lukács, so bourgeois social science tends to generate highly specialized sciences that focus on small groupings of trees while losing sight of the forest. Lukács claims that 'the more intricate a modern science becomes ... the more resolutely it will turn its back on the ontological problems of its own sphere of influence ... The more highly developed it becomes and the more scientific, the more it will become a formally closed system of partial laws'.[12] Surely there is at least a degree of truth in Lukács' claims here. Consider neoclassical economic theory, for example. It combines a complete neglect of ontological issues with extreme formalization into 'closed systems of partial laws'. As a result, neoclassical economists completely ignore fundamental questions about the nature of property, of commodities, of prices, of profits and of the labour-process under capitalism. Typically, they simply accept these things as given and then study mathematical formalizations that trace changes in one variable in relation to another. How the economic actually articulates with the legal, the political, the cultural, the historical, the ideological or the psychical is totally beyond the ken of such theorizing.

Lukács claims that such formalized partial systems cannot begin to understand historical change, since it is the interaction of many social forces within a totality that brings about significant change. As he puts it: 'The greater the distance from pure immediacy, the larger the net encompassing the "relations", and the more complete the integration of the "objects" within the system of relations, the sooner change will cease to be impenetrable and catastrophic, the sooner it will become comprehensible.'[13] For Lukács, 'pure immediacy' implies isolated facts and objects, and since, like Hegel, he thinks objects are fundamentally relational, then they can only be understood when integrated into a system of relations. Moreover, the more encompassing or total the system and the more integrated the objects into the system, the better that system change can be understood. The upshot of this for Lukacs is that the bourgeoisie by and large cannot understand change, because it is not in their class interest to understand the totality; while the proletariat, in so far as it becomes the agent of revolutionary change, comes to understand the change it is making in the process of breaking up the reification of capitalism.

The third dimension of reification I want to explore is its impact on how we relate to use-values in a capitalist society. According to Lukács, 'Marx has often demonstrated convincingly how inadequate the "laws" of bourgeois economics are to the task of explaining the true movement of economic activity in toto. He has made it clear that this limitation lies in the – methodologically inevitable – failure to comprehend use-value and real consumption.'[14] It is, of course, the single-minded focus on the quantitative side of economic life that underlies the neglect of the use-value or the qualitative side of life in bourgeois economics. For example, bourgeois economists and capitalists think only about the effective demand of monied people and not the real demand corresponding to the needs of all the people. Companies are evaluated by their profit rates and not by the social and ecological costs of their profit-making activities. Economists think about market costs, but treat social costs such as ecological costs as externalities. Capitalists try to get away with paying fewer taxes even if it means undermining health, education and welfare. An economy is assessed by its growth in gross domestic product (GDP) even if growing inequality consigns more and more people to lives of desperation and poverty. And one could go on and on about the fixation on the quantitative or value side of things and neglect of the qualitative or use-value side of things under capitalism.

If a capitalist economy is working well from the point of view of capital, it means that the commodity form is totally secure, and as a result capitalists can be totally indifferent to use-value. If workers are not organized, and if unemployment is high, then capitalists may be able to hire and fire workers at will, treating them like any other commodity. If land is readily available at a reasonable price either to buy or to rent, then this use-value can be treated in quantitative terms alone. If the financial system provides low-interest loans, then capital becomes so cheap that it can be utilized for profit-making as an end in itself. If there is no monopoly, then capitalists do not have to worry about the materiality of power that might undermine them. If the state does not intervene, capitalists can ignore the health and safety of workers, environmental regulations, taxes and other use-value annoyances. In short, it is only because we resist capital that it is forced to take use-value into account at all. In a capitalist utopia, where capitalists always got their way, use-value or the materiality or quality of things could be ignored except in the depths of a depression, which always forces capital to face its possible demise.

The fourth and final dimension of reification I shall consider is the connection between reification and subjectivity. Lukács claims:

> Subjectively – where the market economy has been fully developed – man's activity becomes estranged from himself, it turns into a commodity which, subject to the non-human objectivity of the natural laws of society, must get its own way independently of man just like any consumer article.[15]

> The specialized 'virtuoso', the vendor of his objectified and reified faculties does not just become the [passive] observer of society; he also lapses into a contemplative attitude *vis-à-vis* the workings of his own

objectified and reified faculties ... The transformation of the commodity relation into a thing of 'ghostly objectivity' cannot therefore content itself with the reduction of all objects for the gratification of human needs to commodities. It stamps its imprint upon the whole conscious-ness of man; his qualities and abilities are no longer an organic part of his personality, they are things which he can 'own' or 'dispose of' like the various objects of the external world.[16]

In other words, to use recent language, one impact of reification is to 'decentre' the personality. Now, it may be the case that personalities are always decentred to some extent, but what Lukács is suggesting here is that the tendency of capitalism is to radically decentre personalities to the extent that their very capability for agency is undermined. The person becomes a sort of collection of commodity potentials that can be owned or marketed to varying extents. For example, if a woman is beautiful, she has a choice of marketing her beauty in a variety of ways; or if a person is of the 'wrong' race in a racist society, their opportunities to market them-selves may be reduced to only the most menial and low-paying jobs. How you are able to package yourself depends largely on where you are located in the commodity world, and your life chances depend radically on such packaging, whether it is in the marriage market, the education market, or the job market. To the extent that you cannot establish yourself in the world of commodities, you tend to become invisible or subject to treatment in accordance with pre-capitalist social norms that are often embedded in religion or 'traditional' culture.

Postmodernists are no doubt correct that the human personality is less centred and unified than most previous bourgeois thought would have us consider. Indeed, according to bourgeois ideology, we are totally centred egos even as capital's motions decentre us. Indeed, if Lukács is correct, there is an undesirable degree of decentring generated by capitalism, a degree that turns us into 'contemplative' onlookers at our own selves as collections of disparate pieces and faculties that have become objectified as commodities. If we repeat a motion on an assembly line, we are subject to repetitive stress injuries; if we look at computer chips through a microscope all day, we are subject to eye injury; and if we breathe the automobilized and industrialized air of our cities, we are subject to lung diseases. Reification, then, fragments us and weakens our powers to resist even as our bodies are assaulted by a capitalist madness that puts profits before people.

What would be the social/psychic implications of a world in which all objects for the gratification of needs become reduced to commodities? Surely this would have an impact on identity formation in the most funda-mental ways, since it implies that people themselves are reduced to being commodities. A person's desires for all objects, including people, would be channelled in accordance with market-discursive valuings. Needs, then, would become socially constructed as various forms of commodified desire fulfillment, or in other words as the possession of certain objects/persons. A need is always a need for a commodity or a commodified person. A 'star', whether in the cinema, sports, politics or some other arena, is a commodity that has huge value projected on to him/her because most people either cannot possess what they desire or find that their desire is not at all fulfilled when they do possess what they have been led to believe they need. Any of the many needs which cannot be satisfied by possession tend to become invisible or neglected, and this puts a load on possession that it cannot bear, generating a 'star system' fuelled by frustrated need. Moreover, generalized need frustration makes people desperately possessive of those commodities that do seem even slightly need-fulfilling.

Jean-Paul Sartre once argued that Marxist theory treats humans as though they were always adults, and that it must therefore by supplemented by psychoanalytic theory, since our personalities are given their most fundamental shaping in childhood.[17] It is beyond the scope of this chapter to consider the ways in which psychoanalytic theory might contribute to the theory of subjectivity, but in response to Sartre, it is not necessary that Marxian political economy think only of adults. After all, children are raised in families of varying types, but in a society where the economy is predominantly capitalist, capitalist social relations will have a huge impact on the family, and the class location of the family will have a strong influence on the life chances of its children as well as their behavioural predispositions.

Critique

I shall organize my critique of Lukács around the same four themes: reification, totality, use-value, and subjectivity. In this critical section I shall revisit some of the same quotations, only now drawing out some of the problems embedded within them. And, as I have already stated above, the most fundamental problem is Lukács' tendency to confuse the situation of total reification in a purely capitalist society, which is essentially a thought experiment that never exists as any empirical society, with actually existing capitalism where reification is always successfully resisted to some extent and never has the capability 'to penetrate society in all its aspects'.[18]

In Uno and Sekine's theory of a purely capitalist society, we perhaps come closest to Lukács' idealization of total reification. But there is an absolutely crucial difference. Sekine is crystal clear that his dialectic of capital is limited to the socio-economic material reproduction of society in so far as it takes place through a commodity–economic logic alone. Essentially, it is a theory that highlights what capital can do on its own as opposed to what it cannot do, under conditions (total reification) that are most propitious to capital's self-expansion. By reconstructing the necessary inner connections among the fundamental economic categories of capitalism as a dialectical logic, Sekine is able to present a theory of capital's inner logic. Or, to put it a little differently, he is able to reveal capitalistic rationality in its starkest form, and as a result, to demonstrate what capital essentially is. The dialectic of capital can only be completed because, among themselves, value categories can subsume those use-value obstacles that cannot be avoided in any capitalist society – for example, workers, land and tools.

Having a theory of a purely capitalist society is an absolutely crucial starting point for clarifying our thinking about subjectivity and agency. This is so because it makes crystal clear the difference between capital's 'agency' and our 'agency', and hence establishes a basis for thinking about directions that we might choose as alternatives to the general motions of capital. Capital mesmerizes us to identify with its agency, and it is terribly important that we begin to think clearly about alternatives that are not fixed or limited in advance by capital's logic.

While having such a theory can be a huge help in thinking about a society in so far as it is capitalist, no society is totally capitalist, and while capital's logic influences all parts of society, it penetrates some areas more and some less. It never 'remoulds' 'society in all its aspects', as Lukács thinks. Thus it is problematic for Lukács to claim that the factory contains 'in concentrated form the whole structure of capitalist society'. In the theory of a purely capitalist society, we do not know how a factory is organized, except that it is organized around machinery to maximize profits. In contrast, at the level of historical analysis, factory organization may be diverse even within the same country over an identical time span. Furthermore, there has been no time in capitalist history when the majority of working people in the world spent most of their working hours in factories, and, at the time of writing, the influence in the global economy of the classical industrial factory may be shrinking. The problem here, as elsewhere in Lukács' essay, is a tendency to over-totalize, treating some quite variable concrete part as a direct expression or model of the whole.

Thus, while at the highest level of abstraction we can theorize capital's inner logic by assuming total reification, at the level of historical analysis we can never extend this reification to capitalist society as a whole, but instead must in every case explore the ways in which this logic articulates with social forces that have various degrees of autonomy from capitalism, and, of course, included in this relative autonomy is the capacity to resist capital. On the one hand, there is no part of society that totally escapes the influence of capital, and on the other hand, social life is never simply a function of capital's logic. If we accept both of these propositions, then no social forces are totally autonomous from capital, while many social forces are relatively autonomous. For example, a social force such as patriarchy pre-dated capitalism, and while it has been shaped by capitalism, it cannot be reduced to a simple function of capital's logic.

Next I want to revisit the following quotation from Lukács:

> man [*sic*] in capitalist society confronts a reality 'made' by himself (as a class) which appears to him to be a natural phenomenon alien to himself; he is wholly at the mercy of its 'laws', his activity is confined to the exploitation of the inexorable fulfilment of certain individual laws for his own (egoistic) interests. But even while 'acting' he remains, in the nature of the case, the object and not the subject of events.[19]

Other than the sexist use of 'man' as a universal throughout nearly all Western philosophy, the sequentially first thing to note in this quotation is the phrase 'confronts a reality'. I want to be a little picky here in order to make a point. I believe that, for Lukács, we 'confront a reality' because there is quite literally one unified reality created by the universal domination and penetration of the commodity structure. In opposition, I would claim that capital has a unique ontology whose reifying force means that, in the long run, it tends to shape, rather than being shaped by, other social forces, and this is what makes a theory of this unique ontology so important. At the same time, other social forces do shape capitalist history, and to that extent are crucial to understanding that history. It is only in a purely capitalist society that people confront a single reality with a single logic. At more concrete levels of analysis there are social forces that are relatively autonomous, and there may be in some sense relatively autonomous ontologies as well. This would imply a complex articulation of realities in the plural, with capital being the predominant reality in the long run only to the extent that capitalist social relations predominate in the society being studied. Instead of assuming a priori a unified historical reality as a function of capital, I am suggesting that we can only a priori know that capital has a unique ontology that is particularly powerful and will in the long run tend to shape other social forces more than it is shaped by them to the extent that the society in question is capitalist. But without examining actual history, we cannot know a priori how capital articulates with other social forces. Thus my first point is that we do not 'confront a reality', but instead confront a complex of realities articulated with one another in a kind of ensemble of realities that is not necessarily centred or unified. Thus, for example, in a country where capitalism tends to be weak and to be subsumed to a fundamentalist religion, religion may prevail, at least for some time, in shaping some important social realities more than capital. And even where capitalism is well established, patriarchy, racism and heterosexism may predominate in shaping certain social realities.

Next in sequence is the phrase 'a reality "made" by himself (as a class)'. Here, Lukács puts the concept 'made' in quotation marks to note that it is problematic, as indeed it is. I suppose that 'making history' is located somewhere between 'making a cake' and 'making a language'. The latter sounds strange and voluntaristic since, at least in their basic grammars, languages are the product of social interaction over thousands of years. It is for this reason that we think of languages as evolving as opposed to being made. The problem with 'making' is that, in English, it has strongly voluntarist connotations as in the phrase 'self-made man'. I suspect this is part of the reason for all of the debates over agency that usually do not get far past such vacuous phrases as 'structures condition agency and agency transforms structures'. The problem here is that we so often think of a sovereign subject 'making' an object, whereas when considering capitalist history, subjects are always objectified and atomized to the extent that it takes considerable effort to build the kind of collective solidarity that can transform significant structures of oppression. The problem is with the concepts: 'subject', 'agency', and 'making' – concepts that have been made so voluntarist by bourgeois ideology that they can only be used with the utmost caution.

Next let me consider the phrase '"made" by himself (as a class)', in order to address the touchy issue of 'class reductionism'. In some very general and loose sense, capitalism may yet come to an end as a result of struggles by working people to transform it. Lukács, however, tends to confuse thought about class in pure capitalism, where class lines are clear and distinct, with class at the level of historical analysis, where class lines are unclear, and various classes and class fractions are always in the process of coming to the fore or dissolving into the background. Hegemony at local, regional, national, or global levels may be very complex, involving various alliances among class fractions and groups that have contradictory class locations.

In order to be clear about what we mean by 'class', about the dominant forms of class and class struggle during different phases of capitalist development, and about the complexity of class and its articulation with other social forces at the level of history, I believe that it is necessary to have at least three levels of analysis: the theory of capital's inner logic or the theory of pure capitalism, the theory of phases of capitalist development or mid-range theory, and the analysis of history. In *Capital*, Marx mixes up what I have called the 'three levels of analysis' because he is trying to address a popular audience that would find a bare bones rendering of capital's inner logic too bloodless. There is no doubt, however, that capital's inner logic can be theorized as a rigorous dialectic that demonstrates how, under conditions that are ideal for capital, value as capital can be self-expanding. Value cannot be self-expanding if it relies on any outside other; and this entails that value, as a commodity-economic logic, be able to overcome the sorts of use-value obstacles that would be present in any capitalist society, without relying on extra-economic force. It is my contention that Marx's primary aim in *Capital* is to present a theory of capital's inner logic as self-expanding value. Marx himself often describes what he is doing in these terms, or slightly different ones. For example, he also claims that he is tracing the necessary inner connections among the primary economic concepts of capitalism.

The dialectic of capital is basically a dialectic between self-expanding value and the use-value obstacles it must subsume in order to be self-expanding. The dialectic demonstrates that labour-power is the use-value that capital has the most difficulty managing commodity-economically. Indeed, such management implies at least the following: a prior separation of workers from the means of production, an industrial reserve army, and periodic crises. And since all value and surplus value comes from the productive use of labour-power by capital, the secure commodification of labour power is at the core of the expanded reproduction of capital.

In a purely capitalist society where we assume that reification is sufficiently advanced so that capital can operate as a commodity-economic logic without reliance on extra-economic force, we cannot theorize the historically contingent ways in which humans, either capitalists or workers, might organize themselves either to resist or to enforce the law of value. In a society that is ideal from the point of view of capital, all workers are conceived as legal subjects able to sell their labour power for a wage and spend their wage as they will. All workers are free to quit their jobs and look elsewhere for better wages and working conditions, and for this reason, wages and working conditions in a purely capitalist society tend to be averaged. Furthermore, all capitalists, as legal subjects and owners of the means of production, are free not only to buy inputs and sell outputs of the labour and production process and to do what they will with any profits produced, but also to hire and fire at will the workers who provide the labour power from which all profits come. As a result, capitalists must sell what the market dictates through the economic form of a profit rate or go bankrupt, and workers must work for a capitalist where the wages and working conditions are approximately the same among all capitalists, or starve. In short, the much touted bourgeois freedom to buy and sell does not have much substance for the working class.

The theory of capital's inner logic theorizes the fundamental class relation between capital and labour as a structural relationship of exploitation, and in the context of pure capitalism, the concepts of capital and labour are crystal clear, just as assumed by Lukács. At all times capital attempts to extract as much profit as possible no matter what the human or ecological costs.

The dialectic of capital, which is simply a more rigorous version of Marx's theory of capital's inner logic, is the most radical critique of bourgeois freedom ever written. It demonstrates that the economic freedom to buy and sell in a capitalist society must necessarily reproduce class exploitation on an ever-expanding scale. It demonstrates that, if capital were to have its way completely, as is assumed in the theory of a purely capitalist society, then all human values whatsoever, and all use-value considerations whatsoever, would always be sacrificed to short-term profit considerations.

The theory of pure capitalism demonstrates, logically, why in capitalist history there will always be class struggle. Contrary to the thinking of some Marxists, however, it is not necessary, desirable or even possible to theorize class struggle in any meaningful sense in the context of the theory of capital's inner logic. It is not necessary because, by making the structural class relationship crystal clear, the dialectic of capital demonstrates why class struggle will always occur in capitalist history. It is not desirable because the dialectic is the dialectic of capital and not of labour. This implies that the object being theorized is the 'law of value', or, what amounts to the same thing, the law of motion of capital and not the law of motion of labour. Indeed, if labour had a law of motion complementary to capital, then resistance would be futile; and, if not complementary but in opposition, then the ending of capitalism would be automatic. If labour were to resist capital successfully, then the law of value would be altered and we would no longer have a clear conception of it. It follows that including class struggle in the dialectic of capital will hinder the clarity and objectivity of the theory, making it more difficult to distinguish the motions of capital from the motions of class aimed at resisting capital. Thus, well-meaning Marxists who always want to put class struggle at the centre, in fact do it a disservice when they attempt to do this in connection with the theory of capital's inner logic. Finally, theorizing class struggle in the dialectic of capital is not possible because, in order to get a rigorous dialectic of capital, we must assume an atomized society. Resistance implies some kind of class organization, or at least spontaneous solidarity, but at this level of abstraction we cannot specify such historically contingent forms, whether they are shop-floor resistance, bread riots, strikes, factory occupations, mass demonstrations, or revolutions. Such historical contingency clearly does not belong in a theory of 'necessary inner connections' among basic economic categories.

Because Lukács makes reification such a totalizing force, it can only be overcome by an even more totalizing force and, for him, this can only be the proletariat. But as he sets it up, the whole scenario is quite apocalyptic and unlikely. Indeed, if reification were really as strong and complete as Lukács makes it out to be, there would be little chance that the struggle against capitalism could ever be successful. People in capitalist society are not 'wholly at the mercy of its laws', as Lukács claims. This is only true in a context where we assume that the self-abstracting and self-reifying forces of capital are complete, in other words, in a purely capitalist society. In actual history, we always resist the laws of motion of capital, and at least partially as a result of the degree of this resistance, capitalism is transformed continually.

Finally, I want to reconsider the phrase 'appears to him to be a natural phenomenon alien to himself'. The assumption here is that capitalism is analogous to natural phenomena such as photosynthesis or earthquakes, which are both natural and both alien because we do not 'make' or control them. Here, Lukács himself seems to be caught up to some extent into the very subject/object antinomy that his dialectics aims to overcome. For him, capitalism follows its own laws, much like photosynthesis (though it may result in browning instead of greening), but with a communist revolution, we shall overcome our total objectification and in some way become master subjects of our own history. In opposition, it is my claim that neither nature nor history needs to be experienced as alien just because they are not made and controlled by us. Capitalist history neither reduces us to objects nor does communist revolution convert us into sovereign subjects. What is more accurate is to say that we should have more control over our destiny under communism than we do under capitalism, because we shall be able to take more responsibility for our economic life and its outcomes.

I turn now to a reconsideration of Lukács' conception of totality. It is one thing to use this concept negatively to criticize the tendency of much bourgeois social science to consider isolated parts as though they were hermetically sealed off from the whole in which they are embedded; it is quite another to use it positively to claim knowledge of some totality. It is with this latter usage that Lukács gets into trouble. In the first sentence of his essay he claims that Marx, 'set out to portray capitalist society in its totality and to lay bare its fundamental nature'.[20] I believe that it is correct to claim that, in *Capital*, Marx set out to 'lay bare' capital's 'fundamental nature', which, in this case, yields a theory of capital's essence or inner logic. It is very different, however, to claim that Marx 'set out to portray capitalist society in its totality'. I would argue that no society can be portrayed in its totality unless all of its outcomes can be derived from a single inner logic or deep structure. It makes sense to try to understand as many interconnections as possible and avoid studying things in isolation, but Lukács' phrasing fails to express the enormous difficulties in achieving this. It is impossible to be certain that one has grasped accurately the interactions among the main economic forces operating in a particular society at a particular time, much less how these forces interact with, say, religious forces. And yet this kind of analysis can be greatly aided and advanced if we do have a strong theory of capital's inner logic that makes crystal clear what capital is.

Of course, Lukács is right to say that 'the problem of commodities must not be considered in isolation',[21] but then he goes on to make the unsustainable claim that the problem of commodities is 'the central, structural problem of capitalist society in all its aspects'.[22] It is clear that Marx does not attempt to theorize 'capitalist society in all its aspects' in *Capital*; instead, as he asserts time and again, he is only theorizing the necessary inner connections among the economic categories of capital in the abstract and in general. It is not that this theory cannot shed light on many things, but it often can do so only in conjunction with other theories.

For example, Chandra Mohanty demonstrates that the particular exploitation and oppression of women lace-makers in India cannot be fully understood without an analysis of how commodification articulates with local cultural practices that construct gender differences.[23] And while commodification has an impact on the construction of gender differences, we cannot derive an adequate account of these differences from commodification alone.

The central problem with the way Lukács uses the concept totality is that he too easily extends a notion of totality appropriate only to the theory of capital's inner logic to actually existing capitalisms. Consequently, he vastly overstates the degree to which reification takes hold at the level of historical reality. In turn, and as a result, capitalism becomes almost impossible to transform, and its transformation tends to be conceived of as an apocalyptic total revolution in which the proletariat achieves 'knowledge' of the whole. In contrast, it is my claim that we need to study both the general tendencies of capital and the specificity of local forms of oppression in order to build the kinds of collective solidarity that may ultimately transform capitalism. Reification does tend to extend from capital's inner logic throughout actual capitalist societies, but its impact is uneven and partial, not all-encompassing and total.

I turn next to the third dimension of my analysis of Lukács' concept of reification, the use-value dimension of economic life, about which Lukács is again accurate as long as we assume a purely capitalist society, where total indifference to use-value is achieved. At more concrete levels of analysis, use-value obstacles cannot always be overcome by self-valorizing value, but rather require supports that may have at least some autonomy from capital (in some cases, as in the judiciary, their very effectiveness depends upon at least the appearance of relative autonomy).

The continual resistance of working people is a major reason why capital is forced continually to consider use-value even if it would prefer not to. To a very large extent the post-Second World War welfare state was a response to pressures from workers' movements over the course of the ninetieth and twentieth centuries, taking different forms in different geographical locations, just as neoliberalism is to some extent a response to, and cause of, the weakening of workers' movements. Moreover, popular pressure is forcing capital to pay at least some attention to the growing ecological crises, though it would prefer to ignore it if possible, just at it would prefer to ignore all conceivable use-value constraints on the ideal of infinite capital (profit) expansion.

The fourth dimension of my critique engages with the impact of reification on the construction of subjectivity. Because of the excessively totalizing character of Lukács' thought, here as elsewhere, he tends to exaggerate; and yet, on this issue, I am a little more sympathetic, because exaggeration here brings to our attention a much-neglected topic. I believe that the commodification of social relations has a very large impact on the construction of subjectivity, an impact that has hardly even begun to be studied. At the same time, we need to employ levels of analysis to move from the context of a purely capitalist society to historical analysis, and finally to local contexts. A purely capitalist society is totally reified and atomized, and the social relations connecting the atoms are reduced to value relations. It is in this thought experiment that we can consider the implications of a situation where needs are completely satisfied through commodities. In such a society, each individual may appear to be 'self-made', and self-making involves accumulating commodities to satisfy needs, whether real or imaginary. At the same time, as each individual is considered to be 'self-made', all individuals are totally subjected to economic forces beyond their control. The result is a radically frustrating situation where efforts towards 'self-making' are thwarted systematically by totally uncontrollable economic forces that ensure few winners and many losers in the economic 'game'.

It is in this situation of pure capitalism, then, where Lukács' thoughts about subjectivity are most appropriate. It is at more concrete levels of analysis, where identity construction is influenced by many forces other than the commodity structure, that Lukács' views must be used with caution. And it is not that these other forces are not influenced by the commodity structure, but rather that even with this influence they have a relative autonomy. For example, if someone is raised in a patriarchal family that adheres to a fundamentalist Christian sect, this is bound to have an impact on identity formation, even if part of the explanation for the success of the sect has to do with the forces of capitalism.

Conclusions

Mohanty focuses on the actual resistance and transformative possibilities of Third-World working women in ways sensitive to the specificity of their local experience.[24] The main contribution of the political economy I am advocating is a way to theorize capital's logic and capitalism's logics that can avoid economic and class reductionism. Clearly, it would be desirable if, in the future, researchers on the left could achieve greater integration of the sort of work Mohanty is advocating with the sort I am advocating. I want to think about the impact of capital and capitalism on our lives, neither over- nor understating its impact, precisely so that we can better untangle ourselves from its tentacles as we move towards more humane and ecologically sound forms of social life. A first and very important step forward is getting as clear a picture as possible of what capital is, how we collaborate with capital, what impact this collaboration has on us, and how we can break with this collaboration in order to act in more effectively transformative ways in the future. Deep and extended thought using concepts such as 'reification' and 'commodification' offer immense promise in further developing existing theories of subjectivity, in developing new theories of subjectivity, and in developing mediations between political economy in general and theories of subjectivity in general. Equally, we need studies such as Mohanty's that speak to local and specific experience in ways that enable those engaged in local struggles or those experiencing locally specific forms of oppression to see connections with the larger picture.

Lukács' theory of reification provides a good start for bridging this gap from the political economy side, if we limit total reification to the case of a purely capitalist society. By doing this we ground reification in the socio-economic relations of capital's inner logic. At this level of abstraction, reification is worked out in the context of a rigorous dialectical logic that completes itself in such a way that capital can truly be self-expanding value. But because the inner logic of capital never exists in the strong sense of being fully present in any particular historical reality, by adopting the approach I am advocating, the relationships between abstract theory and historical analysis become problematized, and at the same time the relationships between the economic and non-economic spheres of social life become so as well. Neither of these relationships is sufficiently prob-lematized in Lukács, resulting in unacceptable degrees of totalization, essentialism and reductionism. To be clear about reification, we must analyze its degree of penetration into relatively autonomous spheres of social life, and we must analyze ways in which it is resisted and under-mined. Hyperconsumption in the advanced industrial countries at the start of the twenty-first century means that, more than ever, reification, commodification and objectification are very powerful forces, not only in the economic life of those able to access the growing array of commodities but also in that of those excluded. Furthermore, desire is connected to hyperconsumption in ways that penetrate cultural life and the construction of subjectivities even in those parts of the world that seem to be the most remote from the heartlands of capitalism. But it is not enough to state these generalities. It is time to start integrating theories of reification with other theories of subjectivity in order to clarify our thinking about the specific impacts on us of the peculiar capitalist social reality that we are in, precisely so that we can act more effectively in concert to make our social realities more humane and sustainable.

Notes and References

1. Lukács, G., *History and Class Consciousness* (London: Merlin Press, 1971).
2. For an extended discussion of reification and its connection to capital's unique ontology, see Albritton, R., *Dialectics and Deconstruction in Political Economy* (London: Macmillan, 1999).
3. See Fraser, N., 'From Redistribution to Recognition? Dilemmas of Justice in a "Poststructuralist Age"', *New Left Review*, vol. 212 (1995); also Hennessy, R., *Profit and Pleasure* (New York: Routledge, 2000).
4. Lukács, *History and Class Consciousness*, p. 84.
5. Lukács, *History and Class Consciousness*, p. 83.
6. Lukács, *History and Class Consciousness*, p. 85.
7. Lukács, *History and Class Consciousness*, p. 86.
8. Uno, K., *Principles of Political Economy: Theory of a Purely Capitalist Society*, trans. T. Sekine, (Brighton: Harvester Press, 1980).
9. Sekine, T., *An Outline of the Dialectic of Capital*, 2 vols (London: Macmillan, 1997).
10. Lukács, *History and Class Consciousness*, p. 135.
11. Lukács, *History and Class Consciousness*, p. 83.
12. Lukács, *History and Class Consciousness*, p. 104.
13. Lukács, *History and Class Consciousness*, p. 154.
14. Lukács, *History and Class Consciousness*, p. 106.
15. Lukács, *History and Class Consciousness*, p. 87.
16. Lukács, *History and Class Consciousness*, p. 100.
17. Sartre, J.-P., *Search For a Method* (New York: Vintage, 1968).
18. Lukács, *History and Class Consciousness*, p. 86.
19. Lukács, *History and Class Consciousness*, p. 135.
20. Lukács, *History and Class Consciousness*, p. 83.
21. Lukács, *History and Class Consciousness*, p. 83.
22. Lukács, *History and Class Consciousness*, p. 83.
23. Mohanty, C., 'Women Workers and Capitalist Scripts: Ideologies of Domination, Common Interests, and the Politics of Solidarity' in M. J. Alexander and C. Mohanty (eds), *Feminist Genealogies, Colonial Legacies, and Democratic Futures* (New York: Routledge, 1997).
24. Mohanty, 'Women Workers and Capitalist Scripts ...'.

5
Lukács and the Dialectical Critique of Capitalism

Moishe Postone

P16

B51

The historical transformation in recent decades of advanced industrial-ized societies, the collapse of the Soviet Union and of Communism, and the emergence of a neoliberal capitalist global order have drawn attention once again to issues of historical dynamics and global transformations. These historical changes suggest the need for a renewed theoretical concern with capitalism, and cannot be addressed adequately by the post-structuralist and postmodern theories that were hegemonic in the 1970s and 1980s.

Georg Lukács' brilliant essay 'Reification and the Consciousness of the Proletariat' could serve as a point of departure for such a theoretical renewal.[1] In that essay, Lukács develops a rich and rigorous critical analysis of capitalist modernity. Aspects of Lukács' theory, however, are at odds with that very analysis. Nevertheless, as I shall argue, his theoretical approach, if appropriated critically, may form the basis of a sophisticated theory of capitalist society that would be relevant at the start of the twenty-first century. Such a theory could avoid many shortcomings of traditional Marxist critiques of capitalism and recast the relationship of critical theories of capitalism to other major currents of critical social theory today.

The conceptual framework of Lukács' 'Reification' essay differs significantly from most strands of Marxism. As a political and theoretical intervention, Lukács' essay decisively rejects the scientism and faith in linear historical progress of orthodox Second International Marxism. Such positions, for Lukács, were the deep theoretical grounds for the political and world-historical failures of social democracy to prevent war in 1914 and bring about radical historical change in 1918–19. Lukács effects this theoretical break with Second International Marxism by reasserting the Hegelian dimension of Marx's thought, focusing on the importance of subjectivity and the centrality of praxis. His essay recovers Marx's critique of political economy as a powerful social theory – a dialectical theory of praxis.

At the centre of Lukács' theory of praxis is his appropriation of the categories of Marx's mature critique, such as the 'commodity'. Within the framework of this categorial approach, praxis is not simply opposed to structures, it is also constitutive of them.[2] By appropriating Marx's theory of praxis and placing it at the very centre of his critical analysis of capitalism, Lukács argues powerfully for the intrinsic interrelatedness of subjective and objective dimensions of social life. Both are constituted by determinate forms of praxis. That is, Lukács grasps the categories of Marx's mature critique as having a significance that goes far beyond mere economic categories; he interprets them as categories of the forms of modern social life – subjective as well as objective.[3] His approach in this regard parallels Marx's who, in the *Grundrisse*, refers to the categories as *Daseinsformen* (forms of *Dasein*) and *Existenzbestimmungen* (determinations of the mode of existence).[4]

On the basis of this categorial appropriation, Lukács develops a sophisticated social theory of consciousness and of knowledge, which entails a fundamental critique of Cartesianism, of subject–object dualism. His theory of praxis allows him to argue that the subject is both producer and product of the dialectical process.[5] Consequently:

> [t]hought and existence are not identical in the sense that they 'correspond' to each other, or 'reflect' each other, that they 'run parallel' to each other, or 'coincide' with each other (all expressions that conceal a rigid duality). Their identity is that they are aspects of the same real historical and dialectical process.[6]

Within the framework of Lukács' categorial analysis, then, 'consciousness ... is a necessary, indispensable, integral part of that process of [historical] becoming'.[7]

In analyzing the interrelatedness of consciousness and history, Lukács' primary concern is to delineate the historical possibility of revolutionary class consciousness. At the same time, he presents a brilliant social and historical analysis of modern Western philosophy. Such thought, according to Lukács, attempts to wrestle with the problems generated by the peculiar abstract forms of life characteristic of its (capitalist) context, while remaining bound to the immediacy of the forms of appearance of that context. Hence, philosophical thought misrecognizes the problems generated by its context as being transhistorical and ontological.[8] It was Marx, according to Lukács, who first addressed adequately the problems with which modern philosophy had wrestled. He did so by changing the terms of those problems, grounding them socially and historically in the social forms of capitalism expressed by categories such as the commodity.

Recovering this mode of analysis, Lukács formulates a social and historical critique of modern philosophical and sociological thought. In analysing such thought socially and historically, he does not do so with reference to considerations of class interest. Rather than focusing on the function of thought for a system of social domination, such as class domination, Lukács attempts to ground the nature of such thought in the peculiarities of the social forms (commodity, capital) constitutive of capitalism. Lukács' analysis of social form seeks to intrinsically relate social and cultural aspects of life.

This appropriation of Marx's categorial analysis breaks decisively with classical Marxist base-superstructure conceptions. Such conceptions are themselves dualistic – the base being understood as the most fundamental level of social objectivity, and the superstructure being identified with social subjectivity. Lukács' approach also differs from that of the other great theorist of praxis, Antonio Gramsci, inasmuch as it relates intrinsically forms of thought and social forms, and does not treat their relationship as being extrinsic, or in a functionalist manner. Lukács' approach, in other words, can serve as the point of departure for an analysis of the nature of modern, capitalist cultural forms themselves. It not only elucidates the hegemonic function of those forms, but also delineates an overarching framework of historically determined forms of subjectivity within which class-related differentiation takes place.

The approach Lukács develops in the 'Reification' essay not only provides the basis for a sophisticated historical theory of subjectivity, but it also shifts implicitly the focus of the critique of capitalism away from traditional Marxist concerns. In this regard, Lukács' analysis can be understood as an attempt to develop a self-reflexive critical theory of capitalist modernity that would be adequate to the great social, political, economic and cultural changes associated with the development of twentieth century capitalism. It does so in a way that responds to the criticisms of Marxism formulated by classical social theorists.

As is well known, major social theorists such as Max Weber and Émile Durkheim argued at the turn of the last century that, contrary to the critical vision of classical traditional Marxism, modern society cannot be analyzed adequately in terms of the market and private property. Both theorists pointed to what they considered to be more fundamental features of modern society, Durkheim emphasizing the division of labour, and Weber focusing on processes of rationalization and bureaucratization. For both, the abolition of the market and private property would not suffice to transform modern society fundamentally. Indeed, it would simply reinforce its more negative aspects.

Although these theories of modernity may have been reactions to socialist movements and theories, they also sought to grapple with the problems and issues raised by the historical transformation of capitalist society from a liberal configuration in the nineteenth century to an organized bureaucratic, state-centric form in the twentieth century. Viewed in this light, Lukács' approach can be understood as an attempt to grasp the historical changes with which theorists such as Weber and Durkheim were wrestling, by embedding their concerns within a more encompassing theory of capitalism. More specifically, Lukács adopts Weber's characterization of modernity in terms of processes of rationalization and grounds these processes historically by appropriating Marx's analysis of the commodity form as the basic structuring social form of capitalist society. Thus, Lukács begins the 'Reification' essay by arguing that the processes of rationalization and quantification that mould modern institutions are rooted in the commodity form.[9] Following Marx, he characterizes modern, capitalist society in terms of the domination of humans by time, and treats the factory organization of production as a concentrated version of the structure of capitalist society as a whole.[10] This structure is expressed in the nature of modern bureaucracy,[11] and gives rise to a form of the state and of the system of law that corresponds to it.[12] By grounding modern processes of rationalization in this manner, Lukács seeks to show that what Weber described as the 'iron cage' of modern life is not a necessary concomitant of any form of modern society, but is a function of capitalism. Hence, it could be transformed.

Lukács' essay on reification demonstrates the power and rigour of a categorially-based critical theory of modern capitalist society, both as a theory of the intrinsic relatedness of culture, consciousness and society, and as a critique of capitalism. His critique extends beyond a concern with the market and private property – that is, with issues of class domination and exploitation. It seeks to critically grasp and socially ground processes of rationalization and quantification, as well as an abstract mode of power and domination that cannot be understood adequately in terms of concrete personal or group domination. That is, the conception of capitalism implied by Lukács' analysis is much broader and deeper than the traditional one: a system of exploitation based on private property and the market. Indeed, his conception implies that the latter ultimately may not be the most basic features of capitalism. Moreover, Lukács' analysis provides a level of conceptual rigour absent from most discussions of modernity. It indicates that 'modern society' is basically a descriptive term for a form of social life that can be analyzed with greater rigour as capitalism.

Nevertheless, Lukács fails to realize the promise of the sort of categorial critique he outlines. Although the 'Reification' essay presents a critique of capitalism fundamentally richer and more adequate than that of traditional Marxism, ultimately it remains bound to some of that theory's fundamental presuppositions. This weakens Lukács' attempt to formulate a critique of capitalism adequate to the present.

Traditional Marxism

By 'traditional Marxism' I do not mean a specific historical tendency in Marxism, such as orthodox Second International Marxism, for example, but, more generally, all analyses that understand capitalism essentially in terms of class relations structured by a market economy and private ownership of the means of production. Relations of domination are understood primarily in terms of class domination and exploitation. Within this general framework, capitalism is characterized by a growing structural contradiction between that society's basic social relations (interpreted as private property and the market) and the forces of production (interpreted as the industrial mode of producing).

The unfolding of this contradiction gives rise to the possibility of a new form of society, understood in terms of collective ownership of the means of production and economic planning in an industrialized context – that is, in terms of a just and consciously regulated mode of distribution adequate to industrial production. The latter is understood as a technical process that, while used by capitalists for their particularistic ends, is intrinsically independent of capitalism; it could be used for the benefit of all members of society.

This understanding is tied to a determinate reading of the basic categories of Marx's critique of political economy. His category of value, for example, has been interpreted generally as an attempt to show that human labour always and everywhere creates social wealth, and underlies the quasi-automatic, market-mediated mode of distribution in capitalism. His theory of surplus value, according to such views, demonstrates the existence of exploitation by showing that labour alone creates the surplus product which, in capitalism, is appropriated by the capitalist class. Marx's categories, within this general framework, then, are essentially categories of the market and private ownership.[13]

At the heart of this theory is a trans-historical – and commonsensical – understanding of labour as an activity mediating humans and nature that transforms matter in a goal-directed manner and is a condition of social life. Labour, so understood, is posited as the source of wealth in all societies, and as that which constitutes what is truly universal and truly social. In capitalism, however, labour is hindered by particularistic and fragmenting relations from becoming fully realized. 'Labour', understood trans-historically, constitutes the standpoint of this critique – both theoretically and socially. Emancipation is realized in a social form where trans-historical 'labour', freed from the fetters of the market and private property, has emerged openly as the regulating principle of society. (This notion, of course, is bound to that of socialist revolution as the 'self-realization' of the proletariat.)

It should be noted that, within this general framework, form (capitalist relations of production or, expressed categorially, value and surplus value) and content (industrial production or, more generally, 'labour') are related only contingently. A future society would be based on the content coming into its own, stripped of distorting capitalist forms. (As we shall see, however, form and content are related intrinsically in Marx's analysis.)

Within this basic framework there has been a broad range of very different theoretical, methodological, and political approaches. Nevertheless, to the extent that such approaches share the basic assumptions regarding labour and the essential characteristics of capitalism and of socialism outlined above, they remain bound within the framework of what I have called 'traditional Marxism'.

In terms of these considerations, there is an apparent tension in Lukács' thought. On the one hand, his focus on the commodity form allows for a critique of capitalism that explodes the limits of the traditional Marxist framework. But, on the other hand, when he addresses the question of the possible overcoming of capitalism, he has recourse to the notion of the proletariat as the revolutionary Subject of history.[14] This idea, however, is bound to a traditional conception of capitalism, where labour is considered to be the standpoint of the critique. And it is difficult to see how the notion of the proletariat as the revolutionary Subject points to the possibility of a historical transformation of the quantitative, rationalized and rationalizing character of modern institutions that Lukács analyzes critically as being capitalist.

Lukács' theory of the proletariat in the third part of his essay seems, then, to be in tension with the deeper and broader conception of capitalism presented in the essay's first part. This suggests either that Lukács' theory of the proletariat contravenes his categorial analysis, or that his categorial analysis itself is inadequate. That is, it raises the question of whether Lukács' specific understanding of the categories of Marx's critique adequately grounds the rich critical understanding of capitalism he presents in the 'Reification' essay.

I shall argue that Lukács' understanding of the categories is indeed problematic, and that it is consistent with his theory of the proletariat, a theory which others have criticized as being dogmatic and mythological.[15] Nevertheless, his broader conceptions of capitalism and of a categorial analysis are separable from his specific understanding of the categories and his theory of the proletariat. Appropriating the former, Lukács' enormous theoretical contribution, however, requires the critical interrogation of his conception of the commodity, the purportedly fundamental category of modern, capitalist society.

I shall argue that Lukács basically grasps the commodity in traditional Marxist terms and that, as a result, his categorial analysis recapitulates some of the antinomies of bourgeois thought he criticizes. In spite of Lukács' historical-social critique of dualism, his understanding of the commodity is dualistic. It reproduces the opposition of form and content he criticizes and, implicitly, opposes praxis to formalistic social structures in ways that are at odds with a dialectical understanding of praxis as constituting structures that, in turn, are constitutive of praxis.

Another understanding of the commodity would allow for a categorial critique of capitalism that could realize the conceptual rigour and power of the analysis both suggested and undermined by Lukács' remarkable essay. And I shall suggest that, despite the brilliance of Lukács' appropriation of Marx's critique of political economy, Marx's analysis of the commodity in *Capital* differs fundamentally from Lukács', and provides the basis for just such an alternative understanding. Nevertheless, the interpretation of Marx's analysis I shall outline is itself indebted to Lukács' rich general approach, although it contravenes Lukács' specific understanding of the categories.

In order to approach the differences between Marx's understanding of the commodity and that of Lukács, I shall analyse briefly the significantly different ways in which they interpret critically Hegel's conception of the *Geist*, the identical subject–object of history.[16] My intention is not simply to establish that Marx's interpretation is different from Lukács', but to begin elaborating the implications of these differences for understanding the fundamental category of both critical theories – the commodity. By elaborating these differences, I hope to point to the possible appropriation of the power of Lukács' approach in a way that breaks more decisively with traditional Marxism and opens up the possibility of a more adequate critique of capitalism today.

Hegel, Lukács and Marx

As is well-known, Hegel attempted to overcome the classical theoretical dichotomy of subject and object with his theory that reality, natural as well as social, subjective as well as objective, is constituted by practice – by the objectifying practice of the *Geist*, the world-historical Subject. The *Geist* constitutes objective reality by means of a process of externalization, or self-objectification, and, in the process, reflexively constitutes itself. Inasmuch as both objectivity and subjectivity are constituted by the *Geist* as it unfolds dialectically, they are of the same substance, rather than necessarily disparate. Both are moments of a general whole that is substantially homogeneous – a totality.

For Hegel, then, the *Geist* is at once subjective and objective; it is the identical subject–object, the 'substance' which is at the same time 'Subject': 'The living *substance* is, further, that being which is ... *Subject* or, what is the same thing, which is ... actual only insofar as it is the movement of positing itself, or the mediation of the process of becoming different from itself with itself' (translation modified, emphasis added).[17]

The process by which this self-moving substance/Subject, the *Geist*, constitutes objectivity and subjectivity as it unfolds dialectically is a historical process which is grounded in the internal contradictions of the totality. The historical process of self-objectification, according to Hegel, is one of self-alienation, and leads ultimately to the reappropriation by the *Geist* of that which had been alienated in the course of its unfolding. That is, historical development has an end-point: the realization by the *Geist* of itself as a totalizing and totalized Subject.

In 'Reification and the Consciousness of the Proletariat', Lukács appropriates Hegel's theory in a 'materialist' fashion in order to place the category of practice at the centre of a dialectical social theory. Translating Hegel's concept of the *Geist* into anthropological terms, Lukács' identifies the proletariat in a 'materialized' Hegelian manner as the identical subject–object of the historical process, as the historical Subject, constituting the social world and itself through its labour. Relatedly, Lukács analyzes society as a totality constituted by labour, traditionally understood. The existence of this totality, according to Lukács, is veiled by the fragmented and particularistic character of bourgeois social relations. By overthrowing the capitalist order, the proletariat would realize itself as the historical subject; the totality it constitutes would come openly into its own. The totality and, hence, labour, provide the standpoint of Lukács' critical analysis of capitalist society.[18]

Lukács' interpretation of the categories and his reading of Hegel, in particular his identification of the proletariat with the concept of the identical subject–object, has frequently been identified with Marx's position.[19] And it is the case that, in *Capital*, Marx attempts to ground socially and historically that which Hegel sought to grasp with his concept of *Geist*. A close reading, however, indicates that Marx's appropriation of Hegel in his mature works differs fundamentally from Lukács', that is, from one that views totality affirmatively, as the standpoint of critique, and identifies Hegel's identical subject–object with the proletariat. This, in turn, suggests some fundamental differences between their categorial analyses.

In his earlier writings, for example, *The Holy Family* (1845), Marx criticizes the philosophical concept of 'substance' and, in particular, Hegel's conceptualization of 'substance' as 'Subject'.[20] At the beginning of *Capital*, however, he himself makes analytic use of the category of 'substance'. He refers to value as having a 'substance', which he identifies as abstract human labour.[21] Marx, then, no longer considers 'substance' simply to be a theoretical hypostatization, but now conceives of it as an attribute of value – that is, of the peculiar, labour-mediated form of social relations that characterizes capitalism. 'Substance', for Marx, is now an expression of a determinate social reality. He investigates that social reality in *Capital* by unfolding logically the commodity and money forms from his categories of use-value and value. On that basis, Marx begins analysing the complex structure of social relations expressed by his category of capital. He initially determines capital in terms of value, as self-valorizing value. At this point in his exposition, Marx presents the

category of capital in terms that clearly relate it to Hegel's concept of
Geist:

> It [value] is constantly changing from one form into the other without
> becoming lost in this movement; it thus transforms itself into an *auto-*
> *matic subject* ... In truth, however, value is here the *subject* of a process in
> which, while constantly assuming the form in turn of money and of
> commodities, it changes its own magnitude ... and thus valorizes itself
> ... For the movement in the course of which it adds surplus value is its
> own movement, its valorization is therefore self-valorization. ... [V]alue
> suddenly presents itself as a *self-moving substance* which passes through a
> process of its own, and for which the commodity and money are both
> mere forms. (translation modified, emphasis added) [22]

Marx, then, characterizes capital explicitly as the self-moving substance
that is Subject. In so doing, Marx suggests that a historical Subject in the
Hegelian sense does indeed exist in capitalism. Yet he does not identify
that Subject with any social grouping, such as the proletariat, or with
humanity. Rather, Marx characterizes it with reference to social relations
constituted by the forms of objectifying practice grasped by the category of
capital. His analysis suggests that the social relations that characterize capitalism are of a very peculiar sort – they possess the attributes that Hegel
accords to the *Geist*.

Marx's interpretation of the historical Subject with reference to the category of capital indicates that the social relations at his critique's centre
should not be understood essentially in terms of class relations but rather
in terms of forms of social mediation expressed by categories such as value
and capital. Marx's Subject, then, is like Hegel's. It is abstract and cannot be
identified with any social actors. Moreover, it unfolds in time independent
of will.

In *Capital*, Marx analyzes capitalism in terms of a dialectic of development that, because it is independent of will, presents itself as a logic. He
treats the unfolding of that dialectical logic as a real expression of alienated
social relations that, although constituted by practice, exist quasi-indepen-
dently. He does not analyze that logic as an illusion, but as a form of domination that is a function of the social forms of capitalism. Marx, then,
analyzes a dialectical logic of history as a function of capitalism rather than
as a characteristic of human history as such.

As the Subject, capital is a remarkable 'subject'. Whereas Hegel's Subject
is trans-historical and knowing, in Marx's analysis it is historically determinate and blind. As a structure constituted by determinate forms of practice,
capital, in turn, may be constitutive of forms of social practice and subjectivity; as a self-reflexive social form it may induce self-consciousness.
Unlike Hegel's *Geist*, however, it does not possess self-consciousness.

Subjectivity and the socio-historical Subject, in other words, must be distinguished in Marx's analysis.

The identification of the identical subject-object with determinate structures of social relations has very important implications for a theory of subjectivity. As we have seen, Marx does not simply identify with a social agent the concept of the identical subject-object with which Hegel sought to overcome the subject-object dichotomy of classical epistemology. Instead, Marx changes the terms of the epistemological problem from the knowing individual (or supra-individual) subject and its relation to an external (or externalized) world, to the forms of social relations, considered as determinations of social subjectivity as well as objectivity.[23] The problem of knowledge now becomes a question of the relationship between forms of social mediation and forms of thought.

Marx's critique of Hegel, then, is very different from Lukács' materialist appropriation of Hegel. The latter posits 'labour' implicitly as the constituting substance of a Subject, which is prevented by capitalist relations from realizing itself. The historical Subject in this case is a collective version of the bourgeois subject, constituting itself and the world through 'labour'. That is, the concept of 'labour' and that of the bourgeois subject (whether interpreted as the individual, or as a class) are related intrinsically.

Marx's critique of Hegel breaks with the presuppositions of such a position (which nevertheless became dominant within the socialist tradition). Rather than viewing capitalist relations as being extrinsic to the Subject, as hindering its full realization, Marx analyzes those very relations as constituting the Subject. It is because of their peculiar, quasi-objective properties that those relations constitute what Hegel grasped as a historical Subject. This theoretical turn means that Marx's mature theory neither posits nor is bound to the notion of a historical meta-Subject, such as the proletariat, which will realize itself in a future society. Indeed, it implies a critique of such a notion.

A similar difference between Marx and Lukács exists with regard to the Hegelian concept of totality. For Lukács, social totality is constituted by 'labour', but is veiled, fragmented and prevented from realizing itself by capitalist relations. It represents the *standpoint* of the critique of the capitalist present, and will be realized in socialism. Marx's categorial determination of capital as the historical Subject, however, indicates that the totality and the labour that constitutes it have become the *objects* of his critique. The capitalist social formation, according to Marx, is unique inasmuch as it is constituted by a qualitatively homogeneous social 'substance'. Hence it exists as a social totality. Other social formations are not so totalized; their fundamental social relations are not qualitatively homogeneous. They cannot be grasped by the concept of 'substance', cannot be unfolded from a single structuring principle, and do not display an immanent, necessary historical logic.

The idea that capital, and not the proletariat or the species, is the total Subject clearly implies that, for Marx, the historical negation of capitalism would not involve the *realization*, but the *abolition*, of the totality. It follows that the notion of the contradiction driving the unfolding of his totality also must be conceptualized very differently – it presumably does not drive the totality forward towards its full realization, but, rather, towards the possibility of its historical abolition. That is, the contradiction expresses the temporal finiteness of the totality by pointing beyond it.

The determination of capital as the historical Subject is consistent with an analysis that seeks to explain the directional dynamic of capitalist society. Such an analysis grasps capitalism's dynamic with reference to social relations that are constituted by structured forms of practice, and yet acquire a quasi-independent existence and subject people to quasi-objective constraints. This position possesses an emancipatory moment not available to those positions that, explicitly or implicitly, identify the historical Subject with the labouring class. Such 'materialist' interpretations of Hegel which posit the class or the species as the historical Subject seem to enhance human dignity by emphasizing the role of practice in the creation of history. Within the framework of the interpretation outlined here, however, such positions are only apparently emancipatory, for the very existence of a historical logic is an expression of heteronomy, of alienated practice. Moreover, the call for the full realization of the Subject could only imply the full realization of an alienated social form. On the other hand, many currently popular positions that, in the name of emancipation, criticize the affirmation of totality, do so by denying the existence of the totality. Such positions ignore the reality of alienated social structures and cannot grasp the historical tendencies of capitalist society; hence, they cannot formulate an adequate critique of the existent order. In other words, those positions that assert the existence of a totality, but do so in an affirmative fashion, are related to those positions that deny totality's very existence in order to save the possibility of emancipation. Both positions are one-sided: they posit, albeit in opposed fashion, a trans-historical identity between what is and what should be, between recognizing the existence of totality and affirming it. Marx, on the other hand, analyzes totality as a heteronomous reality in order to uncover the condition for its abolition.

Marx's mature critique, therefore, no longer entails a 'materialist', anthropological inversion of Hegel's idealistic dialectic of the sort undertaken by Lukács. Rather, it is, in a sense, the materialist 'justification' of that dialectic. Marx implicitly argues that the so-called 'rational core' of Hegel's dialectic is precisely its idealist character. It is an expression of a mode of social domination constituted by structures of social relations that, because alienated, acquire a quasi-independent existence *vis-à-vis* the individuals and that, because of their peculiar dualistic nature, are dialectical in character. The historical Subject, according to Marx, is the alienated structure of social mediation that is constitutive of the capitalist formation. Lukács' affirmation in social theory of the Hegelian concept of totality and of the dialectic may have provided an effective critique of the evolutionist, fatalistic and deterministic tendencies of the Marxism of the Second International. Nevertheless, within the framework suggested by Marx's initial determination of the category of capital, such a theory does not constitute a critique of capitalism from the standpoint of its historical negation. Rather, it points to the historical overcoming of earlier bourgeois relations of distribution by a form more adequate to a newer configuration of capitalist relations of production – to the supersession of an earlier, apparently more abstract totality by an apparently more concrete one. If the totality itself is understood as capital, such a critique is revealed as one which, behind its own back, points to the full realization of capital as a quasi-concrete totality, rather than to its abolition.

A critique of Lukács' categories

Although both Marx and Lukács appropriate Hegel's concept of the identical subject–object, the differences between them are fundamental. Lukács grasps the concept socially as the universal class, the proletariat, whereas Marx does so as the universal form of mediation, capital. What for Lukács is the basis for emancipation, the future, is for Marx the basis for domination, the present.

This opposition has important implications for the question of an adequate categorial critique. Earlier, I raised the question of whether it is possible to appropriate Lukács' broader conception of capitalism as well as his rigorous categorial analysis of subjectivity by separating them from his specific understanding of the categories and his theory of the proletariat. The differences I have outlined indicate the possibility of such a separation. That Marx initially characterizes the category of capital (that is, self-valorizing value) in the same terms with which Hegel determines his concept of the identical subject–object indicates that the most basic categories of Marx's critical theory can, and should, be read differently than in Lukács' account. It suggests the possibility of the sort of rigorous categorial critique of modernity outlined by Lukács, based on a different understanding of the categories.

How does Lukács understand the commodity? Although he refers explicitly to 'the problem of the commodity ... as the central structural problem of capitalist society' (translation modified), [24] he does not analyze the category itself directly. Nevertheless, it is possible to reconstruct his understanding. As is well known, the commodity, according to Marx, is the most fundamental category of capitalist society; it is characterized by its 'double-character' as a value and as a use-value.[25] What is striking about Lukács' analysis in the 'Reification' essay is that it separates and opposes the quantitative and the qualitative and, relatedly, form and content. These oppositions in Lukács' analysis are bound to his understanding of the relationship of value and use-value and, hence, of the commodity form; they distinguish his understanding of the commodity from Marx's.

As we have seen, Lukács analyzes central aspects of modernity – for example, the factory, bureaucracy, the form of the state and of the law – with reference to processes of rationalization grounded in the commodity form. The commodity as totalizing imparts an apparently unitary character to capitalist society, according to Lukács; for the first time, a unified economic structure and a unified structure of consciousness characterize social life.[26] Lukács describes this unified structure in terms of the subsumption of the qualitative by the quantitative. He argues, for example, that capitalism is characterized by a trend towards greater rationalization and calculability, which eliminates the qualitative, human and individual attributes of the workers.[27] Relatedly, time loses its qualitative, variable and flowing nature and becomes a quantifiable continuum filled with quantifiable 'things'.[28] Because capitalism entails the subsumption of the qualitative under the quantitative, according to Lukács, its unitary character is abstract, general and formalistic.

Nevertheless, although the rationalization of the world effected by the commodity relation may appear to be complete, Lukács argues, it is in fact limited by its own formalism.[29] Its limits emerge clearly in periods of crisis, when capitalism is revealed as a whole made up of partial systems which are only contingently related, an irrational whole of highly rational parts.[30] As such, capitalism cannot be grasped as a totality. Indeed, such knowledge of the whole would amount to the virtual abolition of the capitalist economy, according to Lukács.[31]

Lukács' analysis here entails a sophisticated formulation of a traditional critique of the market from the standpoint of central planning. Rather than elaborating this point, however, I shall pursue further the question of the traditional Marxist dimension of Lukács' thought by focusing on the dualistic understanding of modernity entailed by his opposition of the qualitative and the quantitative. For Lukács, the problem of totality and that of form and content are related. He maintains that the main weakness of the modern sciences is their formalism; their own concrete underlying reality lies, methodologically and in principle, beyond their grasp.[32] This problem of relating form and content is not simply one of inadequate thinking, according to Lukács, but is an expression of the way capitalism is structured. When economic theory, such as the theory of marginal utility, for example, suppresses use-value, it expresses the reality of capitalism: 'the very success with which the economy is totally rationalized and transformed into an abstract and mathematically oriented system of formal "laws" ... creates the methodological barrier to understanding the phenomenon of crisis'.[33]

For Lukács, then, the inability of science to penetrate to its 'real material substratum' is grounded in the nature of capitalism itself. This inability is methodologically inevitable for thought that remains bound to the manifest forms of capitalism.[34] Moments of crisis reveal the reality behind those manifest forms; the surface level is broken through then, and the concrete material substratum of capitalist society is revealed. In such moments, 'the *qualitative* existence of the "things" that lead their lives beyond the purview of economics as ... things-in-themselves, as use-values, suddenly becomes the decisive factor' (emphasis added).[35] The crisis, in other words, reveals that there are qualitative conditions attached to the quantitative relations of capitalism, 'that it is not merely a question of units of value which can easily be compared with each other, but also use-values of a definite kind which must fulfill a definite function in production and consumption'.[36]

Lukács, then, grasps capitalism essentially in terms of the problem of formalism, as a form of social life that does not grasp its own content. This suggests that when he claims the commodity form structures modern, capitalist society, he understands that form solely in terms of its abstract, quantitative and formal dimension – its value dimension. He thereby posits the use-value dimension, the 'real material substratum', as a quasi-ontological content, separable from the form, which is constituted by labour, trans-historically understood.

Within this framework, getting beyond bourgeois thought means getting beyond the formalistic rationalism of such thought; that is, beyond the diremption of form and content effected by capitalism. And this, Lukács argues, requires a concept of form that is oriented towards the concrete content of its material substratum; it requires a dialectical theory of praxis.[37] For Lukács, then, a dialectical, praxis-oriented understanding of the relation of form and content would overcome, on the theoretical level, the abstract formalism associated with the category of value. That is, it would point beyond capitalism.

In order to elucidate such a dialectical understanding, Lukács outlines the course of modern Western philosophy in terms of the problems of totality and of the relation of form and content, culminating in the antinomies of Kant's first critique and the problem of the thing-in-itself. He argues that neither Kant, in his second and third critiques, nor Fichte, nor Schiller, are able to solve these problems theoretically.[38] It is only Hegel, according to Lukács, who points the way to their resolution by turning to history as the concrete and total dialectical process between subject and object. The notion of historical dialectical praxis, of the subject as both the producer and the product of the dialectical process (that is, as the identical subject–object), abolishes the antitheses of subject and object, thought and existence, freedom and necessity.[39] Yet, Lukács claims, although Hegel develops the dialectical method, which grasps the reality of human history and shows the way to the overcoming of the antinomies of bourgeois thought, he is unable to discover the identical subject–object in history, 'the "we" whose action is in fact history'.[40] Instead, he locates it idealistically, outside of history, in the *Geist*. This results in a concept mythology, which reintroduces all the antinomies of classical philosophy.[41]

Overcoming the antinomies of classical philosophical thought entails a social and historical version of Hegel's solution, according to Lukács. This is provided by the proletariat, which is able to discover within itself, on the basis of its life experience, the identical subject–object.[42] Lukács then proceeds to develop a theory of the class consciousness of the proletariat.[43] I shall not discuss this theory at length other than to note that, unlike Marx, Lukács does not present his account with reference to the development of capital – for example, in terms of changes in the nature of surplus value (from absolute to relative surplus value) and related changes in the development of the process of production. Instead, he outlines the objective possibility of a dialectic of immediacy and mediation, quantity and quality, which could lead to the self-awareness of the proletariat as subject. His account is curiously devoid of a historical dynamic. History, which Lukács conceives of as the dialectical process of the self-constitution of humanity, is indeterminate in this essay; it is not analyzed with reference to the historical development of capitalism.

Indeed, Lukács treats capitalism as an essentially static, abstract quantitative form that is superimposed on, and veils, the true nature of the concrete, qualitative, social content. Hence, Lukács' understanding of reification, the form of socially grounded misrecognition characteristic of capitalism, is that the forms of capitalism expressed by the categories veil the 'real' social relations of that society. So, for example, in his critique of Simmel's *The Philosophy of Money*, Lukács cites Marx's analysis of interest-bearing capital as a result of the capitalist process of production that, divorced from that process, acquires an independent existence, as a pure form without content. For Lukács, then, the abstract veils the concrete.[44] He then criticizes Simmel for separating 'these empty manifestations from their real capitalist foundation and ... regarding them as the timeless model of human relations in general'.[45]

The 'real capitalist foundation,' for Lukács, consists of class relations, which exist beneath and are veiled by the surface of capitalist forms. These 'real' social relations become manifest in class struggle. At that point, according to Lukács, 'the "eternal laws" of capitalist economics fail and become dialectical'.[46] Within the framework of this account, the historical dialectic, constituted by praxis, operates on the level of the 'real' social content – that is, class relations; it is ultimately opposed to the categories of capitalism. Those categories, then, veil what is constituted by praxis; they are not themselves categories of praxis. The opposition Lukács draws between 'the developing tendencies of history' and 'the empirical facts', whereby the former constitutes a 'higher reality', also express this under-standing.[47] History here refers to the level of praxis, to the 'real' social content, whereas the empirical 'facts' operate on the level of the economic categories.

How, then, does Lukács deal with capitalism's dynamic? He does refer to the immanent, blind dynamic of capitalist society, which he characterizes as a manifestation of the rule of capital over labour.[48] Nevertheless, Lukács does not ultimately take seriously that dynamic as a historical dynamic, a quasi-independent social reality at the heart of capitalism. Instead, he treats it as a reified manifestation of a more fundamental social reality, a ghostly movement that veils 'real history':

> This image of a frozen reality that nevertheless is caught up in an unremitting, ghostly movement at once becomes meaningful when the reality is dissolved into the process of which man is the driving force. This can be seen only from the standpoint of the proletariat because the meaning of these tendencies is the abolition of capitalism and so for the bourgeoisie to become conscious of them would be tantamount to suicide.[49]

Ultimately, then, the historical dynamic of capitalism is a mere 'ghostly movement', for Lukács.[50] 'Real' history, the dialectical historical process constituted by praxis, operates on a more fundamental level of social reality than what is grasped by the categories of capitalism, and points beyond that society. This 'deeper', more substantive, level of social reality is veiled by the immediacy of capitalist forms; it can only be grasped from a standpoint that breaks through that immediacy. And this standpoint, for Lukács, is a possibility that is available structurally to the proletariat. Within the framework of Lukács' analysis, the 'self-understanding of the proletariat is ... simultaneously the objective understanding of the nature of society'.[51] The historical overcoming of capitalism by the proletariat, then, would involve overcoming the formalistic, quantitative dimension of modern social life (value), thereby allowing the real, substantive, historical nature of society (the dimension of use-value, labour, the proletariat) to emerge openly and come into its own historically.

At this point it should be clear that Lukács presents a positive material-ist version of Hegel's dialectical method. Lukács affirms the dialectical process of history constituted by the praxis of the proletariat (and, hence, the notions of history, totality, dialectic, labour, and the prole-tariat) in opposition to capitalism. This affirmative, materialist appropri-ation of Hegel is effected by a Feuerbachian inversion, which Lukács modifies by adding the dynamic element of history.[52] This approach results in Lukács' identification of Hegel's identical subject–object with the proletariat.

We have seen, however, that Marx interprets the Hegelian identical subject–object with reference to the category of capital. This indicates, as already noted, that precisely what Lukács appropriates from Hegel as critical – the idea of a dialectical historical logic, the notion of totality, the identical subject–object – is understood by Marx with reference to capital. It follows that what Lukács understands as socially ontological, outside the purview of the categories, is grasped critically as being intrinsic to capital by the categories of Marx's critique of political economy.

Towards a critical theory of capitalism

At this point I shall outline briefly a reading of Marx's categories very different from that presented by Lukács. Although indebted to Lukács' focus on the categories, this reading could serve as the basis for a critical theory of capitalism able to overcome the dualism of his specific approach as well as its traditionalist assumptions

Lukács, as we have seen, interprets the commodity as a historically specific abstract form (value) superimposed upon a trans-historical concrete substantive content (use-value, labour), which constitutes the 'real' nature of society. The relation of form and content is contingent in capitalism. Relatedly, a concept of form that is not indifferent to its content would point beyond capitalism.

This, however, is not the case with Marx's analysis of the commodity. At the heart of Marx's analysis is his argument that labour in capitalism, has a 'double character': it is both 'concrete labour' and 'abstract labour'.[53] 'Concrete labour' refers to the fact that some form of what we consider labouring activity mediates the interactions of humans with nature in all societies. 'Abstract labour' does not simply refer to concrete labour in the abstract, to 'labour' in general, but is a very different sort of category. It signifies that labour in capitalism also has a unique social function that is not intrinsic to labouring activity as such: it mediates a new, quasi-objective form of social interdependence.[54] 'Abstract labour,' as a historically specific mediating function of labour, is the content or, better, 'substance' of value.[55] Form and content are indeed intrinsically related here as a fundamental determination of capitalism.

Labour in capitalism, according to Marx, then, is not only labour, as we understand it trans-historically and commonsensically, but is also a historically specific socially mediating activity. Hence its products – commodity, capital – are both concrete labour products and objectified forms of social mediation. According to this analysis, the social relations that characterize fundamentally capitalist society have a peculiar quasi-objective formal character and are dualistic: they are characterized by the opposition of an abstract, general, homogenous dimension and a concrete, particular, material dimension, both of which appear to be 'natural', rather than social, and condition social conceptions of natural reality. Whereas Lukács understands the commodity only in terms of its abstract dimension, Marx analyzes the commodity as both abstract and concrete. Within this framework, Lukács' analysis falls prey to a fetish form; it naturalizes the concrete dimension of the commodity form.

The form of mediation constitutive of capitalism, in Marx's analysis, gives rise to a new form of social domination – one that subjects people to impersonal, increasingly rationalized structural imperatives and constraints. It is the domination of people by time. This abstract form of domination is real, not ghostly. Nevertheless, it cannot be grasped adequately in terms of class domination or, more generally, in terms of the concrete domination of social groupings or of institutional agencies of the state and/or the economy. It has no determinate locus[56] and, while constituted by determinate forms of social practice, appears not to be social at all.

This form of domination, as analyzed by Marx in *Capital*, is dynamic, not static. Examining that dynamic makes it clear that the abstract form of domination that Marx places at the heart of capitalism cannot be understood adequately with reference to the abstract value dimension of the commodity alone. Rather, the unstable duality of the commodity form, as the identity of identity and non-identity, gives rise to a dialectical interaction of value and use-value that grounds the overarching historical dynamic of capitalism. The use-value dimension is very much an integral moment of the underlying structuring forms of capitalism.[57]

Analyzing the dialectic of the two dimensions of the commodity form provides the basis for a critical understanding of capital in terms of a very complex, non-linear historical dynamic. On the one hand, this dynamic is characterized by ongoing transformations of the technical processes of labour, of the social and detail division of labour and, more generally, of social life. On the other hand, this historical dynamic entails the ongoing reconstitution of its own fundamental condition as an unchanging feature of social life – namely that social mediation ultimately is effected by labour and, hence, that living labour remains integral to the process of production (considered in terms of society as a whole), regardless of the level of productivity. The historical dynamic of capitalism generates ceaselessly what is 'new', while regenerating what is 'the same'.

This interpretation of the dialectical process of history differs fundamentally from Lukács'. By grounding that process in the categorial forms, this approach treats the existence of a historical dynamic as a basic characteristic of capitalism, rather than as a feature of human social life that is veiled by capitalism. Within this framework, capitalism is characterized not only by its surface ('facts' for Lukács), but also by a dialectical and dynamic deep structure that Lukács regards as being independent of capitalism ('tendencies'). The existence of a historical dynamic that, while constituted by practice, is quasi-independent of human will and intention is, for Marx, a central feature of the form of abstract domination that characterizes capitalism.

In other words, the quasi-objective structures grasped by the categories of Marx's critique of political economy do not veil the 'real' social relations of capitalism (that is, class relations), just as they do not hide the 'real' historical Subject (that is, the proletariat). Rather, those structures are the fundamental relations of capitalist society. Moreover, they are not static, but historically dynamic.

According to this interpretation, the non-linear historical dynamic elucidated by Marx's categorial analysis provides the basis for a critical understanding of both the form of economic growth and the proletarian-based form of industrial production characteristic of capitalism. That is, it allows for a categorial analysis of the processes of rationalization that Lukács described critically, but was unable to ground theoretically. This approach neither posits a linear developmental schema that points beyond the existing structure and organization of labour (as do theories of post-industrial society), nor does it treat industrial production and the proletariat as the bases for a future society (as do many traditional Marxist approaches). Rather, it indicates that capitalism gives rise to the historical possibility of a different form of growth and of production; at the same time, however, capitalism structurally undermines the realization of those possibilities.

The structural contradiction of capitalism, according to this interpretation, is not one between distribution (the market, private property) and production, between existing property relations and industrial production. Rather, it emerges as a contradiction between existing forms of growth and production, and what could be the case if social relations were no longer mediated in a quasi-objective fashion by labour.

By grounding the contradictory character of the social formation in the dualistic forms expressed by the categories of the commodity and capital, Marx implies that structurally-based social contradiction is specific to capitalism. In the light of this analysis, the notion that reality or social relations in general are essentially contradictory and dialectical can only be assumed metaphysically, but not explained. Marx's analysis, within this framework, suggests that any theory that posits an intrinsic developmental logic to history as such, whether dialectical or evolutionary, projects what is the case for capitalism onto history in general.

The reinterpretation of Marx's theory I have outlined constitutes a basic break with, and critique of, more traditional interpretations. As we have seen, such interpretations understand capitalism in terms of class relations structured by the market and private property, grasp its form of domination primarily in terms of class domination and exploitation, and formulate a normative and historical critique of capitalism from the standpoint of labour and production (understood trans-historically in terms of the interactions of humans with material nature). I have argued that Marx's analysis of labour in capitalism as being historically specific seeks to elucidate a peculiar quasi-objective form of social mediation and wealth (value) that constitutes a form of domination which structures the process of production in capitalism and generates a historically unique dynamic. Hence, labour and the process of production are not separable from, and opposed to, the social relations of capitalism, but constitute their very core. Marx's theory, then, extends far beyond the traditional critique of the bourgeois relations of distribution (the market and private property); it grasps modern industrial society itself as being capitalist. It treats the working class as the basic element of capitalism rather than as the embodiment of its negation, and does not conceptualize socialism in terms of the realization of labour and of industrial production, but in terms of the possible abolition of the proletariat and of the organization of production based on proletarian labour, as well as of the dynamic system of abstract compulsions constituted by labour as a socially mediating activity.

This reinterpretation of Marx's theory thus implies a fundamental rethinking of the nature of capitalism and of its possible historical transformation. By shifting the focus of the critique away from an exclusive concern with the market and private property, it provides the basis for a critical theory of post-liberal society as capitalist, and of the so-called 'actually-existing socialist' countries as alternative (and failed) forms of capital accumulation, rather than as social modes that represented the historical negation of capital, in however imperfect a form. This approach also allows for an analysis of the newest configuration of capitalism – of neoliberal global capitalism – in ways that avoid returning to a traditionalist Marxist framework.

Conclusions

The structural breaks and upheavals of the recent past suggest that theories of democracy, identity or philosophies of the non-identical that do not take into account the dynamics of capitalist globalization are no longer adequate. Nevertheless, the history of the twentieth century suggests that it would be a mistake to resuscitate traditional Marxism. What is required is a more adequate critical theory of capitalism. Lukács opened the way to such a critical theory; at the same time, he remained limited fundamentally by some of his traditional assumptions.

Marx, as is well known, insisted that the coming social revolution must draw its poetry from the future, unlike earlier revolutions that, focused on the past, misrecognized their own historical content.[58] Lukács' critical theory of capitalism, however, grounded in his 'materialist' appropriation of Hegel, backs into a future it does not grasp. It is reminiscent of Walter Benjamin's image of the angel of history, propelled into a future to which its back is turned.[59] Rather than pointing to the overcoming of capitalism, Lukács' approach entails a misrecognition that affirms implicitly the new state-centric configuration that emerged after the First World War.[60] Paradoxically, Lukács' rich critical description of capitalism is directed against precisely this sort of organization of society. His specific understanding of the categories of Marx's critical theory, however, does not ground that critical description of capitalism adequately. Instead, as we have seen, ultimately it contravenes that description. Rethinking Marx through the lens of Lukács' interpretation allows for a critical theory that is adequate to Lukács' description of capitalism and to his idea of a rigorous categorial analysis. By overcoming Lukács' traditionalist assumptions, such an approach could serve as a point of departure for an adequate critical theory of the capitalist order at the start of the twenty-first century.

Notes and References

1. Lukács, G., 'Reification and the Consciousness of the Proletariat', in *History and Class Consciousness*, trans. R. Livingstone (Cambridge, Mass.: MIT Press, 1971).
2. To avoid the misunderstandings that the term 'categorical' might encourage, I use 'categorial' to refer to Marx's attempt to grasp the forms of modern social life with the categories of his critique of political economy.
3. Thus Lukács criticizes Ernst Bloch for missing the real depth of (what he terms) historical materialism by assuming its outlook is merely economic, and attempting to 'deepen' it by supplementing it with (religious) utopian thought. Bloch, according to Lukács, does not realize that what he calls 'economics' deals with the system of forms that define the real and concrete life of humanity. See Lukács, G., 'Reification and the Consciousness of the Proletariat', p. 193.
4. Marx, K., *Grundrisse: Foundations of the Critique of Political Economy*, trans. M. Nicolaus (Harmondsworth: Penguin, 1973), p. 106 (translation modified).
5. Lukács, 'Reification...', p. 142.
6. Lukács, 'Reification...', p. 204.
7. Lukács, 'Reification...', p. 204.
8. Lukács, 'Reification...', pp. 110–12.
9. Lukács, 'Reification...', pp. 85–110.
10. Lukács, 'Reification...', pp. 89–90.
11. Lukács, 'Reification...', pp. 98–100.
12. Lukács, 'Reification...', p. 95.
13. See, for example, Dobb, M., *Political Economy and Capitalism* (London: Routledge, 1940), pp. 70–1; Cohen, G. A., *History, Labour, Freedom: Themes from Marx* (Oxford: Clarendon Press, 1988), pp. 208–38; Elster, J., *Making Sense of Marx* (Cambridge University Press, 1985), p. 127; Meek, R., *Studies in the Labour Theory of Value* (New York/London: Lawrence & Wishart, 1956); Sweezy, P., *The Theory of Capitalist Development* (New York: Monthly Review Press, 1968), pp. 52–3; Steedman, I., 'Ricardo, Marx, Sraffa', in I. Steedman (ed.), *The Value Controversy* (London: NLB, 1981) pp. 11–19.
14. Lukács, 'Reification...', pp. 149–209.
15. Arato, A. and Breines, P., *The Young Lukács and the Origins of Western Marxism* (New York: Seabury Press, 1979), p. 140.

16. This argument was first elaborated in Postone, M., *Time, Labor, and Social Domination* (Cambridge and New York: Cambridge University Press, 1973), pp. 71–83.
17. Hegel, G. W. F., 'Preface to *The Phenomenology of Spirit*', in W. Kaufmann (ed.), *Hegel: Texts and Commentary* (Garden City, NY: Anchor Books, 1966), p. 28.
18. Lukács, 'Reification....', pp. 102–21, 135, 145, 151–3, 162, 175, 197–200.
19. See, for example, Piccone, P., 'General Introduction', in A. Arato and E. Gebhardt (eds), *The Essential Frankfurt School Reader* (New York: Continuum, 1982), p. xvii.
20. Marx, K., *The Holy Family*, in L. Easton and K. Guddat (eds), *Writings of the Young Marx on Philosophy and Society* (Garden City, NY: Doubleday, 1967), pp. 369–73.
21. Marx, K., *Capital*, vol. I, trans. B. Fowkes (Harmondsworth: Penguin, 1976), p. 128.
22. Marx, K., *Capital*, vol. I, pp. 255–6.
23. Habermas claims that his theory of communicative action shifts the framework of critical social theory away from the subject-object paradigm (Habermas, J., *The Theory of Communicative Action*, vol. I, trans. T. McCarthy (Boston: Beacon Press, 1984, p. 390)). I am suggesting that Marx, in his mature works, already effects such a theoretical shift. Moreover, I would argue – although I cannot elaborate here – that Marx's focus on forms of social mediation allows for a more rigorous analysis of capitalist modernity than does Habermas' turn to communicative action.
24. Lukács, 'Reification...', p. 85.
25. Marx, *Capital*, vol. I, pp. 125–9.
26. Lukács, 'Reification...', pp. 99–100.
27. Lukács, 'Reification...', p. 88.
28. Lukács, 'Reification...', p. 90.
29. Lukács, 'Reification...', p. 101.
30. Lukács, 'Reification...', pp. 101–2.
31. Lukács, 'Reification...', p. 102.
32. Lukács, 'Reification...', p. 104.
33. Lukács, 'Reification...', p. 105.
34. Lukács, 'Reification...', pp. 106–7.
35. Lukács, 'Reification...', p. 105.
36. Lukács, 'Reification...', p. 106.
37. Lukács, 'Reification...', pp. 121–42.
38. Lukács, 'Reification...', pp. 110–40.
39. Lukács, 'Reification...', pp. 140–5.
40. Lukács, 'Reification...', p. 145.
41. Lukács, 'Reification...', pp. 145–8.
42. Lukács, 'Reification...', p. 149.
43. Lukács, 'Reification...', pp. 149–209.
44. This, however, is only one form of socially grounded misrecognition, or 'fetish form', that Marx analyzes. What Lukács overlooks is that Marx also elucidates fetish forms in which the concrete dimensions of the social forms veil their abstract, social dimension. So, for example, the commodity appears to be an object – and not, at the same time, a social mediation. Similarly, the process of production in capitalism appears to be a labour process – and not, at the same time, a valorization process. This notion of the fetish, however, is based on an understanding of the categorial forms as two-sided in ways that differ from Lukács' dualistic opposition of abstract (capitalism) and concrete (ontological).
45. Lukács, 'Reification...', pp. 94–5.

46. Lukács, 'Reification...', p. 178.
47. Lukács, 'Reification...', p. 181. The distinction between the tendencies of history and empirical 'facts' is related implicitly by Lukács to the difference in logical levels between Marx's analysis of value and surplus value in Volume I of *Capital* and his analysis of price, profit, rent and interest in Volume III of *Capital*, whereby the latter categories veil the former (see Lukács, 'Reification...', pp. 181–5). What is significant here is that Lukács reads the underlying categories of Volume I such as 'labour' and 'use-value' as being ontological and affirmative.
48. Lukács, 'Reification...', p. 181.
49. Lukács, 'Reification...', p. 181.
50. Lukács' interpretation of Marx is echoed by Habermas, who claims that Marx treated the systemic dimension of capitalism as an illusion, as the ghostly form of class relations that have become anonymous and fetishized (Habermas, J., *The Theory of Communicative Action*, vol. II, trans. T. McCarthy (Boston, Mass.: Beacon Press, 1987, pp. 338–9)). Habermas's reading is significant inasmuch as it underlies his attempt to appropriate critically Talcott Parsons in order to formulate a theory that would be adequate to both what Habermas considers the systemic and lifeworld dimensions of modern society. The reading of Marx I shall outline overcomes Habermas' objection, renders the turn to Parsons unnecessary, and places the critique of capitalism back at the centre of contemporary critical theory.
51. Lukács, 'Reification...', p. 149.
52. Lukács, 'Reification...', pp. 186–94. It is significant that Lukács adopts Feuerbach's anthropological inversion, but criticizes it for being ahistorical. Marx, however, in his mature works, by identifying the identical subject–object with capital, rejects implicitly the anthropological inversion itself.
53. Marx, *Capital*, vol. I, pp. 128–37.
54. Postone, *Time, Labor, and Social Domination*, pp. 123–85.
55. Marx, *Capital*, vol. I, p. 128.
56. This analysis provides a powerful point of departure for analysing the pervasive and immanent form of power that Michel Foucault described as characteristic of modern Western societies. See Foucault, M., *Discipline and Punish* (New York: Pantheon Press, 1984).
57. Postone, *Time, Labor, and Social Domination*, pp. 263–384.
58. Marx, K., 'The Eighteenth Brumaire of Louis Bonaparte', in K. Marx and F. Engels *Collected Works*, vol. 11 (New York: International Publishers, 1979), p. 106.
59. Benjamin, W., 'Theses on the Philosophy of History', in S. Bronner and D. Kellner (eds), *Critical Theory and Society* (New York/London: Routledge, 1989), p. 258.
60. The unintended affirmation of a new configuration of capitalism can be seen more recently in the anti-Hegelian turn to Nietzsche that is characteristic of much post-structuralist thought in the 1970s and 1980s. It could be argued that such thought also backed into a future it did not grasp adequately: in rejecting the sort of state-centric order that Lukács affirmed implicitly, it did so in a manner that, on a deep theoretical level, affirmed, in turn, the neoliberal order that has superseded Fordist state-centric capitalism, in both East and West.

6

From Hegel to Marx to the Dialectic of Capital

John R. Bell

351

P16

An objective account of the operation of the capitalist economy is both necessary and possible because capitalism, unlike any other economic system, systematically reifies or objectifies economic relations as impersonal, anonymous commodity relations. To the degree that workers and capitalists tolerate the existence of a society-wide market for material commodities and commodified labour-power, and do not demand too many heavy or complex use-values that small competitive firms cannot produce, the society-wide competitive market is able to direct human economic activities in such a way that capitalism is reproduced over time, without significant state- or community-based economic policy intervention. Thus, the market, through its commodity-economic logic and not human agency, manages the greater part of economic life.

Commodity-economic logic does not arise inevitably in the history of human societies. While this logic necessarily prevails to the degree that a society-wide capitalist market dominates material economic life, it is a contingent historical development which transforms not only material products but also human labour-power, the ultimate source of productivity, into commodities. This could never have taken place unless the direct producers were first separated from the means of production, and unless traditional economic relations were eroded gradually by impersonal commodity-economic relations. This process occurred slowly over a period of centuries and could, in principle, have been reversed or halted. But, following the Industrial Revolution in late eighteenth century England, capital was finally able to commodify the labour-power it required, while managing the production of use-values as commodities and securing access to land and its resources.[1] The capitalist market could then regulate price, profit and wage levels throughout the economy such that the principal classes of capitalists and workers received the incomes and goods required to support materially the reproduction of both labour power and capital. Social reproduction thus no longer relied on the direct human relations of dominance and subservience that had characterized earlier societies, but increasingly on the operation of the anonymous, impersonal and reified market.

Karl Marx recognized that, during the formative, mercantilist stage of capitalism, in which primitive accumulation occurred, force and fraud were employed routinely. 'Force is the midwife of every old society pregnant with a new one. It is itself an economic power',[2] but in the liberal capitalism of his day, 'direct force, outside economic conditions [was] ... used ... only exceptionally'.[3] Rather, economic actors were subject to the 'dull compulsion of economic relations'.[4] Marx realized that it was neither a trivial nor a simple task to attempt to determine what it was about the nature of the society-wide, competitive, capitalist market that allowed it to reproduce successfully material economic life, including the material requirements of the two major classes, when the state adopted increasingly non-interventionist economic and social policies, as it did in liberal England. It was Marx's intuition that capitalism's survival indicated that the competitive market must operate according to a rigorous logic; indeed, a dialectical logic. I believe the task Marx set for himself in *Capital* was to uncover that logic in its entirety. It was a monumental undertaking and Marx was unable to complete his work before his death. Unfortunately, his discussion of methodology and his passing comments on the debt he owed to Hegel were enigmatic and not altogether illuminating. This has led many Marxian political economists to conclude that Marx's relationship with the Hegelian tradition was casual–amounting to not much more than a flirtation with Hegelian terminology, which Marx employed to add a rhetorical flourish. Others, such as John Rosenthal, have concluded that Marx did employ Hegelian language, concepts and methodology, and that that was precisely the problem.[5] Marx's scientific project in *Capital* was compromised to the extent that he had not freed himself completely from the pernicious, Hegelian influence; consequently, the Hegelian elements in Marx's corpus must be purged to isolate, and thereby to free, the rational and scientific core of his works from these idealistic and pre-scientific 'fetters'. I think, on the contrary, that the structure and argument of *Capital* is quite properly dialectical. If there is any problem in that work it is that it is not as rigorously dialectical as it might have been had Marx's health not deteriorated and had he managed to live long enough to refine and complete *Capital*.

Fortunately, two Japanese Marxian political economists – Kozo Uno and Thomas Sekine – have performed the signal service of correcting and completing the dialectical argument advanced by Marx in *Capital*. The latter has performed the further service of demonstrating not only the correspondences between Marx's work and Hegel's *Logic*, but he has also shown how Marx's exposition of the logic of capital could have been improved greatly if there had been an even greater correspondence with the latter work. On the other hand, Uno and Sekine do not follow slavishly Hegel's lead. If economic reasoning dictates that they part company with Hegel, they do so. It is not even clear when Uno became aware of the correspondence between the dialectic of Hegel and his dialectical theory of capitalism. It may well have occurred to him while he was writing his *Principles of Political Economy*, or, indeed, after he had already completed it. He may well have been influenced unconsciously by his earlier exposure to Hegel as a student when he wrote his *Principles*.

Sekine has argued that Hegel's *Science of Logic* could have been more rigorously dialectical and convincing if Hegel had immersed himself in a study of the dialectical laws of motion of capitalism. This is because use-value, which opposes the organizing principle of value (the most abstract form in which capital presents itself) both in the history and the theory of capitalism, has a substance that is lacking in 'naught' or 'nothing', which opposes 'being' in Hegel's dialectic.[6] Of this, more later in the chapter. What that means is that it is the authority of the dialectic of capital, as articulated by Uno and Sekine, and not the less refined or developed dialectics of Hegel or Marx that should arbitrate if we find that Hegel, Marx and Uno/Sekine seem to be at odds at particular theoretical junctures.

Hegel

For Hegel, logic coincides with metaphysics. I think Hegel intends the dialectical logical categories presented in his two works of logic (*The Science of Logic* and the *Encyclopedia Logic*) to be simultaneously logical and onto-logical categories revealing the presence of the Absolute, both in our thought and in reality. In Sekine's view, however, Hegel's *Science of Logic* does not study the external world, but rather the world of abstract concepts or pure thought forms (that is, his work exposes, at the most general level, the internal operation of the human mind or, more particularly, the Christian *Logos*).[7] I am inclined to see the *Logic* as doing that, certainly, but I suspect that Hegel would have asserted that his metaphysics constitutes not only a science of the way we grasp things in thought, but that it also grasps the categories and logic which the Absolute/Providence/Reason employs to give order and purpose, at the most general/universal level, to the material and social world outside of human thought. In my view, then, Hegel is convinced that his logic coincides with metaphysics not merely as knowing but also as being. Rightly or wrongly, Hegel believes his method uncovers the all-embracing power of reason, not only in human conceptual thought but also in the conceptual organization of the world outside of thought. Hegel would, of course, have conceded that the sublation of the material world to Reason/the Absolute is not as complete in nature as in our thought processes, but I feel confident that he would claim that his method would allow us to grasp 'the essences of things', not merely as they appear in our minds.[8]

According to Sekine, we can enter Hegel's realm of metaphysics by allow-ing our thoughts to universalize themselves so that we arrive at the most pure thought forms – thought forms that have been divested of any partic-ular sensuous, and therefore contingent, connotations. Such universal cate-gories would include the thought forms of infinity, essence, necessity, causality and so on. Sekine reads Hegel as saying that such universal cate-gories are not only free from the contingent factors that might affect our thinking with regard to particular matters, but that they also necessarily form a logically integrated/unified totality. He goes on to point out that the pure, universal metaphysical categories of Hegel are *not* equivalent to the formally abstract, and therefore pure concepts of mathematics or formal logic, because the latter:

> relate themselves not of their own accord but by deliberate agreement among mathematicians in a man-made language. Metaphysics is not an artificial language deliberately constructed to serve a particular purpose. It is a natural and spontaneous language of thought itself. That is why the metaphysical world forms itself without artificially prescribed axioms or sets of rules. The metaphysical system, in other words, is free and self-contained; it hangs together of its own accord, not because it is so designed as to avoid formal inconsistencies. This is the crucial point. Pure thought synthesizes itself by a logic of its own, not by virtue of any arbitrary form imposed on it from outside.[9]

It is the self-synthesizing and self-explaining process of pure thought that Sekine refers to as dialectic. He considers this dialectic to be objective in the inter-subjective sense, in that we can all arrive at a full comprehen-sion of this dialectic if we allow our thought to universalize itself by divesting itself of its sensuous content.[10] I would suggest, however, that Hegel would contend that his dialectic is objective in a second sense. Although Hegel advises us to abstract from that which is sensuous and contingent to arrive at the universal, rational and necessary, he does not advise us to begin the process of universalizing our thought by turning away altogether from the world outside of our thought. Nor does he think the process of self-universalization of thought will, in the end, bracket all that is external to our thought-processes. Rather, he believes that the dialectical process will retain universal concepts and a logic that are reflections in our minds of a conceptual order that has an ontological status outside our minds as well. It only remains for us to draw out in thought the logic that provides the natural, social and thought world with whatever coherence, integration, cohesiveness and unity it has at its most general or universal level of organization.

Perhaps one indication that my interpretation is correct is the fact that *The Logic* does not ignore the work of the natural sciences altogether. With a faith that we cannot share today, Hegel was convinced that these sciences too would soon discover a universal and necessary rational order that would indicate the presence of the Absolute as it penetrates and informs the operation of the natural world.

If I am correct in my reading of Hegel, then Sekine's critique of any and all attempts to produce a materialist dialectic of nature applies with equal force to Hegel's attempt to defend the notion that nature operates according to a rational and dialectical principle, at least to the extent that the Absolute exercises a grasp over the material world. (Hegel's nature has no organizing principle of its own). Following Sekine:

> nature (or matter) does not come forward to tell us its own story. Since it is not 'autobiographical', a dialectic of Nature (or of matter) is an impossibility. Nature passively sits out there and waits to be scrutinised, dissected, analysed and described by us from the outside ... Nature, therefore, has no teleology to reveal to us. We can never know it completely. We can only gain a partial knowledge of its behaviour by constantly observing it from the outside. Nature does not privilege us by selecting us as its agent and letting us play out its logic. Although we belong to Nature, we have not created it. Consequently, we cannot see its logic from the inside, nor can we grasp it as a totality, i.e., as a 'concrete logical idea'. The 'thing-in-itself' of Nature always remains beyond our reach.[11]

Thus, for the foreseeable future we must remain content with 'so far, so good' and, therefore, with tentative hypotheses, conventionally accepted for the present and subject to refutation or falsification by the further progress of natural science, in our attempts to comprehend nature. If, indeed, there is a rational order in nature, Hegel's method did not reveal it, and we are in no position to uncover such an order today. At the time of writing, it appears that whatever relative necessity occurs within nature, ultimately it is trumped by contingency. We should not assume, however, that, in our attempt to comprehend social systems that human beings have created, we shall necessarily confront the same dilemma. In the study of society we should remain open to the possibility that a law governed system could be found.

It would seem that if we wish to apply Hegel's dialectical method of explanation to something that really exists in the material world outside us rather than to something that we only imagine to have an existence that is external to and transcendent of us (for example the Absolute or Christian God), this subject–object must, nevertheless, have many of the properties of Hegel's Absolute. That means the subject–object in question must demonstrate a capacity truly to transcend us even if, at the same time, it is originally our creation, and therefore only an extension of our finite human characteristics in the direction of the Hegelian True Infinite. Such a subject–object could then reveal itself to us even as it develops powers to do infinitely what we can only do finitely. For Sekine, such a subject–object can, and must, be capital as it manages the labour-and-production process of mature capitalism.

We need not be capitalists to understand the capitalist mentality. Even in pre-capitalist societies the wise use of labour and resources was recognized as a virtue in household management. The capitalist differs from the rest of us in that he or she economizes in the pursuit of abstract wealth for its own sake rather than in the provision of use-values. Once the capitalist pursuit of abstract wealth necessarily entails a society-wide production of commodities, the competitive market and its logic enable[12] capital to transcend all of us – not just working people, but also capitalists – in an unceasing pursuit of abstract wealth even as individual capitalists, as finite beings, must sometimes rest or turn their attention to other matters. One does not have to accept the bourgeois conception of capitalistically rational economic man as inherent in human nature generally to recognize that capitalism's uniqueness stems not from the presence of economizing behaviour *per se* but from the ubiquitousness of its employment in the single-minded, unceasing, irrational pursuit of abstract wealth, whatever the social and ecological cost.

The materialist counterpart of the Idea/Providence/the Absolute is capital which, in the liberal era slowly but surely achieved a largely reified, commodity economy which could reproduce itself and material economic life by the operation of its dialectical logic, even as the state increasingly adopted laissez-faire policies. In effect, English capitalism became possessed to an incredible degree by the idea of capital. Liberal capitalism was a society dominated by a principle or idea and its supporting logic. In fact, the compulsion which capital exercises over social actors generally, whether capitalists or workers, demonstrates that capital has powers the Absolute could not approach. In medieval Christendom, the Absolute, as the Christian God, could compel obedience to His will only through human-to-human coercion, but capital's impersonal, market-economic coercion subordinates social actors of the major classes to its chrematistic principle without relying on direct, physical coercion – at least in principle. On the other hand, although Hegel conceives of the Absolute as the True Infinite, we recognize that capital's historical dominion is finite, however much capital might aspire to the status of Hegel's Absolute. Capital can only manage material economic life to the extent that human beings, for whatever reasons, choose not to mount a collective resistance to its commodity-economic logic which is sufficiently strong as to undermine its operation (even as a powerful tendency), and to the extent that society does not require the production of heavy (autos) and complex (information technology) products which capital's logic is incapable of managing. Of this, more later in the chapter.

From Hegel to Marx

I now propose to turn my attention to Marx's uneasy relationship with Hegel. It is commonplace among Marxists that Marx rejected Hegel's idealism but the precise meaning of that rejection is elusive. Rightly or wrongly, Marx is critical of Hegel because the latter:

> transforms the process of thinking into an independent subject, under the name of the Idea, is the creator [*demiurgos*] of the real world, and the real world is only the external appearance [phenomenal form] of the idea' (*Capital* v. I., 102, 1976) ... Hegel fell into the illusion of conceiving the real as the product of thought concentrating itself ... and unfolding itself out of itself, by itself, whereas the method of rising from the abstract to the concrete is the only way in which thought appropriates the concrete [in reality] reproduces it as the concrete in the mind. But this is by no means the process by which the concrete [or real] itself comes into being.[13]

I am not certain that this criticism is entirely fair to Hegel, but the passage does give us an indication of how Marx might attempt to understand capitalism. If the concrete (or real) Marx referred to here is taken to include capitalism as one reasonably self-contained reality, it could be argued that Marx rejects the notion that capital, in its formative stage, had the capacity or power as an operating principle or logic to unfold towards maturity solely by its own self-activity. Nevertheless, Marx believes that a theorist must understand the concrete (real) by reproducing the real in the mind, and this entails moving from the most abstract, general or unspecified categories to the most concrete or fully specified categories. It seems to me that Marx is only justified in using this method to 'appropriate the concrete (or real)' if, at some point in its development towards maturity, that 'concrete' (or real) developed the capacity to 'unfold itself out of itself, by itself'. Furthermore, while I quite agree with Marx that, as a general principle, 'the process of thinking' is not an 'independent subject' capable of reducing the real world to an 'external phenomenal form of the idea', it is my contention that, under the right material or use-value conditions, and, given the prior development of the appropriate social relations, capital can, to a considerable extent, begin to reduce material economic life in capitalist society to the 'external phenomenal form' of the idea of capital, which, by virtue of capital's power of self-abstraction, operating principle or logic manages to subordinate material economic life to the unceasing pursuit of abstract wealth for its own sake. Capital (as profit-seeking activity) may not be able to think mature capitalism into existence, but once mature capitalism has been reached it does demonstrate a pronounced capacity to reproduce the material conditions and social relations necessary to reproduce itself such that it is *as if* capital were thinking or planning its own reproduction. Obviously, Marx does recognize capital's abilities in this area, as will become clear. Unfortunately, he does not do so here. Not only that, he gives the misleading impression that it is legitimate to assume that all of reality – whether social, historical or natural – organizes itself according to dialectical logical principles whether or not these objects have an innate tendency to reveal themselves as dialectically self-organized.

In the *Grundrisse*, Marx states very clearly that to theorize capitalism's inner logic or laws of motion 'it is not necessary to write the real history of the relations of production'.[14] As unsettling as this statement might first appear, Marx tells us that in theorizing mature liberal capitalism:

> the question why this free labourer confronts him in the market, has no interest for the owner of money, who regards the labour-market as a branch of the general market for commodities. And *for the present* it interests us just as little. We cling to the fact theoretically as he does practically.[15]

There are at least two good reasons why Marx does not attempt to incorporate a complete history of labour or labour power into his theory of capitalism. The first is that:

> human labour-power is by nature no more capital than are the means of production. They acquire this specific social character only under definite, historically developed conditions, just as only under such conditions the character of money is stamped upon precious metals, or that of money-capital on money.[16]

Even within capitalism, capital itself does not operate in the same fashion in its formative stage or period as in mature liberal capitalism. According to Marx, 'in the preliminary stages of bourgeois society, trade dominates industry; in modern society, the opposite'.[17] The consequence of this is that, while capital always engages in chrematistic pursuits, mercantile capital operates in a way which is 'directly contradictory to the concept of value'. Prior to the development of the putting-out system 'to buy cheap and sell dear [was] the law of trade'.[18] Consequently:

> where commerce rules industry, where 'merchants' capital promotes the exchange of products between undeveloped societies, commercial profit not only *appears* as outbargaining and cheating, but also largely originates from them ... Merchants' capital, when it holds a position of dominance, stands out everywhere for a system of robbery.[19]

Similarly, money-lending capital, the 'antiquated form' of interest-bearing capital, also depends on 'robbery and plunder'.[20]

The second reason why we are not concerned with such important topics as how labour-power originally became commodified when we are theorizing how capital manages material economic life in a mature capitalist society is that 'production founded on capital is presupposed'[21] and, therefore, the commodification of labour power has already been achieved. Of course, the laying of the foundation for capitalism's management of the labour-and-production process is a worthy topic of Marxian (or other) historical investigation in its own right, but this rich tapestry, which constitutes capitalism's making, must remain:

> among the antediluvian conditions of capital, [which belong] to its historical presuppositions, which, precisely as such historical presuppositions, are past and gone, and hence belong to the history of its formation ... not to the real system of the mode of production ruled by it ... The conditions and presuppositions of the becoming, of the arising, of capital presuppose precisely that it is not yet in being but merely in becoming; they therefore disappear as real capital arises, capital which itself, on the basis of its own reality, posits the conditions for its realization ... As soon as capital has become capital as such, it creates its own presuppositions ... by means of its own production process. These presuppositions, which originally appeared as conditions of its becoming – and hence could not spring from its action as capital – now appear as results of its own realization, reality, as posited by it – not as conditions of its arising, but as results of its presence. It no longer proceeds from presupposition in order to become, but rather it is itself presupposed, and proceeds from itself to create the conditions of its maintenance and growth. Therefore, the conditions which ... express the becoming of capital do not fall into the sphere of that mode of production for which capital serves as the presupposition; as the historic preludes of its becoming they lie behind it.[22]

Recall Marx's earlier criticism of Hegel for 'conceiving of the real as the product of thought ... unfolding itself out of itself'. I suggest that, in the above passage, Marx himself recognizes that the idea of capital can reproduce itself and its real conditions over time once its chrematistic principle activates the labour-and-production process of a society. It appears that Marx is prepared to concede that, under some very peculiar historical and material conditions, the real, as in capitalist reality, can become largely the product of thought – the thought or idea or logic of capital. Capitalism, in its pure form, develops the capacity largely to reproduce itself and its own survival conditions by its own autonomous motion. The theorist who desires to comprehend capitalism, then, must retrace in thought the steps capital takes to ensure that result. The only part of capitalist history that is relevant, and sometimes helpful, here, is the part of capitalism's history in which capitalism displayed this capacity for self-regulation and self-reproduction. The history of how capitalism slowly developed the capacity to reproduce itself is a different story, and one that can lead us astray, because, obviously, an immature capitalism, which has only developed this capacity to a limited degree, must be understood on its own terms, and quite differently.

According to Marx, free competition, and not an economy dominated by monopoly (or corporate oligopoly) in collusion with the state, offers the most solid foundation for the reproduction of capitalism by means of capital's logic, inner laws, or principles. In the mercantilist period, capital's laws operated only as weak tendencies; whereas in mature liberal capitalism, capital's laws operate more like genuine laws. As Marx says:

> Free competition is the relation of capital to itself as another capital, i.e., the real conduct of capital as capital. The inner laws of capital – which appear merely as tendencies in the preliminary historic stages of its development – are for the first time posited as laws; production founded on capital for the first time posits itself in the forms adequate to it only in so far and to the extent that free competition develops, for it is the free development of the mode of production founded on capital; the free development of its conditions and of itself as the process which constantly reproduces those conditions.[23]

Elsewhere, Marx tells us that the further free trade is developed, the 'purer' will be the forms in which [capital's] motion [will] appear'.[24] He also qualifies his remark *vis-à-vis* the operation of capital's laws *as laws*, not merely as powerful tendencies in mature liberal capitalism. He admits that, in history, capital's laws never operate 'in their pure form':

> In reality there exists only an approximation; but this approximation is the greater, the more developed the capitalist mode of production and the less it is adulterated and amalgamated with survivals of former economic conditions.[25]

Marx also identifies the country in which the purest form of capitalism has been achieved:

> No period of modern society is so favourable for the study of capitalist accumulation as the period of the last 20 years [1846–1866] ... But of all countries England again furnishes the classical example, because it holds the foremost place in the world-market, because capitalist production is here alone completely developed, and lastly, because the introduction of

the Free-trade millennium since 1846 has cut off the last retreat of vulgar economy.[26]

Thus Marx uses England as the 'chief illustration in the development of [his] theoretical ideas'.[27] Uno and Sekine follow Marx's lead in that they, too, acknowledge that late liberal capitalism is the purest form of historical capitalism.

As capitalism develops towards maturity, the self regulating, society-wide competitive market, and its commodity-economic logic, demonstrate a progressively greater capacity to manage material economic life such that the liberal state increasingly can adopt laissez-faire policies. For the first time in history, then, the economy stands largely on its own, with relatively little state and ideological intervention to obscure our view of it. The fact that the real or material economic component of economic life, which must be present in any viable economy in history, and the specifically capitalist mode of operating that economic life always appear together in capitalism means that the capitalist economy is not as transparent as we might wish. Not only that, capitalism manages economic life by mediating, and therefore transforming, human-to-human social relations into impersonal, reified, thing-to-thing commodity relations. The power of commodities and money over human beings is genuine, because the economic life of capitalism and the production of goods as commodities are not governed by a co-ordinated and democratic decision process, for example, but rather by the impersonal price-mechanism of the market. Moreover, the reified and impersonal nature of capitalist management makes what is specific to one form of historical society seem trans-historical, natural and therefore unchangeable, while obscuring our view of what really is trans-historical, natural and indispensable – the requirement to maintain the viability of our material/real economic life; that is, the provision of use-values. The intermingling of the commodity-economic and the material-economic confuses not only ordinary citizens but also neoclassical economists. In the absence of a clear grasp of the invisible logic that governs much of their economic life in capitalist society, citizens of that society may accept the liberal dogma that they are unconditionally free as economic agents, or, because they are unable to separate the specifically capitalist economic laws that are historically transient from the general norms of economic life which must prevail in all viable historical societies, they may conclude equally well that the economic laws of capitalism are universal and unchanging (and therefore 'natural') features of the economic life of any society.

Marx is a great admirer of the achievements of the modern natural sciences (Darwin, Newtonian mechanics and so on) but he recognizes clearly that it is neither possible, nor necessarily even desirable, to attempt to study capitalism as if we were in a laboratory. As Marx observes, 'in the analysis of economic forms neither microscopes nor chemical reagents are of use'.[28] Marx adds that 'the force of abstraction' must replace the above method, but that enigmatic comment is not particularly helpful when considered in isolation. Elsewhere, Marx tells us, however, that as capitalism matures it develops its own capacity for self-abstraction:

> Indifference towards any specific kind of labour presupposes a very developed totality and real kinds of labour, of which no single one is any longer predominant. As a rule, the most general abstractions arise only in the midst of the richest possible concrete development, where one thing appears as common to many, to all. Then it ceases to be thinkable in a particular form alone. On the other side, this abstraction of labour as such is not merely the mental product of a concrete totality of labours. Indifference towards specific labours corresponds to a form of society in which individuals can with ease transfer from one labour to another, and where the specific kind is a matter of chance to them, but labour in reality has here become the means of creating wealth in general, and has ceased to be organically linked with particular individuals in any specific form.[29]

Thus labour may be as old as humanity itself but, before the modern concept of 'abstract labour' can be grounded objectively or scientifically, one requires the development of the capitalist labour market and 'indifference towards specific labours'. In other words, although productive activity is essential in all societies, it is the chrematistic form of capital that simplifies productive labour to the maximum degree compatible with the prevailing level of technology and, in so doing, establishes the labour theory of value both as a scientific concept and as the organizing principle of the commodity-economy.

Capitalism's power of self-abstraction always runs into some form of use-value resistance in history (even in late liberal England). Thus we cannot be certain in that environment that we have understood capital's self-definition and the precise limits of its powers completely. We must find some way to examine capital's process of self-abstraction in an ideal environment in which capital may reveal itself completely, or we shall encounter the identical dilemma that natural scientists and their emulators meet in the neoclassical school of economics. Sekine explains:

> it is necessary that the process of abstraction should be sufficiently complete to reveal in the end the motivating force or the generator of those principles themselves, the generator or the motivating force being the materialistic counterpart of the Idea or Providence. [The self-abstracting and self-synthesizing logic of capital as it organizes material economic life.] Principles that lack their own generator have to be derived from a

set of unrelated axioms; and the model of the real world thus constructed axiomatically cannot be other than partial, static and lifeless.[30]

To expose totally the logic of capital in theory it is necessary to construct a dialectical model of the system rather than an axiomatically detached one, such that capitalism is confirmed not as an arbitrary, entirely dubious formalization of a supra-historic 'reality' but as the only valid theoretical abstraction of a hitherto existing, and largely self-abstracting, historical capitalism. The dialectical model is complete only when capital's power of self-abstraction is itself completely exposed. Such a theory takes us beyond one-sided, simplified, 'external' descriptions of capitalism, viewed as a 'thing-in-itself', which are constructed by theorists who rely on their intuition to separate the necessary from what is only contingent. Marx tells us in numerous places that, in his theory of capitalism as it is developed in *Capital*, 'it is assumed that the laws of capitalist production operate in their pure form',[31] that individual capitalists, and landlords are 'personifications of economic categories', 'agents of capital', or 'personifications of capital',[32] and that the capitalist is 'the soul of capital' with 'one single life impulse, the tendency to create value and surplus value'.[33] He also tells us that, 'a scientific analysis of competition is not possible before we have a conception of the inner nature of capital'. We must understand capitalism's real motions, motions that 'are not perceptible by the senses'[34] and this, in turn, entails 'evolving the different forms' of capitalism 'through their inner genesis'.[35]

From Marx to Uno and Sekine

I am convinced that *Capital* represents Marx's attempt to develop a theory of pure capitalism. As we shall see, however, Marx's pure theory is not as convincing as it could be, because Marx does not make explicit his dialectical methodology – although he claims to be employing a materialist inversion of Hegel's method.[36] More seriously, Marx does not adhere to his dialectical approach in political economy as consistently as he ought to have. This has unfortunate theoretical consequences, which will become obvious. We thus turn to the work of Kozo Uno, and especially Thomas Sekine, who have employed Marx's Hegelian method much more consistently than Marx himself in order to produce a reconstruction of *Capital* which is therefore much more convincing. Sekine has performed the additional service of acknowledging explicitly the close correspondence between the dialectical structure of his *Outline of the Dialectic of Capital* (as well as his earlier work, *The Dialectic of Capital*) and the structure of Hegel's small *Logic*.

Uno and Sekine theorize a purely capitalist economy in which all material use-values are produced as commodities that are sold in a society-wide market by competing capitalist firms, which purchase material commodities in the form of production inputs, together with 'commodified' labour-power purchased in that same market, in order to carry on their profit-seeking activity. In order to theorize pure capitalism and expose capital's laws as laws rather than as tendencies, it is necessary to presuppose an ideal use-value space that will allow capital to produce all use-values as commodities. As capitalism developed in the direction of a mature liberal capitalism in England it was fortuitously the case that competitive capitalist firms became capable increasingly of producing the light use-values that society required with the technologies that were readily available to them. Moreover, the workers who supplied labour-power to capital did not collectively offer the kind of organized, sustained resistance to capital that would have posed a serious threat to capital's management of the economy or the capitalist's management of the workplace. Nevertheless, there was always some use-value and human resistance that capital's impersonal commodity economic logic could not overcome by applying its 'dull compulsion' on capitalists and workers alike. The state had to support capital in those instances in which market coercion failed, or capitalism's future would have been put in question. This means that, in any historical capitalist society, capital's laws operate as tendencies, albeit powerful ones. In the pure theory of the Uno school, we abstract from any resistance that capital's commodity-economic logic cannot overcome in order to see capital's logic or laws of motion with perfect clarity and in order to determine definitively just what use-value and human resistance capital can overcome by its own motion. Use-value resistance that capital cannot overcome is first confronted in a mid-range stage theory which mediates between pure theory and empirical studies of capitalist societies. The stage theory is an indispensable component of any attempt to explain capitalism's operation in history, and we shall touch on its importance later. For now we are only interested in explaining why it is advantageous to provide capital with an ideal use-value space in which it can demonstrate clearly both its cunning and its limits (or fragility). It cannot be overemphasized that Unoists do *not* assume away *any* and *all* resistance to capital. Moreover, although pure capitalism is, in theory, not a clone of liberal capitalism in England, it is not such a departure from that society that we do not recognize it immediately as being depressingly familiar, given our experience with historical capitalism.

In such an ideal environment, capital can dialectically define or synthesize itself such that it reveals itself to us completely. Indeed, for a dialectical subject–object, the truth is the whole. Such a subject–object, must have a logic inherent in it such that it can explain or reveal itself completely rather than having a logic arbitrarily imposed upon it from the outside. It must be, in Hegel's terms, a concrete logical idea. The construction of a purely capitalist society as a dialectical system in thought is therefore justified, and is possible only if our object of investigation (that is, capitalism that occurs in history) has an innate tendency to define, regulate and reveal itself. Indeed, this inner logic could never be constructed arbitrarily in one's mind and imposed upon the external world. All such attempts have produced one-sided definitions of capitalism that are never logically complete. If a natural or historical object of investigation is not dialectically self-managing and self-abstracting, then the decision to view that object as a logically synthesized totality can only be subjective and arbitrary.[37]

The dialectical theory of capital is possible because the dialectical theorist can reactivate in theory capitalism's power of self-regulation which hitherto existed as an objective reality. When the theorist performs this operation, he or she ends up retracing the path or steps by which capital went about organizing economic life, and so allows capital to reveal its laws of operation in their entirety. This is a unique feature of capitalism which sets it apart, not just from natural systems but also from all other social systems.

A dialectical self-definition of a subject – object explains a complex and layered reality to us step by step, moving from what is logically prior, empty, immediate, insufficiently specified and abstract to what is increasingly more adequately specified, or determined. Indeed, an identical concept appears many times and, each time, it is specified in greater detail until all its logical components or necessary inner connections are revealed. This movement is *not* a movement from the abstract-general to the real, empirical or historical concrete. Rather, when the theory is fully developed, the subject–object reveals itself to be concrete-synthetic in the sense that it has specified itself fully, exposing all of its inner determinations.

By the time the dialectician is ready to present the self-definition of a dialectical subject–object he or she already knows how the explanation will finish or reach closure. It is known, in other words, how the broad contours or spaces provided by the abstract categories that were begun with are going to be fully elaborated or specified by all the details necessary to provide a complete explanation of the system when the dialectical account reaches closure. It is a characteristic of the dialectic that it always presupposes a complex, fully specified totality as its subject-matter, but cannot exhibit all of that totality's concrete features or specifications at once. The logic of the system can only be revealed by a gradual unfolding. As Hegel says, 'it is precisely the truth in the form of a result that we are gradually making apparent'.[38]

As the dialectical unfolding proceeds, it should become obvious that what appears to be a progressive movement is simultaneously a retrogressive grounding of the beginning, so that any feeling that we might have had that the beginning was chosen somewhat arbitrarily by the dialectical theorist is replaced by a growing recognition that the beginning was itself derived or mediated, as we learn progressively more about the determinations that provide more and more of the specifications of that initially empty concept with which we began. According to Hegel:

> Each step of the advance in the process of further determination, while getting further away from the indeterminate beginning is also *getting back nearer* to it ... What at first sight may appear to be different, the retrogressive grounding of the beginning, and the progressive further determining of it, coincide and are the same. The method, which thus winds itself into a circle, cannot anticipate in a development in time that the beginning is, as such, already something derived ... and there is no need to deprecate the fact that it may only be accepted provisionally and hypothetically.[39]

We now come to the vexing issue of dialectical contradictions. Unfortunately, a lot of misleading disinformation has circulated in Marxian circles to the effect that dialectical reasoning is a logic of contradiction or a negative logic. It must be stated emphatically that thinking dialectically does not entail embracing formal, logical contradictions.

Dialectical contradictions arise when a particular kind of complex subject–object appears before us without adequate specification or determination. This subject–object can be specified more adequately if we can relate its present inadequate specification to its other possibility or negation. The resulting synthesis yields a more adequate specification of the subject–object. However, each time a new specification is introduced, the level of abstraction changes and the dialectic is compelled to recognize and overcome a new form of the contradiction, the synthesis of which amounts to a richer, more complete, and therefore concrete specification of the totality.

The dialectic thus proceeds by synthesizing contradictions through recurring triads. Each triad is composed of a thesis, an antithesis or negation, and a synthesis. When the dialectic finally reaches closure there are no more contradictions left to impel the logic forward, for, indeed, the subject-matter needs no further specification. The dialectic, in other words, returns to the starting point of its exposition in possession of all the 'concrete' details that are necessary to fill the original emptiness and abstractness of the concept. A dialectic ends with a fully synthesized totality, which Hegel refers to as the 'absolute idea'. It is at this point that the subject-matter completely, and therefore absolutely, reveals all its inner connections.

In the case of the dialectic of capital, the dialectical subject–object presents itself initially in the form of a commodity in possession of value, which is the most abstract or immediate representation of the presence of capitalism. A dialectical contradiction arises immediately between the value or capitalist social aspect of the commodity and its other possibility, its potential use-value aspect. A synthesis occurs when value adopts the form of exchange value to prevail over its use-value aspect; however, use-value resistance to value returns in a new form, and value must again adopt a new form in order to continue to prevail. Successive triads, as a process of capital's self-synthesis, eventually move capital's self-definition towards closure when capital has fully explained its inner logic/laws of motion and totally subdued use-value resistance (in theory). When this dialectic reaches closure, with the form of interest-bearing capital, which necessarily entails the conversion of capital into a commodity, we have returned to our starting point, the commodity form, but this time with a full comprehension of the essence of a society which tends to produce all use-values as commodities with commodified labour-power. This circular movement is a characteristic of any genuine dialectic, as was pointed out earlier.

If we have truly achieved complete knowledge of the system's inner laws of motion (that is, how it is 'programmed' to operate), then our theoretical explanation of capitalism as an object of investigation will be identical with the logical self-exposition of capital as subject. The theory of pure capitalism is genuinely dialectical, because the theory merely reactivates in thought the dialectical laws that tended to prevail increasingly in liberal capitalism once the competitive capitalist market and its attendant reification of social relations enabled capital to exercise its 'dull compulsion' over economic agents. This is no less true even if we recognize that capitalism's appearance on the world stage was a contingent historical development and not the result of dialectical laws operating in history as a whole (nor the result of a 'necessary' unfolding of the World Spirit), and even if the historical process of progressive mechanization, reification and purification was interrupted before a pure capitalism was realized completely. If, for Hegel, logic corresponds with metaphysics; for the Uno/Sekine dialectic of capital, logic corresponds with the economic theory of pure capitalism.

In my article, 'Dialectics and Economic Theory',[40] I explored the correspondence between Hegel's *Encyclopedia Logic* and Sekine's *Dialectic of Capital*. The article did not receive much attention or criticism, positive or otherwise, but eventually I became somewhat dissatisfied with my presentation of the case for correspondence. Having subjected my earlier attempt to as rigorous a critique as I could, I rewrote the correspondence as my contribution to this collection; however, I found that, because of its length, space did not permit its inclusion here. Whatever my reservations, now, about that article, I would still defend Sekine's version of the correspondence, as opposed to C. J. Arthur's, though I am delighted that he too believes that some kind of correspondence exists between the dialectical logic of Hegel and the dialectic of capital. In my article I attempted to defend Sekine's claim that the Doctrines of Being, Essence and the Notion in Hegel's *Logic* correspond to the Doctrines of Circulation, Production and

Distribution in the dialectical theory of capital, and that in both dialectics the logics employed in each of the three doctrines were 'becoming' (or 'transition'), 'internalization' and 'unfolding'. I am still comfortable with Sekine's schema outlining the correspondence, which is as follows:[41]

Dialectic of Capital		*Hegel's Logic*	
I	The Doctrine of Circulation	I	The Doctrine of Being
	1　The Commodity-form		1　Quality
	2　The Money-form		2　Quantity
	3　The Capital-form		3　Measure
II	The Doctrine of Production	II	The Doctrine of Essence
	1　The Production-Process of Capital		1　Ground
	2　The Circulation-Process of Capital		2　Appearance
	3　The Reproduction-Process of Capital		3　Actuality
III	The Doctrine of Distribution	III	The Doctrine of Notion
	1　The Theory of Profit		1　The Subjective Notion
	2　The Theory of Rent		2　The Objective Notion
	3　The Theory of Interest		3　The Idea

Notes and References

1. For the best discussion in English of the development of historical capitalism in the light of the dialectical theory of capitalism, see Albritton, R., *A Japanese Approach to Stages of Capitalist Development* (London: Macmillan, 1991).
2. Marx, K., *Capital,* vol. I (Moscow: Progress, 1971), p. 751.
3. Marx, *Capital,* vol. I, p. 737.
4. Marx, *Capital,* vol. I, p. 737.
5. Rosenthal, J., 'The Escape from Hegel', *Science and Society,* vol. 63, no. 3 (Fall, 1999).
6. Sekine, T., 'The Dialectic, or Logic that Coincides with Economics', pp. 4–5 unpublished but revised.
7. Sekine, T., 'Capitalism and the Dialectic,' unpublished, pp. 2–3.
8. Hegel, G. W. F., *The Encyclopaedia Logic,* trans. T. F. Garaets, W. A. Suchting and H. S. Harris (Indianapolis: Hackett, 1991), pp. 24, 81.
9. Sekine, 'Capitalism and the Dialectic', pp. 3–4.
10. Sekine, 'Capitalism and the Dialectic', pp. 3–4.
11. Sekine, T., *Marxian Theory of Value – An Unoist Approach,* unpublished manuscript (1993), pp. 25–6.
12. For a more detailed discussion, see Sekine, 'Capitalism and the Dialectic'.
13. Marx, K., *Grundrisse,* trans. M. Nicolaus (Harmondsworth: Penguin, 1973), p. 101.
14. Marx, *Grundrisse,* p. 59, pp. 92–3.
15. Marx, *Capital,* vol. I, p. 169.
16. Marx, K., *Capital,* vol. II (Moscow: Progress, 1967), p. 35.
17. Marx, *Grundrisse,* p. 858.
18. Marx, *Grundrisse,* p. 856.
19. Marx, *Capital,* vol. III (Moscow: Progress, 1971), pp. 330–1.
20. Marx, *Capital,* vol. III p. 593

21. Marx, *Grundrisse*, p. 459.
22. Marx, *Grundrisse*, pp. 459–60.
23. Marx, *Grundrisse*, p. 650.
24. Marx, *Grundrisse*, p. 651.
25. Marx, *Capital*, vol. III, p. 175; see also p. 23.
26. Marx, *Capital*, vol. I, p. 648.
27. Marx, *Capital*, vol. I, p. 90.
28. Marx, K., 'Preface to the first German Edition', *Capital*, vol. I, p. 8.
29. Marx, *Grundrisse*, pp. 103–4.
30. Sekine, T., 'Uno-Riron: A Japanese Contribution to Political Economy', *Journal of Economic Literature*, vol. XIII, p. 860.
31. Marx, *Capital*, vol. III, p. 175.
32. Marx, *Capital*, vol. I, pp. 10, 233, 316, 546; *Capital*, vol. III, pp. 373–4, 819.
33. Marx, *Capital*, vol. I, pp. 233, 546.
34. Marx, *Capital*, vol. I, p. 316; *Capital*, vol. III, pp. 373–4.
35. Marx, *Capital*, vol. I, pp. 101, 108.
36. Marx, *Capital*, vol. I, p. 103.
37. For a more detailed discussion, see Sekine, 'Capitalism and the Dialectic'.
38. Hegel, G. W. F., *Philosophy of Right*, trans. T. M. Knox (Oxford: Clarendon Press, 1967), p. 233.
39. Hegel, G. W. F., *Science of Logic*, trans. A. V. Miller (Atlantic Highlands, NJ: Humanities Press, 1969), p. 841.
40. In Albritton, R., and Sekine, T. (eds), *A Japanese Approach to Political Economy* (London: Macmillan, 1995).
41. Albritton, R., *A Japanese Reconstruction of Marxist Theory* (London: Macmillan, 1986), p. 187.

7
The Dialectic, or Logic that Coincides with Economics

Thomas T. Sekine

In the course of my training as an economist I have learned that true economic theory should take the form of *the dialectic of capital*, whose structure is a mirror image of Hegel's logic. My reason for writing this chapter is to explain to you what all that means. With this preamble-caveat, I wish to begin with a personal episode relating me with Hegel.

Kozo Uno (1897–1977) taught me economic theory when I was an undergraduate. But he never related his approach to economic theory to Hegel's logic. Nor did he, unlike Lenin, ever recommend his students to familiarize themselves first with the Hegelian logic in order to understand correctly Marx's *Capital*. Much later, when I finished my doctoral dissertation in neoclassical economics at the London School of Economics (LSE), I had not the faintest idea of what 'scientific method' was all about. I did not even know of Karl Popper, who was then still lecturing at LSE. But upon arriving at Simon Fraser University, I met Larry Boland, who introduced me to Popper. I read a few of his writings. Though I was not so terribly impressed by his ideas, I learned for the first time what 'scientific method' involved, and took some interest in the subject. A few years later I had a sort of intellectual crisis in that I could no longer live with seriously, let alone enjoy, neoclassical economics. It was then that I met Uno again after many years of lapsed contact. I tentatively threw at him some logical positivist and Popperian ideas to see his reaction, only to find out that he was totally unperturbed. In fact, his aloofness to that sort of discussion impressed me greatly, for it was so complete and total. This made me suspect that Uno was hiding a scientific method of his own behind his economics, a kind that was not shared by any Western-trained scholar in social science around at that time. It took me a while before I worked out that it was indeed the Hegelian logic.

Uno claimed, on numerous occasions, that Marx's economics was a 'science' and not a mere 'ideology'. By this he meant that it constituted an objective knowledge that should make sense to anyone regardless of class or ideology. This greatly angered some Marxists who stuck to the 'partisan character' of Marxism, but pleased others who believed in its universal scientific validity. This 'science-but-not-ideology' thesis of Uno's soon became a holy canon of all his followers. But few, even into the twenty-first century, have inquired seriously into what Uno in fact meant by 'science' or 'objective knowledge', despite his strenuous (but alas not so successful) efforts to insist on a (scientific) method peculiar to Marxian economics. The commonsensical view, promoted vigorously by the positivists, that only natural science constitutes a genuinely objective knowledge, is still quite widespread and persists even among Unoists. Perhaps to some extent Marx himself was responsible for this, as he never stinted praise of Newtonian mechanics as a model of science. Yet it is my belief that what Uno called '[scientific] method peculiar to Marxian economics' was nothing other than the Hegelian dialectic, which, I believe, does not apply to natural science. I regard this to be a matter of vital importance methodologically, epistemologically and ontologically in our apprehension of the Marxian scientific tradition. First, I wish to explain why social science needs its own method distinct from that of natural science.

Natural science

Let me begin by reviewing the widely accepted idea that a knowledge of nature is *predictive, prescriptive* and *prospective*. This comes from the fact that nature exists out there (that is outside of ourselves, human beings), so that we cannot know it totally. It, in other words, jealously guards its *thing-in-itself* and never reveals itself totally. In consequence, our knowledge of nature is bound to be *empirical* and *partial*.

All natural scientific propositions take the *predictive* form: $(a, b, c, \ldots) \rightarrow x$, meaning that, if the conditions $a, b, c, \ldots$ materialize, the event x will occur. Mathematical theorems too are always formulated in this way, except that the conditions and the event are axiomatic in mathematics, whereas they are factual in natural science. For example, 'if water is heated to 100 degrees centigrade, it vaporizes' would be a natural-scientific statement. This kind of statement refers to a phenomenon pertaining to an aspect or a phase of nature, and gives us only a *partial* knowledge of nature. Because, if we ask how condition a did in fact materialize, we must seek to establish another proposition such as $(a_1, a_2, a_3, \ldots) \rightarrow a$, and, if we further ask how a_1 did the same, we must again verify a conjecture such as $(a_{11}, a_{12}, a_{13}, \ldots) \rightarrow a_1$, and so on ad infinitum. Clearly, there can be no end to this type of inquiry. Furthermore, there is also the tricky issue (known as Hume's problem) that a factual verification of both the conditions and the event is never conclusive, so that the truth of a natural-scientific proposition is always tentative, being relative to the existing state of knowledge. Even the widely accepted, factual proposition that water vaporizes at 100 degrees centigrade is only a so-far, so-good hypothesis, and is never established conclusively. For there is no assurance that it will not be overthrown in the next experiment. In other words, its truthfulness is never at par with that of an axiomatic proposition such as 'the inner angles of a triangle add up to a straight line'.

All this means that, no matter how much we accumulate this type of knowledge, we can never hope to know nature itself *in toto*, and hence that its inner logic, its integral programme or its ultimate software will for ever remain unknown to us. This is the case even though we benefit enormously from accomplishments in the natural sciences. The more we know of natural phenomena, the easier and the more convenient our lives can become. The reason is that the *predictive* form of knowledge lends itself easily to technical (that is, *prescriptive*) applications. So long as these applications are conceived correctly, they always benefit human beings. In this sense, our increasing knowledge of nature can be described as *prospective*. Unfortunately, however, in the present age of accelerated progress in 'science and technology', frequently we are humbled by devastating misapplications of natural-scientific knowledge working ultimately against our own well-being. This, it seems to me, is a convincing proof that our knowledge of nature always remains *partial*, so that, as soon as we forget our limitations and arrogate to ourselves the power to reshape nature radically to suit our needs, our hubris will be punished. This being so, what we should learn from natural science is how we should conform to nature, and not how we should make it conform to us. It is a matter of practical wisdom on our part to comply with nature and to piggy-back on its forces to improve our living conditions as we protect ourselves from natural disasters.

Social science

Social science cannot share the same method with natural science. Its object of study, society, is wholly unlike nature. Society does not exist outside ourselves, the human beings who constitute it. Consciously or unconsciously, we ourselves make up our society. Therefore, we can, and must, know this object of study *totally*, by laying bare its inner logic, its programme and its ultimate software. Instead of conforming blindly to the existing order of society, we must, if need be, seek to reshape and change it radically. Applying to the study of society the empirical method of natural science is tantamount to sanctifying it as absolute and immutable; that is, as something that dictates our conformity. Such a premise is from the beginning marred by an ideological bias and cannot possibly be regarded as objective. Society does not lie out there as a 'real world' which allows us only to observe its disconnected features and let us formulate hypothetical propositions in the predictive form to be tested empirically. If so, however, we clearly need to establish a scientific method fit for our needs, quite distinct from that used in the study of nature. What sort of scientific method will it be? My claim is that the dialectic is the method appropriate to social science. In particular, it applies to economics that forms the core of social science, whence the title of this essay: 'The Dialectic, or Logic that Coincides with Economics'. Of course, I am here echoing Hegel's own dictum that 'Logic coincides with Metaphysics'.[1]

What characterizes dialectical knowledge is that it is *'post-dictive'* (or *grey*), *self-reflective* and *retrospective*. One should here remember Hegel's celebrated metaphor of the owl of Minerva, 'which spread its wings with the falling of the dusk'. 'Philosophy comes on the scene too late to give instruction as to what the world ought to be', says Hegel. For 'only when actuality is already there cut and dried, does the thought of the world appear'; 'only when actuality is mature does the ideal apprehend this world in its substance, and build it up for itself into the shape of an intellectual realm'.[2] In other words, we comprehend our own world only *retrospectively* as we get older (more mature) and capable of reflecting on what we have thus far done and therefore what we are. This kind of knowledge predicts nothing; it rather 'post-dicts', if one may coin such a word. Nor does it lend itself to technical applications, for it prescribes nothing. Being *self-reflective*, it is only good for the self-discovery and self-comprehension (that is, knowing oneself) of human beings. Instead of being prospective, it is retrospective; for, as Paul Valéry once said, aptly, 'we enter the future by stepping backwards' (*nous entrons dans l'avenir à reculons*).

These are the properties essential to dialectical knowledge. Yet frequently they are half understood and, consciously or unconsciously, evaded because of the deeply entrenched popular notion that knowledge that does not lend itself to technical applications must be useless to humanity. As has already been explained, natural-scientific knowledge permits technical applications because it takes the predictive form. The virtue of its predictability is not always an unqualified boon. Because of its necessarily partial character, technical applications can be good or bad. Yet the spectacular achievement of 'science and technology' in recent years has scarcely been doubted, giving them much credit. Under the circumstances, the fact that social-scientific knowledge permits no technical application appears to be rather disappointing. One therefore tends to resist this fact, conceding to the vulgar soul to which it is nothing but a sign of the weakness and underdevelopment of social relative to natural science. Thus, Marx is often praised for having prophesized a future course of events accurately, just as he is depreciated for having failed to do so. Many Marxists claim themselves to be in possession of better 'predictive' power than are bourgeois economists. These, to me, are indications of a gross misapprehension of the dialectic. Granted that bourgeois economists predict poorly, that does not make Marxists any better equipped with clairvoyance with regard to the future.

Materialist dialectics

Marxists' errors began with a wrong critique of Hegel based on the fancy that his dialectic could be grafted mechanically on to 'materialism'; that is, on to the highly doubtful materialism such as is often represented by the trite dictum 'matter precedes idea', where 'matter' itself is an abstract idea. The Engelsian invention that matter (or nature) could simply be substituted for Hegel's Absolute is a pure non-starter, because matter is not a subject–object that can be induced to recount its own story. Elsewhere I stated that a dialectic needs an autobiographical subject or a storyteller who can be induced to tell his story from within, and that such a subject should transcend we human beings.[3] The reason why Hegel could develop his dialectic successfully is that its subject, the Absolute, both originates in human beings and transcends them. My reasoning here is based on the Feuerbachian thesis of 'anthropomorphism', which says that man creates God (the Absolute) in his own image rather than God creating man in His image. Man has many virtues but, being trapped in his finiteness, cannot pursue any one of them without limits; that is, unboundedly. But man, unlike animals, can undo his own bounds in his imagination and thus create God (the Absolute). Only a human quality, rendered absolute or infinite, in the sense of transcending human bounds, can be a dialectical subject. This is the point that orthodox Marxists have failed consistently to understand.

But if one reads *Capital* without preconceived ideas, be they political, ideological or revolutionary, one can see through its imperfections that it does indeed intend to be a dialectic of capital in the same sense as Hegel's *Logic* was a dialectic of the Absolute. This is how Uno read *Capital*. Just as Hegel's logic coincided with metaphysics, the dialectic of capital should coincide with economic theory – economic theory in the sense of the definition of capitalism by capital itself. Just as Hegel (according to Ludwig Feuerbach) reached his Absolute by undoing the boundedness (or finitude) of human virtues, we can reach capital by pushing human 'economic motives' (the jargon I inherit from Karl Polanyi) to their limits. Indeed, capital is the god of 'economic motives'; that is, the human propensity to maximize gains and minimize losses. All human beings are endowed with economic motives, which, however, they pursue only within limits. Scrooge and Eugenie Grandet, who seek abstract rather than concrete wealth, embody more of the capitalist spirit, but they are to that extent suspected of being 'inhuman'. Capital goes further, and wholly transcends human feelings and corporeity. The dialectic of capital, or economic theory, is the logical system in which capital synthesizes itself. Capital reveals itself completely by defining what capitalism in its pure form might be like.

From the above follows the meaning of 'materialist' dialectic. What makes the dialectic of capital materialist and non-idealist is not that capital is 'matter as opposed to idea', whatever that may mean. Capital is certainly a 'software' and not a hardware, and, in that, it is no different from the Absolute. What makes the difference between them is the circumstances under which the software has developed. As Feurerbach pointed out aptly, human beings, unlike animals, tend to create religion, presumably *under all material conditions* though he did not say it in so many words. In contrast, human beings do not always create capitalism. Capitalism comes into being only when products can easily take the form of commodities, that is, *only when material conditions (pertaining to what to produce and how) are right.* We all know that such material conditions evolved first in seventeenth century England and not before. I use the phrase 'use-value space' frequently for the material conditions on which the economic life of a society is built. Capitalism occurs when capital takes over (or subsumes under it) a 'use-value space' suitable for organization under its logic. In other words, we need the right kind of hardware ('use-value space') to enable the software (the logic of capital) to fully work itself out.

Dialectics and social science

This way of understanding capitalism, which is inherent in Marx, is never more clearly expressed than by Uno, according to whom capitalism comes into being when the *form* of capital 'grasps' or 'seizes upon' the *substance* of use-value space. This, by the way, parallels closely Karl Polanyi's idea of capitalism.[4] In fact, the explanation of capitalism as an *uncertain* union of the form of value and the substance of use-value space constitutes the hall-mark of all non-liberal (that is, non-bourgeois) approaches to economics, in sharp contrast to classical and neoclassical views, which presuppose a com-plete fusion of the form and the substance. Under this presupposition, 'eco-nomic man' would be eternal, for 'the propensity to truck, barter and exchange one thing for another' would be inherent in human nature, so that human society would always be a virtual capitalist society, the form of capital and the substance of economic life being in permanent and insepa-rable union. Yet many Marxists unwittingly allow themselves to be trapped into such bourgeois ideology, by believing that the substance determines its own appropriate form. By failing to understand capital correctly as a form or 'software', one can easily be led astray.

Economics and the other social sciences, once bundled together and called political economy, are the products of the modern (capitalist) age, and are therefore inevitably laden with bourgeois-liberal preconceptions. This means that even with a strongly motivated anti-capitalist ideology one can easily be duped into embracing, rather than exorcizing,the presupposi-tions of bourgeois ideology. The most effective antidote to that, to my mind, is to grasp firmly the 'materialist' dialectic as the method of social science. By pointing out that the circumstances under which capital developed as 'software' differed from the case of the Absolute, I have contrasted the 'materialist' dialectic with the old Hegelian dialectic. The same contrast carries into that between the two characteristic 'contradictions' which set the dialectic into motion. The dialectic of capital synthesizes itself by solving the 'contradiction between value and use-value', while Hegel's dialectic of the Absolute undergoes its spiral march by overcoming the 'contradiction between being and naught'. Here 'value' represents abstract-mercantile wealth which capital seeks, and 'use-value' the concrete-material side of society's economic life. Thus capitalism synthesized as value prevails over the resistance put up by use-value restrictions. In the case of Hegel, 'being' indicates the presence of the Absolute, and 'naught' its absence. By prevailing over naught, being proceeds to establish the divine realm of reason. In this way, the structure of the dialectic is the same. But a fundamental difference seems to me to exist between 'use-value' and 'naught'. Although from the point of view of the materialist dialectic, value representing capital, its subject, prevails over use-value in order to synthesize capitalism, the real implication is that this can be done only in so far as the use-value side permits it. For capitalism is historically transient. This means that the real winner in the end is use-value (concrete wealth for human beings), which will remain even after the death of value (abstract wealth sought by capital). This is different from the implication of Hegel's dialectic of the Absolute. Once being succeeds in synthesizing fully the Absolute, naught (the absence of divine wisdom) is conquered and suppressed forever. In other words, Hegel's naught is strictly empty and passive; it is meant to be subdued forever by being. Since naught offers hardly any real resistance to the progress of being, the triumph of being over naught is a foregone conclusion in Hegel. This, it seems to me, renders his idealist dialectic somewhat lopsided, and explains why his reasoning validating the dialectical progress (from abstract-unspecified to concrete-synthetic) appears at times to be rather forced and unnatural. Needless to say, the materialist dialectic of value and use-value, as formulated by Uno, is more even-handed and free from such mental acrobatics. This, to my mind, is because use-value can exist outside the dialectic of capital as it does inside it.

Materialism and idealism

This point seems to me to give us a real clue in contrasting materialism to idealism in dialectics. To Hegel, the establishment of divine wisdom and the kingdom of reason was the ultimate aim of the dialectic. Once this was done, it only remained to see how that infinite reason of the Absolute manifested itself in nature, human beings (finite spirit) and history. There was clearly no question of abolishing the Absolute. That made Hegel's 'dialectic of history' completely determinist, allowing no freedom to choose or even to err in the future course of humanity's evolution. In the materialist dialectic, in contrast, we let capital synthesize itself *in logic* precisely for the purpose of abolishing it later *in history*, and of thus emancipating ourselves, human beings, from the sway of its abstract universality. *Logic belongs to capital, but history is ours*. This we can say because use-value will never be completely assimilated to value, that is, because 'use-value space', the material conditions on which the economic life of a society stands, maintains its own ontology.

In fact, even under capitalism, the subsumption of the use-value space under the logic of capital is never perfect; there are always remaining 'externalities'. Real capitalism exists when these externalities (that is, parts of the use-value space that do not submit to the logic of capital) can be 'internalized' by economic policies of the bourgeois state. But the dialectic of capital, or economic theory in the sense of the definition of capitalism by capital itself, must presuppose an ideal use-value space. A use-value space is ideal when no part of it resists or exceeds subsumption under the logic of capital. Only by presupposing such an ideal use-value space, can we let capital synthesize pure capitalism, a theoretical definition of capitalism. The way in which this kind of economic theory is synthesized is, in fact, quite simple. In this ideal use-value space we need only specify a particular situation or context, before asking capital 'Now what do you want to do?' We always get the right answer from capital, and economic theory is no more than an ordered totality of such answers. But how do we know that capital's answer is always true? Because the truth is already in ourselves. Recall that capital originated in us before it transcended us. Since capital is our 'economic motives' made infinite, we are in fact asking the question of ourselves and answering it. There is nothing inside ourselves that we do not know.

In other words, the truthfulness of the dialectic of capital has no epistemological ambiguity. Every dialectical proposition can, in fact, be confirmed *introspectively* and requires no further external verification (empirical test) to be validated, as would be the case with an axiomatic proposition. This, I believe, is an important conclusion pertaining to the nature of economic theory, which both bourgeois economics and orthodox Marxism fail to understand. Axiomatic propositions are derived logically from arbitrary axioms or postulates whose truthfulness remains open to doubt. Therefore, in principle, they cannot be accepted as being conclusively true before verification. Yet, as was also pointed out, no verification is conclusive in natural science, so that the latter cannot claim anything more than so-far, so-good truth, and not conclusive truth of the kind that the dialectic of capital can claim. Economic theory, whether neoclassical or Marxist, which wants to be natural-scientific, will also be deprived of the self-assurance of the materialist dialectic.

The dialectic of capital and history

The fact that there are such things as 'externalities', so that the logic of capital can never completely assimilate a use-value space even under capitalism, holds the key to the emancipation of humankind and socialism. For it means that capitalism can exist only to the extent that externalities are manageable by policies of the bourgeois state. If they are so rampant as to exceed the control of the bourgeois state, capital will no longer be able to function as the determining software of the society. Capitalist society must then give way to its successor, which may or may not be socialism, depending on whether it is progressive or retrogressive in terms of the emancipation of humanity. But all this involves what Uno once called the 'dialectic of history' and the 'dialectic of revolution'.

When the dialectic of capital synthesizes itself fully, defining capitalism, we must then see how capital asserts itself in real, that is, non-idealized use-value spaces. Here the theme is 'negotiation' between capital and the use-value space, which is quite unlike the unilateral self-imposition of divine reason on human contingencies as in Hegel's philosophy of history. In the Unoist doctrine, concrete-empirical use-values are reintroduced very carefully, first as types such as wool, cotton and steel, which were dominant in the three world-historic developmental stages of capitalism. For example, the liberal stage of capitalism is conceived as one in which all or most use-values are like cotton products, and produced with technology similar to that employed by the nineteenth-century English cotton industry. Thus, in the stages-theory, use-values remain controlled as 'types' so as to bring out the mode of negotiation whereby capital manages to regulate a use-value space of a particular kind. Naked and multifarious use-values as they exist in real history are introduced at another level, the level of historical analysis. If we deal with an historical period of capitalism, the stage-theoretic determinations mediate between theory and reality. For a study of a non-capitalist period, such a mediation cannot be counted on. But, in either case, there is no place for historical determinism. Every episode in capitalist history is full of contingencies and freedom, and is informed by the logic of capital only in broad outlines and in part. The history of a non-capitalist era is even less subject to the logic of capital.

In explaining the three distinct levels of analysis, Uno referred to three kinds of necessity: the necessity of decennial crises, the necessity of an imperialist war, and the necessity of a revolution. The first of these is dictated by the logic of capital and is fully determinate. The second occurs at the stages-theoretic level. When the logic of capital asserts itself at the stage of development of capitalism typified by heavy industries such as steel and chemicals, bourgeois states are compelled to resort to imperialist economic policies, the consequence of which is a war between major powers for economic hegemony. This necessity is not explained completely by the logic of capital, but involves human factors reflected in policies of the bourgeois states. The third necessity refers only to the likely collective choice of human societies. Human beings must be protected from the brute force of the self-regulating capitalist market, as Polanyi says. This means that there comes a point where the capitalist pursuit of abstract-mercantile wealth becomes intolerable to the well-being of humankind, and that at or near that point the latter will choose to terminate the rule of capital. It is, in other words, a prognosis of human behaviour that is essentially free and contingent. In deference to the historicist tradition of Hegel and Marx, Uno talked of the dialectics of history and revolution. But clearly he did not subscribe to the eschatological biases of that tradition.

Conclusions

I would like to conclude this paper by drawing out the implication of this last statement. When the dialectic identifies a subject–object which spins its story (that is, the software that defines an operating system), the next step is to see how it actually works or manifests itself in reality. In Hegel's case, his logic, which coincided with metaphysics, defined the Absolute (the Christian *logos*, divine wisdom, reason, or whatever) as the subject–object. The Absolute then asserted its sway completely over nature and human beings in such a way that no contingency and freedom would remain after its establishment. It is this that made his dialectic 'idealist'. In contrast, the subject–object of the materialist dialectic, capital, is much less powerful in its actual working. For we can identify it as the software of capitalism only by imagining an idealized use-value space. In other words, real use-value spaces can never be subordinated completely to the logic of capital. There always remain 'externalities' that escape the sway of capital. It is therefore 'use-value' and not 'value' that wins eventually. From our human point of view, we always need a use-value space, but we tolerate the dictates of capital only under certain circumstances. To me, it is this fact that makes the dialectic of capital 'materialist' and not 'idealist'. The materialist dialectic synthesizes capital as software, in just the same way as the Hegelian dialectic does the Absolute. At this level there is a complete parallel, almost a homomorphism. The distinction arises in what the software does. The Absolute insists on being omnipotent always, permitting no freedom for human beings to choose their own destiny, whereas capital wants to be omnipotent only when it can – that is, *only when material conditions are right* – thus assuring complete freedom for human beings to go beyond it.

Notes and References

1. Hegel, G. W. F., *Logic*, trans. W. Wallace (New York: Oxford University Press, 1975), p. 24.
2. Hegel, G. W. F., *Philosophy of Right*, trans. T. M. Knox (Oxford University Press, 1967), Preface.
3. Sekine, T., *An Outline of the Dialectic of Capital*, vol. I (London: Macmillan, 1997), pp. 5–7. See also Sekine, T., 'The Dialectic of Capital: An Unoist Interpretation' in *Science and Society*, vol. 62, no. 3 (1998).
4. Polanyi, K., *The Great Transformation* (Boston, Mass.: Beacon Press, 1957), pp. 40–5.

8
The Problem of Use-Value for a Dialectic of Capital

Christopher J. Arthur

P16
B51

Towards a dialectic of capital

It is well known that Marx's *Capital* was influenced profoundly by Hegel's dialectical logic; this goes well beyond Marx's flirting with Hegelian expressions. However, the deep structure so influenced is not immediately visible. Moreover, it is almost certain that the appropriation of Hegel's logic by Marx was inconsistent and obscure even to him. We are forced therefore to start anew with the problem of how to construct a 'dialectic of capital'. When one speaks of a 'dialectic of capital' it is necessary to explain why and how this object of study may be expected to have a dialectical character in the first place. Given that the great exponent of modern dialectics, namely Hegel, was an idealist, and given the implausibility of Engelsian 'materialist dialectic', the suspicion must arise that dialectical arguments are peculiarly suited to illuminating the logical structure of systems of ideas, and then to such social forms as may be represented as the 'embodiment' of such logical relations.

As the Uno–Sekine school of thought in the Marxist tradition has pointed out, the unique ontology of capitalism provides the most plausible case for such a dialectically informed social theory. In particular, the phenomenon of exchange of heterogeneous commodities, which are yet posited as identical in value, introduces, it seems, an objective separation between the realm of use-value founded in material particularity, and the realm of value, a quasi-universal attribute of commodities which develops logically from commodity exchange to other value forms such as money, and capital defined as self-valorizing value. T. Sekine writes: 'The so-called "contradiction" between value and use-values ... means that the abstract-general (infinite) principle of capital represented by "value" and the concrete-specific (finite) reality of human economic life represented by "use-values" do not mix naturally.'[1]

K. Uno says: 'The commodity-economy ... arises ... from the exchange-relation between one production process and another. The forms ... peculiar to commodity exchange then influence the production processes by reaction, sink slowly into them, and finally take possession of them.' Despite the historical flavour of this claim, Uno reformulates it as a logical requirement: 'It is for this reason that the pure theory of capitalism cannot begin with a doctrine of production, despite the widely-held view to the contrary that political economy should first examine the process of production – which forms the real basis of any economic process.' Thus the primary concept in 'pure theory' is not the product but the commodity form. I agree with this. I agree again with Uno when he concludes, contrary to Marx, that the labour theory of value must not be put at the head, because commodity production must be capitalist, and this means that labour should be introduced 'only after the conceptual development of the form of commodity into that of capital'.[2]

At the level of circulation, because capital *itself* is indifferent to it, there is no need for theory to address the specificity of use-value – it is objectively present only as a support for value. But I will argue that this 'indifference' cannot be sustained when production is thematized. The Idea of capital is the unity-in-difference of the value form springing *from* exchange relations and the production of commodities *for* exchange. The distinction between the two must be held fast if utter confusion between the relevant dimensions of the capital system is to be avoided. The distinction has relevance for the scope of the dialectic in question. With respect to the development of the value form, the problem is to achieve the grounding of value on itself, in the form of capital, and the contradictions involved in the general formula of capital are intrinsic to its form. With respect to production, a new set of contradictions between the value form in general and the sphere of use-value come into play, requiring value to find a way of coping with the obstacles thrown up by use-value.

The occlusion of use-value

The problem for capital is not only that value and use-value do not fit naturally together but also that its conceptual filter (the 'bottom line') allows it to cognize only value. It becomes conscious of use-value considerations, in consumption and (more importantly) in production, only in so far as they accelerate or impede valorization. This is why it cannot function without human agents such as managers, salesmen, engineers, foremen and the like, with a foot on both sides of this divide, measuring everything by its contribution to profit but attending to material reality sufficiently so as to be able to produce use-value solutions to use-value problems with a view to facilitating valorization. But in the pure form of capital, such problems are outside its terms of reference; no thought is taken as to *how* results are obtained, only *that* capital is accumulated through production and exchange.

It is tempting here to separate the life of capital in psychological terms into its *consciousness*, wherein it demands that an income stream arises simply from its own self-determination, and an *unconsciousness* comprising all the knotty problems of production arising from two repressed others of capital, labour-power and land, each recalcitrant in different ways to capital's view of them as moments of itself as it appropriates them under the value forms, wage and rent.

In this way, the dialectic of capital has a certain homology with Hegel's system in that, for Hegel too, the self-transparency of the logic is not capable of registering in their own terms the non-logical spheres of nature and society, but simply reduces them to the objectification of *logical* categories. In so far as their non-logical character as realities is recognized, it is only so as to give the logic a *body* for itself (as Marx remarked acutely of Hegel's political philosophy).

At all events, whatever one thinks of Hegel, I believe the dialectic of capital has to be traced through two stages, or on two levels. At one level, theory must attend to the forms that capital requires to formulate its aim of self-determination, to constitute a self-grounded totality. Here, the categories of Hegel's logic are demonstrably useful. But at another level capital must be psychoanalysed, so to speak, by theory, so as to uncover the hidden roots of its self-expansion of value in the expropriation and wastage consequent on its incarnation in the use-value sphere, and the latter's possible irruptions into capital's dream world of frictionless circulation and growth.

The exposition of the dialectic of capital proceeds most conveniently by developing the value form up to the general formula of capital as if the use-value sphere posed no problem, precisely because this is implied in the forms themselves, which really abstract from use-value, and in particular represent the production process only as a reified result, without noting the mediations of industry vanished in its result. Then the exposition must study to what extent these forms take charge of production, form-determining it as a valorization process. While capital, by and large, has proved itself successful in this aim, it would be a mistake at this level of theory to take capital at its own estimation as incorporating unproblematically use-value as the bearer of valorization; rather, theory must identify the key contradictions between value and use-value with a view to seeing how capital actively overcomes use-value.

In 1859, Marx made an inexact remark – which I believe has affected the reception of his work from the earliest time. He first states that use value is not affected by the social form under which it was produced, and then lets slip the comment: 'Use Value as such lies outside the sphere of investigation of political economy'. Immediately he qualifies this by continuing: 'It belongs to this sphere only when it is itself a determinate [economic] form'.[3] But it was possible to take the first remark out of context and ignore the importance of studying the phenomena in which use-value *does* enter into the determinations of economic forms. The misunderstanding started in Marx's own lifetime with the polemic against him by Adolf Wagner. This led Marx, in his 'Notes on Wagner', to respond angrily, stating how wrong it was to say *'use-value* plays no part' in his work; crucially, he stresses 'that *surplus-value* itself is derived from a "specific" *use-value of labour power* belonging to it exclusively'.[4]

Earlier, in the *Grundrisse,* he had said similar things – for example, that nothing is more erroneous than to think that, if the distinction between use-value and exchange-value lies 'outside' the forms characterizing simple circulation, it does so in general. He continues: *'Use value itself plays a role as an economic category* [my emphasis]. Where it plays this role is given by the development itself.'[5] Certainly 'use value does not lie dead as a simple presupposition'.[6] He goes on to demonstrate the interchanges of the categories in the circuit of capital: 'From the standpoint of capital (in circulation), exchange appears as the positing of its use value, while on the other side its use (in the act of production) appears as positing for exchange, as positing its exchange value.'[7]

In *Capital,* Volume II, the whole theme of social reproduction mediated through exchange between departments makes the theorization of specific use-values essential:

> The transformation of one part of the product's value back into capital, the entry of another part into the individual consumption of the capitalist and the working classes, forms a movement within the value of the product in which total capital has resulted; and this movement is not only a replacement of values, but a replacement of materials, and is therefore conditioned not just by the mutual relations of the value components of the social product but equally by their use-values, their material shape.[8]

The texts just reviewed show that, if Marx's theory is primarily a 'social economics', the key categories being 'the theoretical expressions of the social relations of production', it must not be forgotten that not only is the production and distribution of use-values an essential context for the production and circulation of value, but also that certain economic determinants spring from use-value itself, the use-value of labour-power playing a unique part in valorization.

If it is supposed that the form of value appropriates the production process painlessly, reducing the material interchanges to its vehicle, then the dynamic of capital accumulation is unproblematically *immanent* in the form of self-valorizing value, and may plausibly be represented as a dialectical development of the concept of capital whose completion is not impeded by the matter subsumed under it. Attempts to illuminate 'the dialectic of capital' from this standpoint must find the problem of use-value is a stumbling block, because it turns out that the particularities of the sphere of use-value production pose obstacles to the free movement of capital. Once the infinite aspiration inherent in the form of capital accumulation descends to finitude to grapple with the otherness of use-value in order to ground valorization on production, then use-values can no longer figure as mere place-holders for value. Capital, in its phase as production capital, has to move under the burden of exogenous determinants (whether these are construed as contingent or necessary). At a minimum, appropriate means of production and labour powers for the making of specific use-values must be selected. More importantly, there is one such element of the production process that cannot be considered as if it were integrated into capital's self-development unresistingly. This is labour itself, living labour, the *sine qua non* of capitalist production.

The form of capital as inherently infinitely self-expanding value makes capitalism utterly different from any other mode of production. In all modes of production it is possible to seek ways of improving the productivity of labour and all exploitative modes rely on some form of 'pumping out' surplus labour. *Only* capital is *in point of form* as such *driven* to accumulate 'wealth'. But if it were not for the real historical existence of labour-power as a commodity, and of the reality of surplus labour that makes possible its exploitation, then there would be no self-expansion of value. Once the problem of grounding the systematic surplus presupposed in the general formula of capital arises, then the dialectic must turn to production to resolve the contradictions in the general formula referred to by Marx. It is when the problem of production is posed, that Marx's anticipation that specific economic forms spring from use-value determinants arises.

First, we address the special contribution of labour. As noted earlier, Marx gives the example of the specific use-value of labour-power when rebutting the misinterpretation of his work. Second, we address the contribution of nature: for two reasons – it is underplayed by Marx; and it problematizes any unthinking stipulation that only labour time determines the magnitude of value.

The contribution of labour

In trying to explicate the dialectic of the capital relation, I think it is useful to attend to some intriguing passages in Marx's *Grundrisse,* in which we find a transition from labour as capital's *other* to labour as a *moment* of capital itself; clearly, if both theses are to be maintained this indicates the deeply contradictory character of the capital relation.

To begin, let us note that Marx draws our attention explicitly to the importance of this topic for the issue (mentioned earlier) of use-value as an economic form. The passage is important enough to quote at length:

'The *use value* which confronts capital as posited exchange value is *labour*. Capital ... exists ... only in connection with *not-capital*, the negation of capital, without which it is not capital; the real *not-capital* is *labour*. If we consider the exchange between capital and labour, then we find it splits into two processes which are not only formally but also qualitatively different, and even contradictory:

(1)   The worker sells his commodity, labour [power], which has a use value ....
(2)   The capitalist ... obtains the productive force which maintains and multiplies capital, and which thereby becomes ... a force belonging to capital itself ....

In simple circulation, this double process does not take place ... The using-up of the commodity ... destined to be consumed ... falls entirely outside the economic relation. Here, by contrast, *the use value of that which is exchanged for money appears as a particular economic relation*, and the *specific utilisation of that which is exchanged for money forms the ultimate aim of both processes. Therefore, this is already a distinction of form between the exchange of capital and labour, and simple exchange – two different processes.*[9]

Marx stresses earlier the oppositional character of this relationship: 'In the relation of capital and labour, exchange value and use value are brought into relation; the one side (capital) initially stands opposite the other side as *exchange value*, and the other (labour) stands opposite capital, as *use value*.'[10] But capital takes charge of the developing relationship such that: 'Labour is not only the use value which *confronts* capital, but, rather, it is the *use value of capital* itself' (my emphases).[11] 'As use value, labour exists only *for capital*, and is itself the *use value* of capital, i.e. the mediating activity by means of which it realizes itself.'[12] Indeed, labour-power exists *only* for capital, since it is incapable of acting here except when placed by capital in connection with the means of production. Then it must act as 'a moment of capital itself'.[13]

But, because of the contradictory form of the relationship, capital finds that it is confronted by a special difficulty: the repressed 'subjectivity' of the worker poses unique problems. The other 'factors' of production, land, machinery and materials enter with their productive potential *given*, known in advance; only with labour is productivity contestable and contested, known only in the upshot of the working day. Capital is limited by the extent to which it can enforce the 'pumping out' (Marx) of labour services. The basis of this special feature of labour is that the relation between capital and labour is intrinsically antagonistic in that the workers are actually or potentially recalcitrant to capital's effort to exploit their labour. This is why, for a theory grounded on the *social form* of the economy, labour is to be correlated with value. New value is the successful reification of living labour. Thus, whereas at the start of *Capital* Marx assumes there is no problem about labour appearing as reified in value, really this is consequent only on the success (partial and always contested) of the struggle to subsume labour under capital. Value is the reward for capital's success in achieving the subsumption of labour under its forms; *the struggle to reify labour in value is what capital is all about.* It constitutes itself as what it is, as a peculiar mode of pumping out surplus labour, in this endlessly renewed struggle.[14]

Capital realizes itself in an entire circuit of movement: M—C ... P ... C' – M' (M = money; C = commodity; P = production; M' = M + Δm). In this, the phase '...P...' is not a formal metamorphosis of commodities, as are the flanking phases. It is a material transformation of one use-value into another, albeit intended for commodity exchange. Use-values, such as means of production and labour power, are what is aimed at in the first metamorphosis 'M—C'. While they are acquired under the relevant commodity form (price and wage) their exploitation *as use-value* is a different matter. Here, their specific adequacy for the task of production is relevant to the success of capital's valorization. If the capital circuit is taken only as a formal metamorphosis borne silently by use-value, then the process of production '...P...' lies as a 'black box' at its heart. That other 'black box', where capital has to rely on the self-production of the working class in the domestic sphere, while part of *capitalism*, is not part of *capital*. But it is precisely '...P...' that lies at the heart of capital, and which it must manage materially, and not just formally. This clearly involves exploiting the use-value of labour-power – that is, 'pumping out' (Marx) living labour against the recalcitrance of the workers.

The tendency for capital to confuse the purchase of labour-power with the acquisition of its use is refuted rudely by the counter-tendency of the workers to resist yielding up its use. I am not thinking only of organized resistance here, but of everyday shirking, skiving, sabotaging, or even mere lack of enthusiasm for the task. Capital has to employ an entire army of foremen and other supervisors to try to overcome this. Theory must take account of this simply to grasp capital as a social relation. In Chapter 1 of *Capital*, Marx began the exposition 'after the harvest' with an already-produced commodity, stated to embody labour, but without reference to the labour process that has vanished in this result. The commodity then appears as a form in which labour is reified. But it had to be produced in conditions in which labour was *not* reified. Let us be more precise: labour-power as a quasi-commodity sold like any other may be said to be a reified shape of the human bearer but its *use* involves precisely the coming into play of labour itself, bound up with the labourer, of course, who is imbued with a complex set of desires, on the one hand to keep a job, and on the other to do as little work as possible.

There is a deep fallacy in taking capital's dream world of frictionless circuitry to be meaningful in any sense, even for a high level of abstraction from the concrete, because subjection to exploitation cannot plausibly be represented as the completion of *an inherent tendency to reification*. The tendency to reification is a function of the interpellation of commodities as values *after* production, when they are anointed in exchange as *inherently* being values through distancing and occluding the facts of their production; in other words, labour is *represented* as being reified in value, but this does not mean it was *really* reified in the production of value. Capital would like labour to be yielded uncomplainingly by the 'commodity' they have bought and hence 'possess'. But labour-power is not a standard commodity, just because it can be separated from its original possessor only by a legal fiction but not in material reality. The capitalist does not expand biologically when he hires a hundred 'hands' to work for him or her; he or she has to force the hands to work by threat, bribe, or the very design of the production process. But in no case can the workers be reduced to robots.

At the level of the forms of circulation, capital's natural element, so to speak, the value product sublates the process of its production in such a manner that the human and natural mediators of its production vanish from view. But the reified forms of value must not be read back into production itself so as to presuppose living labour as simply being an appendage of the machine. Such a tendency may be present, the more so as capital develops, but it is met by an equally real *counter-tendency*. This is the resistance of living labour to its putative, or tendential, reduction to a robotized shape. This is not a contingent externality but exists as a potential inherent to the capitalist mode of production always and everywhere. The fact that resistance waxes and wanes historically may be accepted without disturbing the general point. If the specificity of labour is disregarded, exploitation is itself unrecognized in the material sense, leaving only the distributional sense (in that those who labour get only part of the product, while those who do not labour get the other part). One would rather have surplus product appearing as the result of the entire use-value operation as if there had been total automation. If the specificity of living labour is lost sight of, capitalism really could be reduced to 'production of commodities by means of commodities'! Marx writes: 'In my presentation, profit is ... *not* simply "a *deduction* from or 'robbery' of the worker". On the contrary, I depict the capitalist as the necessary functionary of capitalist production and show at great length that he not only "deducts" or "*robs*", but enforces the *production of surplus-value*, thus first helping to create what is to be deducted.'[15]

It is, of course, the case that capital is 'dead labour', but in conceptualizing it we must go beyond this characterization of capital simply as a *result* of its intermediation with labour to include the process *constituting* it, namely the appropriation of *living* labour. From the point of view of capital itself, this is a distinction without a difference, because it conflates the labour process and the valorization process in its concept of itself, as if living labour was nothing but a 'speaking instrument' of its own action. It thinks itself to be productive of itself because it cognizes all factors of production under their various value forms and cannot admit its dependence on land and labour-power as being necessary to its determination, but not reducible to aspects of itself.

The contribution of nature

In the first instance, capital can be studied as pure form, prior to addressing the questions of the content regulated and the determinants of magnitude. As pure form, it already has its 'measures'; in the circuit M–C–M' it measures itself against itself through the moment at which its abstract identity with itself is posited explicitly, namely money; but it is inherent to the concept of capital that the proportionate increase registered there serves only as a presupposition of further expansion; mere increase is therefore sublated, and the true measure is the *rate* of accumulation. That is the measure that is appropriate to the quality of quantitative expansion.

It follows that when capital grounds itself on production it seeks a content capable of generating an *excess* over itself, and that *time* is of the essence of self-valorization. The time of value-positing might seem, then, to correspond immediately with the time of production. However, having turned to production in order to see how to measure this time, a peculiar issue arises. As we know, Marx distinguished within the time of production, labour time and non-labour time. The latter is accounted for by the time necessary for certain natural processes to occur, such as ripening, cooling, fermenting and so on. But if Marx allows explicitly for an 'excess' of production time over labour time, then, given that he stipulated that only the latter 'creates' value, this has peculiar consequences for use-value. Because Marx had already presupposed at the start that value was founded on labour, he has to say that such extra time during which capital is tied up in use-value production is not value creating, although it does represent possible claims on the value product in the same way as socially necessary circulation time does.

Let us first examine the relevant passages of *Capital*, Volume II. Marx concedes that one reason why there is 'an excess of production time over the working time' is that there are 'intervals in which the object of labour is exposed to the action of physical processes, without further addition of human labour'. Nature itself transforms use-values from one condition to another (following Baruch Spinoza, we call this 'nature naturing' by analogy with 'labour labouring'). Marx continues: 'The means of production are here placed by labour itself in conditions in which they undergo by themselves certain specific natural processes, the result of which is a specific useful effect or a changed form of their use-value.' Marx, of course, in line with his stipulative labour theory of value, claims 'nature naturing' creates no value: 'hence this is no valorisation of the productive capital, as long as this finds itself in that part of its production time that is in excess of the working time, no matter how inseparable these pauses may be from the accomplishment of the valorization process'. An interesting point is that, in effect, Marx does not merely say the 'excess' is unproductive; in the context of competition it shows up as an actual deduction. Along with all other non-productive times in which capital circulates, this has a 'negative effect' in that it slows up valorization. He says: 'What political economy sees is only the appearance, i.e. the effect of circulation time on the valorisation process of capital in general. It conceives this negative effect as positive, because its results are positive.'[16]

Marx does not in fact equate the excess of production time over working time with circulation time, but there is no doubt that within his conceptual scheme it too would be a 'negative effect' appearing as something 'positive' where valorization rather than use-value is the issue.

I think it too easy to say that only labour is productive, and that any interruption in the labour process made necessary by the need for certain physical processes to take place is time wasted. For there is a very important difference from circulation considered narrowly here. As far as the production of use-value is concerned, circulation not only adds nothing, it even threatens deterioration. But corn ripening, wine maturing, or even steel cooling, are not cases of capital being tied up uselessly; they are essential to the very production of commodities.

Thus any attempt to base the claim that labour is value-creating because it has a *unique* role in the production process of the goods to be valued is dubious. One can well imagine a 'green' argument to the effect that, not only does nature provide labour with its materials, but also that 'nature naturing' is an important productive activity to set alongside 'labour labouring': such an argument might conclude that, as such an essential activity, the substance of commodities working on itself, so to speak, it is impermissible to set it aside where the time determining value is calculated.[17]

One way of dealing with the problem that production time is longer than labour time might be to assume an identity of the two times on the basis of an idealizing simplification. It might be argued that the labour theory certainly does not work in agricultural systems, because nature's time outweighs human time, and that it would not work in a totally automated system in which human activity was reduced to a trouble-shooting role, for the same reason, although here it would be a 'second nature', the self-acting machinery, taking time. But industry, at the present time, it might be said, is primarily a system of labour processes with natural and mechanical processes under the continual control of the workers. While this argument has its merits, it does not go to the root of the matter. Even in modern industry the distinction between production time and labour time remains significant, and in any case requires conceptualization if possible rather than being treated as negligible.

As long as the focus is on the side of material relations rather than on social relations, there is no refutation of Karl Popper's old accusation that Marx believes in 'the holiness of human labour'. He says:

> The strange thing about Marx's value theory is that it considers human labour as fundamentally different from all other processes in nature, for example, from the labour of animals. This shows clearly that the theory is based ultimately upon a *moral* theory . ... We can call this the doctrine of the *holiness of human labour*.[18]

And he objects that this is not the right basis for economic analysis.

Marx responded directly to a proto-Popper. A reviewer of *Capital*, Karl Rössler, wanted to know why it should be that 'the food in the stomach of a worker should be the source of surplus value, whereas the food eaten by a horse or an ox should not'. Marx commented that 'Mr. Rössler obviously thinks if a horse works longer than is necessary for the production of its horse power, then it creates value just as a worker would who worked 12 instead of 6 hours [necessary labour]. The same could be said of any machine.' Such 'productivity' of horses or machines is certainly relevant to the use-value output, but not to value; because, Marx stresses, 'the value of things is nothing other than the relations in which people stand to each other'.[19] In his *Grundrisse*, Marx again provides the following anticipation of Popper's attempt to conflate the labour of humans and animals:

> Basically the appropriation of animals, land etc. cannot take place in a master–servant relation, although the animal provides service. The presupposition of the master–servant relation is the appropriation of an alien *will*. Whatever has no will, e.g. the animal, may well provide a service, but does not thereby make its owner into a *master* ... The master–servant relation ... is reproduced – in mediated form to be sure – in capital.[20]

As it stands, this does not seem adequate in that animals do have a will, they are stubborn and have to be driven; none the less, they cannot formulate an alternative aim to that of the owner; so what I suggest is a three-level conceptual scheme:

(i) Nature naturing even if manipulated and distorted by humanity, for example, cows bred to produce unnatural amounts of milk;

(ii) Human and animal recalcitrance requiring them to be *driven* to produce; and

(iii) Labourers as potential counter-subjects threatening a determinate negation of capital itself, which latter is hence conceptualizable as a negation of its negation in a strong sense, not just as overcoming recalcitrance.

What this last indicates is that labour is not merely a technical factor of production; it is itself a social subject employed in a certain social form of production. Within capitalism, there is every reason to see it as unique on that account. Labour is actively involved in the production process as a potential *counter-subject* to capital, whereas nature 'naturing' is a process of the matter that is not in itself capable of actively resisting its manipulation for human purposes, although it may frustrate them, unknowingly, for material reasons.

So here is a clear case where use-value is an important form determination, because only the use-value distinction between labouring and naturing allows us to justify restricting valorization to the former. Thus it is important for 'pure theory' to make a distinction between labour time and production time, but this distinction is a use-value distinction in so far as it relates to the *agent* of production, which must be articulated theoretically only on the basis that labour and nature have relevant differences. It is a distinction of *economic form* – just the kind of thing that Marx said we had to anticipate when we turn from circulation to production. In this way, the labour theory of value may be defended against alternative 'green' theory.

The 'others' of capital

In the last two sections I have shown that labouring and 'naturing' are the use-value basis of the production process. I insist that the way in which these use-value processes are themselves effective as economic forms (whether recognized by value as a 'positive' – labouring; or a 'negative' – naturing) cannot be dispensed with in the 'pure theory' of capital. In particular, the problem of their management by capital must not be obscured by a rather different issue, namely that capital succeeds in bringing within the commodity form the two inputs it requires for production to begin, namely labour-power and land. The two questions may, however, be related in the following way. I call labour and nature 'capital's others'. They each appear in the whole movement of capital as product and process. Let us address each in turn.

As product, labour is 'labour-power'. This presupposition of capital originally appears outside it, but is now reproduced within it; it is capital's 'internal other'. It is not, of course, reproduced immediately by capital, but in the domestic sphere. Nevertheless, the domestic sphere may be treated as a 'black box' within capitalism in that the 'value' emerging from it may properly be equated in magnitude with the values absorbed by it (notwithstanding that capital therewith gets something for free in the interim). The domestic sphere absorbs commodities necessary for its reproduction and supplies in commodity form labour-power to capital. Once hired by capital, the use-value of wage-labour is potentially appropriated as the process of labouring. But I have stressed that the recalcitrance of the workers to yielding this use is constitutive of the exploitative character of the capital relation.

Nature is a product of the history of our planet. In its passive aspect it appears as land, and other resources such as wind and water, that capital subjects to a commodity form, namely rent. I call nature the 'external other' of capital. Even though 'original' nature scarcely exists anywhere, and it is rapidly being destroyed by capital, this transformation is effected through use-value interactions, and in this way is different from the way in which the domestic sphere interfaces with values.

Rent is a contingent and external deduction from the product of capital, because there is nothing in the concept of capital itself that would suggest that there must be permanent scarcity relative to demand in an element of its factors of production; it is none the less subject to such a material contingency; so rent is a necessary form of its actual existence. Rent, then, is a product of a contingency that, however important materially for the capitalist mode of production, is, from the strictly *logical* standpoint of capital, a *distortion* of its reproduction because of the element of non-reproducibility that enters as a determining economic form.

Nature appears 'outside' production as a given precondition. But as active, and transformative, it also appears within production as nature 'naturing'. Capital counts non-labour production time as a negative quantity, as we established earlier. But it need not count reproduction time at all if nature is awaiting appropriation. For example, it only takes a short time to cut up a hardwood tree, which may well have taken a century to grow.[21] Contrary to neoclassical claims that capital handles scarce resources well, generally the exact opposite is true. It is profligate with scarce natural resources and wastes them – for example, oil, natural gas, and rainforests.

The idealization of capital

Sekine argues for the methodological legitimacy of abstracting from the problem of use-value for the sake of theorizing capital in its purity so as to exhibit its 'inner logic'.[22] This assumes a theory of capital's inner logic in which indifference to use-value is realized completely. In R. Albritton's gloss on this 'thought experiment': 'At the level of pure capitalism the motion of value is allowed to overcome all use-value obstacles including the special use-value labour-power. That is, the reifying force of capital securely commodifies labour-power with the implication that class struggle is temporarily quieted at this level of theory.'[23] According to Albritton, in pure theory all worker resistance has to be theorized as 'overridden by the self-expansion of value'.[24] Moreover, the fact 'that labour power is capable of agency' is said not to be a problem. But it *is* a problem for capital precisely because it *cannot* be reified. Tendencies to turn workers into machines cannot be completed even in principle (to act as robots they have to be forced or bribed to do so).

As part of his argument for excluding class struggle from the dialectic of capital, Albritton conflates abstraction from the historical specificity of such struggle with abstraction from it altogether. He argues that 'the law of value is the inner logic of capital' but 'class struggle is historical'. He illustrates the point with a reference to the struggle over the length of the working day: 'From the point of view of pure theory, the length of the working day is simply given. Thus pure theory looks at what variations in the length of the working day mean to the law of value without going into the conjunctural determinants of a working day of a certain length.'[25]

In my opinion, however, the dialectic of capital is entitled to draw attention to the fact that the determination of capital here is such that it is necessarily contestable; but the development is subject to contingencies, the study of which pertains more to history than to system. I agree that much in Marx's chapter on the subject is not part of the systematic development of the idea of capital, being illustrative and empirical. But it seems to me that the very concept of surplus value *production* can hardly be properly articulated without reference in a general way to its determination through struggle. This is all part of grasping capital as a unity of value and use-values, the latter being pressed into the shape of the former precisely because they do not fit naturally, as we saw Sekine observe. But the central case where the *specificity* of use-value cannot be rendered indifferent to *value* is that of labour-power. The exploitation of just this agent of production is defining of capital. Of course, again, there is a history of the labour process to be written, to which Marx and Harry Braverman have signally contributed, but one way or another this particular use-value must be appropriated by capital, and the peculiar recalcitrance it has, actually or potentially, to such subsumption is the defining moment of the Idea of capital.

It may be possible to argue on purely methodological grounds for a two-stage model, first developing capital as if it were coherent and complete in itself, and then developing the reality of use-value obstacles. But, in my view, this is rather undialectical – better to follow capital in its own effort to subsume labour, and allow the limits to show within the presentation itself. Moreover, such a procedure still allows the perspicuousness of a purely logical stage of development of the concept, since beginning with the form of circulation allows the possibility of bracketing use-value in so far as circulation itself does so through the bending back on itself of exchange value in the general formula for capital (M—C—M'). Probing the conditions of existence of this form both reveals its dependence on production and forces us into a confrontation with certain peculiar use-values that are economic forms in their own right (for example, surplus product).

It is true that capital has its own concept of itself in so far as it is constituted through a radical inversion of the relation between the universal and the particular; for all the specificity of use-value is ignored when commodities are considered by capital as so many bearers of value and surplus value. Similarly, capital recognizes in production only its production of itself, albeit through the mediation of the use-values it effectively idealizes. This idealization of reality effected through the structure of capital results in the development of a false totality.[26]

Our own concept of capital must certainly include recognition of the objective reality of this totalizing power of capital bent on idealizing reality, but we also must include within our concept of capital this equally essential hidden truth of its dependence on what it mediates itself in. Allowing capital to complete its ideality in thought (in dreams, rather!) is precisely allowing it to tell a story that *represses* its truth. Our method must not only *listen* to capital[27] but also simultaneously *interrogate it* so as to make visible the repressed others, namely its dependence on, and exploitation of, labour and nature.

Conclusion: beyond capital

In both Hegel's philosophy, and in capital, everything stands on its head. Hegel presents the categories he abstracted from reality as the logical basis of that reality such that nature has its truth outside itself in the Logic. Similarly, capital presents the form of value as the real being of the economy, reducing use-value to its non-being, such that the 'truth' of the production process is the valorization process, and living labour and nature naturing are posited as moments of capital's own circuit. Moreover, this inversion is objectively valid for the capitalist epoch; it can be removed only in practical action. In the history of philosophy, L. Feuerbach could dispel Hegel's idealist illusion by arguing that, to give itself reality, logic must mediate itself in nature and therefore depends on it, but nature itself has immediate validity and stands in no need of mediation by some abstraction. In a parallel – but practical – way, throwing off the shackles of that self-moving abstraction, capital, allows reality to be put back on its feet in so far as production is reorganized for need, not profit, and use-value flourishes in its own right. Under the rule of capital, production processes are posited as the worldly phenomena of which valorization is the truth that lies beyond, but since valorization in fact *depends* on production and exploitation, whether of labour or nature, our criticism takes the Feuerbachian road and says that, if valorization requires mediation in the production of use-value, it is really better seen as the alien form of the material immediacy of surplus production. Social action can start from the immediacy and get rid of the abstraction of value, since use-value does not require it.

Epochally, the being of value encloses its non-being, use-value, taking it into its *possession*, and exploiting it materially with a view to valorization. But use-value production, that is labouring, cannot be understood as enclosing value. It can only constrain the above-mentioned imputation of itself as nothing but value's material support. Value subordinates to its own law the extremes of the use-value spheres (for example, production and consumption) it supposedly mediates. Yet, just in so far as value *has* to alienate itself by thus sinking from its infinite self-satisfaction in the monetary circuits (M–M′ or M—C—M′, where M′ = M + Δm) to the humbling passage through finitude (real production by/through/of use-values), it confesses involuntarily both its dependence on use-value and the latter's potential liberation from it.

Unlike Feuerbach's critique of Hegel, which could be accomplished in the sphere of ideas, we have to admit that capital is epochally hegemonic in practice, and pose the task of its practical critique once theory has comprehended it. This revolution liberates both labour and nature, currently the repressed 'others' of capital, to embark on the process of their *own* Becoming.[28]

Appendix on the uses of Hegel's *logic*

The issues discussed in this chapter have a bearing on larger philosophical problems in relation to the conceptualization of capital. Both in my own view, and that of Sekine and Albritton, it is important to draw on the resources available to us in Hegel's dialectic when attempting to reconstruct Marx's *Capital* in systematic terms, developing each category of capital out of the previous ones with a view to exhibiting the architectonic of capital.

The differences between the Sekine–Albritton theory and my own may be summarized as shown below:

(i)   The Sekine–Albritton view is that it is best to secure a homology between the structure and categories of Hegel's *Logic* and those of the three volumes of Marx's *Capital* (suitably redrawn); my view is that the appropriate homology with Hegel's *Logic* is to be sought in the dialectic of the value form up to the general formula for capital; the turn to production (to solve the contradictions implicit in the general formula) is parallel to the turn in Hegel's philosophy from its logical principles to the reality principled by them.

(ii) Since the Sekine–Albritton approach takes the dialectic of capital to be essentially logical in character, it follows that it is *closed*; truth cannot remain undecidable in a coherent and complete logical system. My view, corresponding to Hegel's, is that in reality there is always a gap between conceptual truths and the object domain, namely, as Hegel would put it, the realm of finitude, or as we have it in the homology, the sphere of use-value which capital can never completely conquer.

(iii) The Sekine–Albritton theory of pure capitalism secures its logical coherence and completeness through 'quieting' the use-value sphere generally, and in particular bracketing the resistance to valorization that might be expected to arise from the exploited class. This is said to be a necessary strategy, since the aim of this part of the theory is to show capital in its truth. Only after this has been accomplished is it relevant for the theory of pure capitalism to give way to a new study, in which the previous methodological closure is relaxed and disruptive influences from use-value considered.

On my account, the contradiction between value and use value is *constitutive* of capital. This is connected to the first two points in that I restrict the purely logical development to the 'inner' dialectic of capital as a value form where value moves freely in its own element. The sphere where the pure forms of logic are likely to find their homomorphs is surely the sphere of circulation; in such phenomena as price, and the metamorphoses of commodities and money, value deals only with itself in its various expressions. Then, in treating the further concretization of capital in production and accumulation in accordance with an 'external' dialectic of value and use-value, considered as 'real extremes' no matter in how sophisticated a manner the structure capital evolves to mediate them, a central place would be accorded to capital's strategies of securing its existence through 'negating its negation' (that is, its putative 'gravediggers').

The following lists[29] exhibit the homologies with Hegel's *Logic* that I propose.

Hegel's *Encyclopaedia Logic* §83:

Logic is subdivided into three parts:
 I the Doctrine of Being
 II the Doctrine of Essence
 III the Doctrine of the Notion and Idea

That is, into the Theory of Thought:
 I In its immediacy: the notion implicit and in germ.
 II In its reflection and mediation: the being-for-self and show of the notion.
 III In its return into itself, and its developed abiding by itself: the notion in-and-for-itself.

Arthur:

The dialectic of the value form is divided into three parts:
I Commodity
II Money
III Capital

That is, into the theory of exchange:
I In its immediacy: value implicit and in germ.
II In its reflection and mediation: 'value-for-itself', the showing forth of value.
III In its return into itself, and its development of itself: value-in-and-for-itself.

Hegel: *Logic*	Arthur: *Dialectic of the Value Form*
I The Doctrine of Being	I Commodity
A Quality	A Exchangeability of commodities
B Quantity	B Quantity of commodities
C Measure	C Exchange value of commodities
II The Doctrine of Essence	II Money
A Ground	A Value-in-itself
B Appearance	B Forms of value
C Actuality	C Money
III The Doctrine of Notion	III Capital (General Formula)
A The Subjective Notion	A Price
B The Objective Notion	B Metamorphoses of money and commodities
C The Idea	C Capital

Notes and References

1. Sekine, T., *An Outline of the Dialectic of Capital,* 2 vols (London: Macmillan, 1997), p. 9.
2. Uno, K., *Principles of Political Economy: Theory of a Purely Capitalist Society*, trans. T. Sekine (Sussex: Harvester Press, 1980) pp. xxiv–xxviii.
3. Marx, K., 'Contribution to the Critique of Political Economy', in K. Marx and F. Engels, *Collected Works* (*CW*), vol. 29 (London: Lawrence & Wishart, 1987), p. 270.
4. Marx, K., 'On Wagner' in K. Marx and F. Engels, *Collected Works* (*CW*) vol. 24 (London: Lawrence & Wishart, 1989), pp. 545, 546.
5. Marx, K., *Grundrisse,* trans. M. Nicolaus (Harmondsworth: Penguin, 1973), p. 646 (*CW* 29, p. 34). See also p. 881 (*CW* 29, p. 252).
6. Marx, *Grundrisse,* p. 320.
7. Marx, *Grundrisse,* p. 647 (*CW* 29, p. 35).
8. Marx, K., *Capital,* vol. II, trans. D. Fernbach (Harmondsworth: Penguin, 1978), p. 470.
9. Marx's emphases; Marx, *Grundrisse,* pp. 274–5.

10. Marx, *Grundrisse*, pp. 267–8.
11. Marx, *Grundrisse*, p. 297.
12. Marx, *Grundrisse*, (Marx's emphases) p. 305.
13. Marx, *Grundrisse*, p. 364.
14. This paragraph draws on my 'Value, Labour and Negativity', *Capital & Class*, no. 73 (Spring 2001).
15. Marx, 'On Wagner', *CW* 24, (Marx's emphases) p. 535.
16. Marx, *Capital*, vol. II, pp. 201, 202, 204.
17. I do not think that Marx's argument is threatened by this point, but I do think that at the level the argument is put, namely use-value, there is indeed a good case against Marx's discourse, as Ted Benton has argued: Benton, T., 'Marxism and Natural Limits: An Ecological Critique and Reconstruction', in T. Benton (ed.), *The Greening of Marxism* (New York and London: Guilford Press, 1996).
18. Popper, K., *The Open Society and its Enemies*, vol. II, 3rd edn (London: Routledge, 1957), p. 347, n. 24. It is amusing to read in Smith: 'In the price of corn ... one part pays the ... wages or maintenance of the labourers and labouring cattle [NB] employed in producing it'. Smith, A., *The Wealth of Nations* (Chicago: University of Chicago Press, 1976), p. 57.
19. I take this story from White, James D., *Marx and the Origins of Dialectical Materialism*, (London: Macmillan, 1996), p. 234.
20. Marx, *Grundrisse*, pp. 500–1.
21. T. Brennan rightly points out that price is not determined by the time of reproduction of use values but by their *speed of acquisition* by capital: Brennan, T., *Exhausting Modernity* (London and New York: Routledge, 2000), pt 2.
22. I relegate a discussion of the logical issues to an Appendix: see pp. 146–8.
23. Albritton, R., *A Japanese Reconstruction of Marxist Theory* (London: Macmillan, 1986), p. 13.
24. Albritton, R., *Dialectics and Deconstruction in Political Economy* (London: Macmillan, 1999), p. 37.
25. Albritton, *A Japanese Reconstruction of Marxist Theory*, p. 33.
26. The idea of a 'false totality' is articulated in Arthur, C. J., 'The Spectral Ontology of Value', in A. Brown *et al.* (eds), *Critical Realism and Marxism* (London: Routledge, 2002).
27. Sekine, *An Outline...*, pp. 27–8.
28. These use-value categories are employed here purely abstractly. At a more concrete level it would be necessary to discuss the ways in which labour, machinery and nature itself have been transformed thoroughly by the penetration of capital; for the most part in unfortunate ways – for example, the division established between mental and manual labour. So a considerable reworking of the use-value sphere would be necessary before a socialist mode of production could take root.
29. Based on Arthur, C. J., 'Hegel's *Logic* and Marx's *Capital*, in F. Moseley (ed.), *Marx's Method in 'Capital'* (Atlantic Highlands, NJ: Humanities Press, 1993).

9

(K. Marx|

Things Fall Apart: Historical and Systematic Dialectics and the Critique of Political Economy

Patrick Murray

P16
B51 331

> In its mystified form, the dialectic became the fashion in Germany, because it seemed to transfigure and glorify what exists. In its rational form, it is a scandal and an abomination to the bourgeoisie and its doctrinaire spokesmen, because it includes in its positive understanding of what exists a simultaneous recognition of its negation, its necessary destruction; because it regards every historically developed form as being in a fluid state, in motion, and therefore grasps its transient aspect as well; and because it does not let itself be impressed by anything, being in its very essence critical and revolutionary.[1]

Social form and 'the illusion of the economic'

Things Fall Apart, the title of Achinua Achebe's classic novel, expresses the nightmare side of the question that weighed on Marx's mind throughout his life: how does human life, which is irreducibly social in character, reproduce itself?[2] Humans are mortal, needy beings who reproduce sexually and meet (changeable) needs by engaging in definite, socially-structured transformations of the partly natural and partly already historically worked-up settings in which they find themselves. This production of wealth in the form of useful goods is a common factor in the reproduction of human life. Though it is a *general*, and rather banal, truth that to reproduce themselves humans must produce the things that answer their needs, *there is no production in general*.[3] Or, as Marx expressed concisely the seminal idea of historical materialism, 'All production is appropriation of nature on the part of an individual *within and through a specific form of society*' (my emphasis).[4]

Here lies Marx's fundamental contribution to the critique of political economy (or economics, as we now call it). It is also the taproot of both historical and systematic dialectics. 'Political economy is not technology ... production ... is always a certain social body, a social subject, which is active in a greater or sparser totality of branches of production'.[5]

Production always has a definite *social form and purpose*.[6] What I call the 'illusion of the economic' is oblivious to this basic phenomenological truth. The 'illusion of the economic' is the notion that there is production in general, and that there is a generic 'economy', as opposed to this or that historically specific mode of production. This illusion forms the basis of economics. Because it purports to offer a scientific account of production in utter abstraction from the specific social forms and purposes of actual modes of production, forms such as the commodity, money, capital, surplus-value and wage labour, economics must be judged to be a pseudo-science. Consequently, Marx's critique of political economy or economics is not to be understood as a criticism of this or that 'economic' doctrine – though Marx is full of those sorts of criticism too – but as a rejection of the horizon of inquiry that defines the discipline. As Paul Mattick, Jr, puts it, 'Marx's critique – his "scientific revolution" – therefore involved not merely reworking of economic categories but the construction of another set of concepts, explicitly social and historical ones'.[7] In excluding historically specific social forms and purposes from its foundations, economics makes a mockery of any attempt to understand actual modes of production. The problem, then, comes to this: *economics is missing an object of inquiry*. For there is no 'production in general'; there is no 'economy'. There are only historically determinate modes of production and distribution, none of which can be understood on the basis of the few banal truths that in fact do cut across the many different historically specific modes of production.[8] Marx, then, was not a radical economist, but a radical critic of economics. Strictly speaking, terms such as 'Marxist economics' or 'Marxist political economy' are oxymorons.

The 'illusion of the economic' usually takes the form of mistaking the capitalist mode of production for 'production in general'. So it is typical for texts in economics to bait and switch. They pretend to analyze 'the economy' and then quickly smuggle in the characteristic social forms and purposes of bourgeois society and the capitalist mode of production.[9] For example, an introductory microeconomics text used at Creighton University obliviously reproduces the Trinity Formula on page seven. 'Appreciating the power of the "illusion of the economic", Marx felt obliged to lead with his trump when he got to the final part of his three-volume book *Capital*':

> We have seen how the capitalist process of production is a historically
> specific form of the social production process in general. This last is both
> a production process of the material conditions of existence for human
> life, and a process, proceeding in specific economic and historical
> relations of production, that produces and reproduces these relations of
> production themselves, and with them the bearers of this process, their
> material conditions of existence, and their mutual relationships, i.e. the
> specific economic form of their society.[10]

Economics fails to grasp this basic truth because it is stuck in the 'illusion of the economic'.[11] In the *Poverty of Philosophy*, Marx expressed the dreary outlook of this way of thinking, 'Thus there has been history, but there is no longer any.'[12] Economics would bring history to a standstill, but history is not so obliging.

Systematic and historical dialectics and their relation

'The relation between a systematic and historical dialectic is obscure', writes Chris Arthur.[13] But not just their relation! Many questions arise regarding each term of the relationship and what place, if any, each has in Marx's thought. In this chapter I will try to identify and answer some of the most important of these questions. Let me briefly state in advance the chief conclusions that I reach:

1. *Specific social form and purpose* are the heartbeat of both systematic and historical dialectics. Consequently, we can expect no contribution to either systematic or historical dialectics from economics – except when it forgets itself.[14] To understand why things fall apart, we need to scrutinize the social forms and purposes involved in the various ways that the appropriation of nature to meet human needs have been organized and oriented socially.
2. 'Historical dialectics' is a phrase that points to aspects of necessity in historical change. I take it that the phrase refers to the sort of thing Marx was getting at in his remark that *human beings make history but under circumstances not of their own choosing*. As such, historical dialectics is a blunt concept, but I believe that it can be articulated further according to types of historical necessity. I distinguish five: (i) the historical dialectic involved in transformations from one mode of production to another; (ii) the historical dialectic involved in the actualization of a mode's social forms, entrenching their dominance; (iii) the historical dialectic involved in the emergence of new forms, new necessities, as a dominant social form (mode of production) matures; (iv) the historical dialectic involved in the contradictory tendencies within a mode of production that destabilize it and push it apart; and (v) the historical dialectic involved in the struggles of participants in a particular mode of production, those within that mode of production and those against it.
3. Historical dialectics and systematic dialectics are not the same; neither is one reducible to the other. Mixing up the two has been the source of many problems.
4. Against those who contend that *Capital* is a work in *Hegelian* systematic dialectics, I argue that *Capital* is a work of *Marxian* systematic dialectics. Marxian systematic dialectics, I argue, distinguishes itself from the

Hegelian (at least as Marx conceived of it) by recognizing the limits of a dialectical presentation, specifically by recognizing the natural and historical presuppositions of a systematic dialectical presentation, therewith rejecting the strictly Hegelian ideal of a purely 'presuppositionless' science.

5. Against those, such as John Rosenthal and Paul Mattick, Jr, who reject systematic dialectics, I argue that Marx does offer a systematic dialectical account in *Capital*.

6. Since Marx distinguishes between the method of *inquiry* and the method of *presentation*, we may wonder whether or not there is a 'dialectics of inquiry' in addition to a (systematic) 'dialectics of presentation'. I argue that there is not, though one can prepare the mind for inquiries that result in a systematic dialectical presentation.

7. The stages in a systematic dialectical presentation are stages of a *conceptual* development that move from the *abstract* to the *concrete*; they are not *actual* stages, and their order should not be confused with the order of historical stages, even when the two orders sometimes overlap.

8. Theories of historical tendencies, historical stages or different 'regimes' of capital accumulation (for example, 'Fordism' or 'flexible accumulation') involve contingencies from which systematic dialectics abstracts; such theories depend upon systematic dialectics, while supplementing it.

9. Talk of historical dialectics is pointless apart from a guiding conception of the human species as perfectible – Rousseau and Kant pioneered such thinking in the eighteenth century – and definite ideas regarding what human perfection involves. The question of the moral telos of humanity that sparks charges of 'Eurocentrism' cannot be sidestepped by Marxian theory.

Historical dialectics

Since 'dialectics' spells necessity, doesn't the very phrase 'historical dialectics' turn human freedom into a paper tiger? Doesn't such terminology imply that historical materialism offers a deterministic 'science of history' (a phrase crossed out in the manuscript of the *German Ideology*)? Such a reaction represents a basic misunderstanding of what Marx is driving at with his conception of historical materialism. For Marx, necessity is an ingredient in history, but its presence does not exclude the exercise of human freedom. As Marx puts the point in his third thesis on Feuerbach, 'The coincidence of the changing of circumstances and of human activity can be conceived and rationally understood only as revolutionizing practice.'[15] Human beings 'make history', but they do so under circumstances that are not of their own making. The idea of a 'historical dialectic' begins with the thought that, in the human changing of human circumstances, the already given mode of production always plays a role:

> It is superfluous to add that men are not free to choose their productive forces – which are the basis of all their history – for every productive force is an acquired force, the product of former activity. The productive forces are therefore the result of practical human energy; but this energy is itself conditioned by the circumstances in which men find themselves, by the productive forces already acquired, by the social form which exists before they do, which they do not create, which is the product of the preceding generation.[16]

The already existing social form of production conditions human actions; here we see the link between Marx's fundamental insight into the significance of the specific social form and purpose of the reproduction of human life with his conception of historical dialectics:

> Because of this simple fact that every succeeding generation finds itself in possession of the productive forces acquired by the previous genera-tion, which serve as the raw material for new production, a coherence arises in human history, a history of humanity which takes shape is all the more a history of humanity as the productive forces of man and therefore his social relations have been more developed.[17]

This grounding of historical dialectic in the ongoing entrenchment, trans-formation, and even revolutionary overthrow, of these social forms of the provisioning process invites us to discriminate between different types of historical dialectic with different degrees of necessity.

For heuristic purposes, I propose to differentiate five sorts of necessity that can be grouped under the concept of 'historical dialectics':

(i) The transition from one mode of production to another is condi-tioned by the former mode of production and its problems in repro-ducing itself – the reasons why it falls apart – but here we find the greatest opportunity for freedom and creativity. Taking advantage of such opportunities requires a revolutionary leap, not only in circum-stances but also in consciousness. Looking forward to the demise of the capitalist mode of production and the birth of communism, Marx and Engels write:

> Both for the production on a mass scale of this communist con-sciousness and for the success of the cause itself, the alteration of men on a mass scale is necessary, an alteration which can only take place in a practical movement, a revolution; the revolution is neces-

sary, therefore, not only because the ruling class cannot be over-thrown in any other way, but also because the class overthrowing it can only in a revolution succeed in ridding itself of all the muck of ages and become fitted to found society anew.[18]

(ii) The actualization of the social forms bound up with a mode of pro-duction that is entrenching itself as dominant, spreading itself, deep-ening its hold, involves necessities that tend to be very strong, though the power of these social forms and the ways they work will depend on the particular mode of production in question and on pre-existing conditions. As the rhetoric of the *Communist Manifesto* proclaims, capitalist social forms are uniquely dynamic and expansive by nature.

(iii) Beyond the entrenchment and expansion of the social forms consti-tuting a particular mode of production, there can be a growth of new forms, new necessities, as a mode matures. Here, too, the necessities may be quite strong, but they will, again, depend upon the particular dynamism of the mode of production in question and pre-existing conditions.

(iv) As a historian, Marx was impressed with how things fall apart; as a dialectician he was keen to discover the extent to which the demise of a mode of production was a consequence of its pulling itself apart: 'Just as, on one side the pre-bourgeois phases appear as merely histori-cal, i.e. suspended presuppositions, so do the contemporary condi-tions of production likewise appear as engaged in suspending themselves and hence in positing the historic presuppositions for a new state of society.'[19] The strength of these self-destabilizing tenden-cies varies with the mode of production in question and, of course, their power grows as a mode of production's inner antagonisms grow.[20]

(v) Marx's assessment of the actual modes of production up through the capitalist one is that they have provided only either a narrow satisfac-tion, as in the case of the pre-capitalist modes, or no satisfaction, as in the case of the capitalist mode.[21] Dissatisfaction caused by a society's members chafing against the social forms and purposes of a certain mode of production leads to forms of opposition that mark a fifth sort of necessity involved in Marxian 'historical dialectics'. Some such conflicts involve inevitable features of the mode of production in question and take place more or less within its social forms. For example, in the capitalist mode of production, conflicts over the wage (which contains a historical and 'moral' ingredient), and over the length and intensity of the workday are unavoidable; they belong to how these forms function. Beyond these unavoidable conflicts, there is vast scope for opposition to the workings of capitalist social forms.

For example, the insecurity of employment can be challenged in various ways – by, say, demanding state-enforced unemployment insurance. Commodification can be challenged by demands for the public provision of education, health care or other goods, or by restricting the commodification of naturally or of culturally significant sites. These challenges can range from the mildly reformist to the revolutionary, at which point we circle back to item (i).

In the *Great Transformation*, Karl Polanyi was so shocked by the woes of unencumbered market society that he hypothesized its emergence as a 'double movement', the simultaneous creation of a 'disembedded' market society along with a host of restrictive reactions to it.[22] Within the Marxian tradition, Felton Shortall, working from the Uno–Sekine conception of the 'dialectic of capital', writes of the 'counterdialectic' of the working class to the impositions of capital.[23] Shortall's term 'counterdialectic' seems problematic, however, given that he conceives of the 'dialectic of capital' as a systematic dialectic. 'Counterdialectic' suggests that the opposition of wage labourers to capital involves the sort of systematic necessities found in the 'dialectic of capital'. This appears to misclassify the sort of necessity involved in the opposition of wage labourers to capital's rule; the contingency, freedom and creativity involved in labour's 'counterdialectic' place it outside the scope of systematic dialectics, though not outside 'historical dialectics'.

A contrary problem with the (Uno–Sekine) approach adopted by Shortall requires a cautionary note regarding the distinction between items (iv) and (v). Given Marx's insistence on conceiving of 'revolutionizing practice' as 'the coincidence of the changing of circumstances and of human activity', we should not split item (v) from item (iv), even if we can distinguish between them. Now the problem with the opposition between the 'dialectic of capital' and the 'counterdialectic' of the working class is the opposite of the one just considered. Instead of too much necessity, now there is too little. Splitting the circumstances from the reaction against them underplays the disintegrative forces internal to capital and deflects attention from the ways these 'changing circumstances' shape forms of opposition to capital's dominance.[24] The less the 'dialectic of capital' discloses disintegrative tendencies, the more the 'counterdialectic' of the working class seems to be unhinged from 'changing circumstances'.[25]

Systematic dialectics

The focus of systematic dialectics is *one* mode of production, considered (with qualifications to come) *synchronically*. The point of a systematic dialectical presentation of a mode of production is to identify and present in the most compelling way the essential moments of that mode of production, that is, those moments that are necessary for its reproduction.[26] *Capital* is, I argue, a systematic dialectical presentation of the capitalist mode of production. Marx worried that his systematic dialectical presentation in *Capital* would be mistaken for the sort of '*a priori* construction', for which he criticized 'German ideology'.[27] He was so concerned that, in December 1861, he wrote to Engels that the continuation of his *Contribution to the Critique of Political Economy* (1859) 'will nonetheless be much more popular and the method will be much more hidden than in part 1'.[28] 'Hidden' implies present.

For Marx, a systematic dialectical presentation cannot be arrived at by 'applying' a pre-established 'dialectical logic' to some domain of inquiry. The only way to achieve a proper systematic dialectical presentation is through a rigorous, experience-based inquiry into the subject matter at hand. Such an inquiry 'has to appropriate the material in detail, to analyse its different forms of development and to track down their inner connection'.[29] I call such an inquiry 'phenomenological', for it goes beyond the ordinary empirical collection of facts organized under 'ready-made' concepts. It probes the concepts themselves, testing for 'inner connections'.[30] Only on this basis can the forms of the subject matter at hand be represented in a systematic dialectic of concepts.

The 'systematic' in 'systematic dialectic' refers to a presentation's being orderly, coherent and complete. (With that last qualifier in mind, it is evident that there is at least one sense in which *Capital* fails to come up to the standard for systematic dialectics.) The orderliness requirement echoes René Descartes' writings on method – as does the *Grundrisse* section on method – by calling for the introduction of concepts *synthetically*; that is, in the order of their conceptual concreteness: simpler categories come before more complex ones. What 'systematic dialectics' adds to Descartes' account, and which greatly increases the systematicity of such a presentation, is that in such a presentation *the structure of presupposition runs in both directions*.[31] Not only do the complex categories presuppose the simple ones, which is the familiar point about synthesis; the simple categories also presuppose the complex ones, which is the phenomenological point. This two-way directionality of dialectical systematicity expresses the phenomenologically ascertained inseparability of multiple aspects of the object under examination. The dialectical movement from simpler to more complex categories reveals the latter to be presupposed by, and implicit in, the former. For example, the more complex category of commodity-capital, which figures in the circuits of capital, treated in Part I of Volume II of *Capital*, is implicit in the simpler category of the commodity, with which *Capital* begins. It is one of the most significant developments of Marx's systematic dialectical presentation that the generalization of simple commodity exchange is shown to presuppose the capitalist mode of production: commodities are produced as commodity-capital.

So far, Marx's conception of systematic dialectics follows Hegel's. What, then, do we make of Marx's lifelong criticism of Hegel's dialectic as 'mystifying'? In the Postface to the second edition of *Capital*, Marx memorably contrasts his dialectic with Hegel's, while affirming that Hegel had the basics right:

> My dialectical method is, in its foundations, not only different from the Hegelian, but exactly opposite to it. For Hegel, the process of thinking, which he even transforms into an independent subject, under the name of 'the Idea', is the creator of the real world, and the real world is only the external appearance of the idea. With me the reverse is true: the ideal is nothing but the material world reflected in the mind of man, and translated into forms of thought ... The mystification which the dialectic suffers in Hegel's hands by no means prevents him from being the first to present its general forms of motion in a comprehensive and conscious manner. With him it is standing on its head. It must be inverted, in order to discover the rational kernel within the mystical shell.[32]

Faced with those metaphors, let me propose an interpretation of how Marx sees his dialectic differing from Hegel's. Hegelian dialectic, at least as Marx conceives of it, recognizes no dependence of its object upon anything outside thought, no historical or material presuppositions limiting thought. It prides itself on its 'presuppositionlessness'. *Marx's dialectic differs from Hegel's precisely in insisting on weaving material presuppositions, namely, historical presuppositions and those picked out by the 'general phenomenology' of the human condition, into the systematic dialectical presentation.*[33] For example, in his opening account of the capitalist production process, in Chapter 7 of *Capital*, Volume I, Marx begins with an account of the general features of human labour processes, and, in solving the mystery of the source of surplus value, Marx makes it clear that the existence of 'free' wage labourers is a factual, historical presupposition that is a condition for the systematic dialectical presentation of capital.[34]

We can summarize the chief features of Marxian systematic dialectics, then, as follows: (i) a systematic dialectical presentation will have identifiable premises or presuppositions given by nature and history; (ii) it will represent the moments of the object under study in their inseparability as uncovered by phenomenological inquiry into that object, and in so doing it discloses the essence of what is under study; (iii) in introducing those moments, the presentation will proceed from the conceptually simpler to the conceptually more complex; and (iv) though the conceptual development proceeds from the conceptually simpler to the conceptually more complex, the former are presented, at least implicitly, as presupposing the latter: there is a structure of mutual presupposition among the simpler and more complex categories.

The myth of systematic dialectics?

Recent works by Paul Mattick Jr and John Rosenthal deny that *Capital* is a work of systematic dialectics.[35] Rosenthal regards dialectics as altogether a myth, while Mattick argues that 'Marx's dialectic' is strictly historical: there is no systematic dialectical presentation in *Capital*. For a defence of systematic dialectics against Rosenthal, I refer the reader to the critical review of his book *The Myth of Dialectics* by Tony Smith.[36] Here I shall make just a few points in reply to Mattick. Mattick maintains that Marx's dialectic 'is identified not with a logic of theory construction, but with the idea of the essentially historical character of social formations'.[37] This reduces any appearance of a systematic dialectic of presentation to historical dialectic. For Mattick, *Capital* is a systematic critique of the ideology of classical political economy, not a systematic dialectical presentation of the capitalist mode of production. I do not believe that these two purposes are mutually exclusive.

Mattick seems to think that, if *Capital* is making a systematic dialectical presentation, it must be applying a 'dialectical logic' like Hegel's to its subject. The trouble there is that, for Mattick, there's really nothing to apply since 'even in the best cases, it must be said, the *necessity* ... of the transition between categories in the Hegelian dialectic – and hence of its being a logic – has not been convincingly made. Hegel, at any rate, simply asserts it'.[38] A 'logic' that lacks necessity is no logic at all.

On this score, I think that Marx and Mattick are on the same wavelength, as Marx was always wary of efforts to 'apply' any abstract 'dialectical logic' to any subject matter. In his *Critique of Hegel's 'Philosophy of Right'*, Marx rebuked Hegel for attempting to impose an abstract, pre-fabricated 'dialectical' logic on his subject matter rather than let the necessities flow from a thoroughgoing empirical investigation of his subject matter. For Marx, only the phenomenologically ascertained necessities of the matter under investigation can warrant a systematic dialectical presentation, not some abstract 'dialectical logic'. Interestingly, when Mattick looks at Marx's argument in section 3 of Chapter 1 of *Capital*, for why value *must* appear as money, he concludes: 'The insufficiency of the simple form is not logical but practical and material: It would not suffice as a mode of representation of value'.[39] What is this 'practical' necessity, but the engine of Marxian systematic dialectics in *Capital*, which is rooted not in some 'dialectical logical' necessity but in the capitalist mode of production's requirements for reproducing itself?

While Mattick's position captures the critical side of Marx's relation to Hegel's dialectic, it strikes me as unconvincing with regard to Marx's repeated affirmations to the effect that Hegel was 'the first to present its general forms of motion in a comprehensive and conscious manner'.[40] Moreover, there is so much in *Capital* that fits with the claim that it provides a systematic dialectical presentation of its subject matter, in particular the structure of mutual presupposition of categories, to which Marx often calls attention.

Finally, I interpret the epigram to the present chapter to mean that the deepest outcome of the systematic dialectical presentation of the capitalist mode of production is the recognition of its transience.

A 'dialectics of inquiry'?

Marx made a point in the introduction to the *Grundrisse* and again in the Postface to the second edition of *Capital* of distinguishing between the method of *inquiry* and the method of *presentation*, writing of the latter, 'Of course the method of presentation must differ in form from that of inquiry. The latter has to appropriate the material in detail, to analyse its different forms of development and to track down their inner connection. Only after this work has been done can the real movement be appropriately presented'.[41] We may wonder, then, if we should think in terms of two kinds of dialectics, a dialectics of investigation and a dialectics of presentation. The title and contents of Bertell Ollman's book *Dialectical Investigations* recommend that approach to us.[42]

I believe that it is preferable to conceive of the phase of investigation as *phenomenological*, where that is understood, as Marx suggests, to include the work of analysis and the work of phenomenology construed more narrowly as ascertaining which aspects of the object of study are inseparable and essential ('their inner connection'). Phenomenological inquiry is what makes systematic dialectical presentation possible. As has already been indicated, we can identify definite features of the structure of a dialectical presentation, but the method of investigation cannot be so set in advance. I am reluctant to put much weight on the idea that Marx has a method of investigation.[43] Marx seems to agree with Aristotle and Hegel that the method of inquiry must take its lead from the object being investigated.[44] To say too much in advance is to beg the important questions.

In the *German Ideology*, Marx and Engels criticized German idealism's *a priori* handling of history:

> The difficulties begin only when one sets about the examination and arrangement of the material – whether of a past epoch or of the present – and its actual presentation. The removal of these difficulties is governed by premises which certainly cannot be stated here, but which only the study of the actual life-process and the activity of the individuals of each epoch will make evident.[45]

Marx returned to this thought in an 1858 letter to Engels regarding Ferdinand Lassalle:

> I see from this one note that the fellow plans in his second great work to present political economy Hegel-like. To his detriment, he will come to

learn that it is a wholly other thing to bring a science for the first time to the point of being able to present it dialectically, through critique, than to apply an abstract, finished system of logic to hunches of just such a system.[46]

Though it makes sense to be wary of positing a 'dialectics of investigation' alongside Marx's conception of systematic dialectical presentation, one can prepare the mind for phenomenological inquiry. In that spirit, Hegel called the study of logic 'the absolute education and breeding of consciousness'.[47] In addition to the study of logic, study of the history of philosophy and of the sciences helps to prepare the mind of the investigator. But these preparations function like physical training for quickness, speed, flexibility and strength; none guarantees that you can hit a curve ball or head a crossing soccer ball into the corner of the net. There is no substitute for the encounter of scientific investigators with the actual movements of their object of inquiry.

Mix-ups of historical and systematic dialectics

The slurring of systematic and historical dialectics has caused Marxian theory problems for a long time. Here I shall note briefly four varieties. The first is the most infamous, Engels' influential conflation of the systematic and the historical into 'logical-historical method' – the exact phrase comes from R. L. Meek – according to which, the method of presentation tracks the historical order stripped of accidentals.[48] At the root of this confusion lies a serious mistake that has misled badly even readers of *Capital* who avoid the 'logical-historical' conflation. The mistake is to conceive of the various stages in the systematic presentation in *Capital* as describing *actualities* rather than various *levels of abstraction from actuality*. Eugen Böhm-Bawerk's complaint of a 'contradiction' between Volume I's theory of value and Volume III's theory of prices of production, and the misbegotten 'transformation problem' (transforming values into prices of production) are among the most egregious consequences of that misconception.[49]

The second type slurs the difference between a 'stage' or 'regime' theory of capitalism and a systematic dialectical theory of the capitalist mode of production. Such theories, while desirable, may obscure the distinction between contingent and necessary features of capitalism. Consequently, as Geert Reuten nicely puts it, 'When the regime goes into crisis, so does the theory.'[50]

A third variety overlooks the difference between a tendency and a trend. Systematic dialectical theory can identify tendencies (and often counter-tendencies), but it is usually a matter of historical contingency when, or sometimes if, a tendency will result in an observable, historical trend. A systematic dialectical account of wage labour can identify a *tendency* to 'deskill' labour in order to cheapen it (the Babbage Principle); and this might lead one to posit a secular, historical *trend* towards 'deskilling', making Marxian theory unfairly vulnerable to refutation by disproving the existence of such a trend.[51]

A fourth mix-up has been pointed out by Tony Smith. The error here is to confuse primacy in systematic dialectical presentation with explanatory primacy in historical explanation. Against this misstep, Smith offers the proposition, 'There is an unbridgeable gulf between systematic dialectics and historical theorizing such that explanatory primacy in the former does not imply explanatory primacy in the latter.'[52] Applying this in the context of the debate over Robert Brenner's 'The Economics of Global Turbulence', Smith argues that the primacy of the class relationship between capital and wage labour in Marx's systematic dialectical theory in *Capital* in no way assures that class conflict, and not inter-capitalist competition, is the primary cause of the global downturn after the 'Golden Age' that followed the Second World War.

Historical dialectics in systematic dialectics?

Systematic dialectics ordinarily is contrasted with historical dialectics as the synchronic to the diachronic. I question whether that way of thinking does not let something important fall between the cracks – namely, the *historical dialectics implicated in systematic dialectics*. According to the usual conception, systematic dialectics provides a snapshot of a historically determinate mode of production (say, the capitalist mode of production), while historical dialectics takes up transitions from one mode of production to another, (say, the feudal to the capitalist). *Capital*'s treatment of 'The So-called Primitive Accumulation' would thus be an excursion into historical dialectics supplementing a systematic dialectical presentation. Marx seems to encourage the synchronic conception of systematic dialectics:

> In the succession of the economic categories, as in any other historical, social science, it must not be forgotten that their subject – here, modern bourgeois society – is always what is given, in the head as well as in reality, and that these categories therefore express the forms of being, the characteristics of existence, and often only individual sides of this specific society, this subject, and that therefore this society by no means begins only at the point where on can speak of it as such; this holds for science as well. This is to be kept in mind because it will shortly be decisive for the order and sequence of the categories.[53]

This pointed passage nicely debunks the old idea of the order of a systematic development tracking that of historical development, but there is something fishy about it. Was 'modern bourgeois society' really 'given' in

1857? 'Yes', because essential forms of 'modern bourgeois society' were present at that time and flexing their muscles; but also 'no', in that, in 1857, the world, even England, was far from answering to the description of capitalist societies that *Capital* offers. To take a simple but important example, *Capital* is written as if the ordinary form of labour was wage labour, but that was far from being the case in 1857.[54] Then, in *Capital*, Volume I we read of rampant 'Freedom, Equality, Property and Bentham' in the wonderfully ironic paragraph wrapping up the 'wisdom' of simple commodity circulation,[55] yet battles for basic freedoms, equalities and rights to property have raged since.

A later passage in the *Grundrisse* provides a more accurate picture:

> While in the completed bourgeois system every economic relation presupposes every other in its bourgeois economic form, and everything posited is thus also a presupposition, this is the case with every organic system. This organic system itself, as a totality, has its presuppositions, and its development to its totality consists precisely in subordinating all elements of society to itself, or in creating out of it the organs which it still lacks. This is historically how it becomes a totality. The process of becoming this totality forms a moment of its process, of its development.[56]

In other words, the systematic dialectic of *Capital* tells us not only what the capitalist mode of production *is* but points *where it is going*.[57] One cannot bleach the historical aspect out of systematic dialectics.

Historical dialectic, then, is implicated in the systematic dialectic of the social forms, the value forms (the generalized commodity, money, capital, wage labour and so on), presented in *Capital*. In the section on historical dialectics, I discriminated three sorts of necessity ((ii), (iii) and (iv)) that pertain here (see page 155). Several related aspects of the historical dynamism posited by the capitalist mode of production may be mentioned here.

In the unfinished manuscript *Results of the Immediate Production Process*, Marx identified different forms of the subsumption of labour under capital, notably *formal* and *real* subsumption. Formal subsumption of labour under capital simply involves subjecting it to capital's purpose, the production of surplus value, while real subsumption of labour involves changing the technique or organization of the labour process in order to increase surplus value. Marx writes that it is only with real subsumption that we can speak of a 'specifically capitalist form of production'.[58] The historical dynamism of the capitalist mode of production is to keep expanding both formal and real subsumption. With the ongoing expansion of real subsumption, the mismatch between the capitalist measure of wealth (value, and more particularly, surplus value) and the mass of use-values produced, grows.

It is only with the global reach of capital that the value forms actually become what the systematic dialectic of *Capital* posits their nature to be:

> Abstract wealth, value, money, hence abstract labour, develop in the measure that concrete labour becomes a totality of different modes of labour embracing the world market. Capitalist production rests on the *value* or the transformation of the labour embodied in the product into social labour. But this is only [possible] on the basis of foreign trade and of the world market. This is at once the precondition and the result of capitalist production.[59]

We should entertain the further possibility that, with the maturation of a mode of production, systematic dialectics may have to be responsive to the emergence of new necessities, and new social forms. Perhaps the credit card, the ATM (Automatic Transaction Machine) card and the debit card represent necessary new monetary instruments. If today's mass advertising can add use-value to 'finished' products, perhaps adjustments in the account of circulation costs in Volume II of *Capital* are called for. Perhaps maintaining a moderate rate of inflation has become a necessary tendency, as Geert Reuten argues in this volume.

Marx on purpose in history: a eurocentric view?

Marx's historical materialism, though a breakthrough in the scientific study of history, does not provide a template for a 'science of history'. Marx warns us not to 'metamorphose my historical sketch of the genesis of capitalism in Western Europe into an historical-philosophical theory of the general path every people is fated to tread'.[60] Marx's distaste for *a priori* theorizing about history comes through strongly when he ridicules the very idea of a 'general historico-philosophical theory' providing a 'master key', 'the supreme virtue of which consists in being super-historical'.[61]

Still, things fall apart, and we want to know why. I believe that Marx responds to this question in various ways and on various levels. At the level of philosophical anthropology, Marx adopted Rousseau's conception of humanity from the *Second Discourse*: the essence of humanity is perfectibility. Our hearts are restless as long as the capacities for intelligent self-direction with which humans are endowed remain bottled up or perverted. The phenomenology of the human involved at this level of abstraction establishes a horizon within which more determinate explanations of historical change are situated. Marx has some quite general observations regarding the dynamics of historical development. Retooling a point Kant makes in his essay 'The Speculative (or Conjectural) Beginnings of Mankind', the following passage from the *German Ideology* envisions a spiralling dialectic of human needs and the measures taken to satisfy needs:

'The satisfaction of the first need, the action of satisfying and the instrument of satisfaction which has been acquired, leads to new needs; and this creation of new needs is the first historical act.'[62] In the *Grundrisse*, Marx returns to this thought, but puts something of a Malthusian–Darwinian spin on it:

> If the community as such is to continue in the old way, the reproduction of its members under the objective conditions already assumed as given, is necessary. Production itself, the advance of population (which also falls under the head of production), in time necessarily eliminates these conditions, destroying instead of reproducing them, etc., and as this occurs the community decays and dies, together with the property relations on which it was based.[63]

Things fall apart

Moving to a less general level, Marx recognizes a bond between *private property and individualism*, and furthermore sees this pair as being corrosive of traditional societies. In particular, in the *German Ideology*, Marx and Engels see the gradual emergence of private property within the ancient communal mode of production as setting off a dynamic of dissolution: 'the whole structure of society based on this communal ownership, and with it the power of the people, decays in the same measure as, in particular, immovable private property evolves'.[64] Private property, of course, plays a crucial role in Marx's sketch of the historical dynamics of the decline of feudalism and the emergence of capitalism. The historical dynamism Marx attributes to private property and individualism appears too in his explanation of why the so-called 'Asiatic mode of production' is so resistant to change: 'The Asiatic form necessarily survives longest and most stubbornly. This is due to the fundamental principle on which it is based, that is, that the individual does not become independent of the community; that the circle of production is self-sustaining, unity of agriculture and craft manufacture, etc.'.[65] Obviously, this sort of immediate, unreflective and compulsory coincidence of the individual and the community is not Marx's cup of tea. The absence of private property and the stifling of the individual that Marx claimed to find in China, and more particularly in India, combine to jam history. Unsurprisingly, Marx associates this shutdown with a short-circuiting of the dialectic of new needs we considered above: 'Absence of wants and predilection for hereditary modes of dress, are obstacles which civilized commerce has to encounter in all new markets.'[66] Here, again, we see Marx's philosophical anthropology making itself felt. In the purported stagnancy of the Asiatic mode of production, Marx does not detect counter-evidence to his Rousseau-inspired assertion of the human conatus of perfectibility; rather, he judges the Asiatic mode of production to be the sort of fetter on humanity that he and Engels described in the *German Ideology*: 'This fixation of social activity, this consolidation of what we ourselves produce into an objective power above us, growing out of our control, thwarting our expectations, bringing to naught our calculations, is one of the chief factors in historical development up till now'.[67] Where 'up till now' includes capitalism, of course.

If there is some rough teleological dialectic in the West leading from the emergence of private property and individualism towards bourgeois society and the capitalist mode of production, with the establishment of capitalism as the dominant mode of production on the face of the earth the teleology and dynamics of history become much more definite and pushy. Capitalism knows where it is going – everywhere – and what it is going to do once it gets there – remake whatever's there into its own hectic form of life.[68] As Marx and Engels put it in the *Communist Manifesto*, the bourgeoisie 'draws all, even the most barbarian, nations into civilization. The cheap prices of its commodities are the heavy artillery with which it batters down all Chinese walls, with which it forces the barbarians' intensely obstinate hatred of foreigners to capitulate. It compels all nations, on pain of extinction, to adopt the bourgeois mode of production ... to become bourgeois themselves. In one word, it creates a world after its own image'.[69]

In its own perverse way, though, capitalism discloses several shortcomings of prior human history, while moving in contradictory ways towards overcoming them. As Marx sizes up capitalism's historic mission:

> The bourgeois period of history has to create the material basis of the new world – on the one hand the universal intercourse founded upon the mutual dependency of mankind, and the means of that intercourse; on the other hand the development of the productive powers of man and the transformation of material production into a scientific domination of natural agencies.[70]

Capitalism illuminates and addresses: (i) the narrowness and despotism of earlier social formations; (ii) their material poverty and the stifling of what David Hume fondly called the 'refinement' of human needs; (iii) their ignorance and superstition; and (iv) their subjection of humans to blind nature.

Why are pre-capitalist social formations destined to fall apart? Because they are too narrow, too parochial and too confining for humans. Marx harps on the narrowness and fixity of all pre-capitalist social formations:

> In all these forms the basis of evolution is the reproduction of relations between individual and community *assumed as given* – they may be more or less primitive, more or less the result of history, but fixed into tradition

– and a *definite, predetermined objective* existence, both as regards the relation to the condition of labour and the relations between one man and his co-workers, fellow-tribesmen, etc. Such evolution is therefore from the outset *limited*, but once the limits are transcended, decay and disintegration ensue.[71]

Marx adds, 'But free and full development of individual or society is inconceivable here, for such evolution stands in contradiction to the original relationship'.[72] (It turns out that capitalism also rests on too narrow a foundation for human flourishing, and that this poses problems for its capacity to keep reproducing itself.)

As Marx looks back over human history in the face of the emergence of a capitalist world market, the options have been (i) narrow satisfaction, in pre-capitalist societies; or (ii) lack of satisfaction in capitalist society – which turns out to be based on its own very peculiar kind of narrowness. Capitalism's miserly pursuit of wealth as an end in itself suffers by comparison: 'The ancient conception, in which man always appears (in however narrowly national, religious, or political a definition) as the aim of production, seems very much more exalted than the modern world, in which production is the aim of man and wealth the aim of production'.[73] Marx continues his thought: 'Hence in one way the childlike world of the ancients appears to be superior; and this is so, in so far as we seek for closed shape, form and established limitation. The ancients provide a narrow satisfaction, whereas the modern world leaves us unsatisfied, or, where it appears to be satisfied with itself, is *vulgar* and *mean*'.[74]

Where, then, does this leave Marx? Standing with Kant and Hegel, it appears:

> England, it is true, in causing a social revolution in Hindostan, was actu-ated only by the vilest interests, and was stupid in her manner of enforc-ing them. But that is not the question. The question is, can mankind fulfill its destiny without a fundamental revolution in the social state of Asia? If not, whatever may have been the crimes of England she was the unconscious tool of history in bringing about the revolution.[75]

Writing in 1968, with these and similar passages in mind, Shlomo Avineri passed the following judgement: 'Marx's sole criteria for judging the social revolution imposed on Asia are those of European, bourgeois society itself'.[76] Surely this remark, and the label 'Europocentric', with which he then tags Marx, are intended to be pejorative.

I am not prepared to defend Marx's harsh judgement of mid-nineteenth-century Indian village life; but I would like at least to question Avineri's assertion, which he makes no effort to support, that Marx's criteria are European in a pejorative sense. I believe that the criteria to which Marx appeals in making his harsh judgements of both the British and the Indians may be found in the following passage:

> when the narrow bourgeois form has been peeled away, what is wealth, if not the universality of needs, capacities, enjoyments, productive powers, etc., of individuals, produced in universal exchange? What, if not the full development of human control over the forces of nature – those of his own nature as well as those of so-called 'nature'? What, if not the absolute elaboration of his creative dispositions, without any preconditions other than antecedent historical evolution – i.e. the evolution of all human powers as such, unmeasured by any *previously established* yardstick – an end in itself?[77]

To assess Marx's ideas about purpose in history, it would help to know what, if anything, is pejoratively European about this, and why.

Notes and References

1. Marx, K., *Capital*, vol. I, trans. B. Fowkes (New York: Vintage, 1977), p. 103.
2. 'The human being is ... not merely a gregarious animal, but an animal which can individuate itself only in the midst of society. Production by an isolated individual outside society ... is as much of an absurdity as is the development of language without individuals living together and talking to each other. There is no point in dwelling on this any longer' (Marx, K., *Grundrisse*, trans. M. Nicolaus (Harmondsworth: Penguin, 1973), p. 84).
3. Marx, *Grundrisse*, p. 86.
4. Marx, *Grundrisse*, p. 87.
5. Marx, *Grundrisse*, p. 86.
6. On this point that specific *social forms* are bound up with definite *social purposes*, see Campbell, M., 'Marx's Concept of Economic Relations and the Method of *Capital*', in F. Moseley (ed.), *Marx's Method in 'Capital'* (Atlantic Highlands, NJ: Humanities Press, 1993), pp. 145–6. The idea that any social organization of production is purposive and that the purposes will vary with the form of that social organization of production sounds obvious enough. However, the rise of markets and capitalism has given rise to the illusion, seized upon by liberals, that free market societies lack any organizing social purpose or have a social purpose only in the equivocal sense of being organized to address the individually determined schedules of needs of their members. I say that this is an illusion because, as Marx has shown, the truth of a market society is that it is a capitalist society. (This is because making a profit is the only reasonable explanation why goods and services are produced as commodities.) The endless accumulation of capital is the compulsory social purpose of market societies. The real task for defenders of market societies, then, is not met by arguing, as F. A. Hayek does, that a market society is just precisely because it has no compulsory collective purpose. They have the more difficult task of showing that the endless accumulation of capital is the best achievable social purpose.
7. Mattick, P. Jr, 'Marx's Dialectic', in F. Moseley (ed.), *Marx's Method*, p. 124.
8. See Murray, P., *Marx's Theory of Scientific Knowledge* (Atlantic Highlands, NJ: Humanities Press, 1988), ch. 10.

9. See Marx's criticism of J. S. Mill in Marx, *Grundrisse*, p. 87.

10. Marx, K., *Capital*, vol. III, trans. D. Fernbach (London: Penguin, 1981), p. 957.

11. Why is the 'illusion of the economic' so common? Marx addresses this problem in his characteristic, historical materialist way. That is, he explains how specific features of the society under consideration give rise to it. One of the peculiarities of the capitalist production process is that it presents itself in ways that encourage mistaking it for production in general. The specific social forms of capitalist society seem to be written across it in invisible ink. For a detailed account of how capitalist social forms promote 'the illusion of the economic', see my 'The Illusion of the Economic: the Trinity Formula and the "Religion of Everyday Life"', in G. Reuten and M. Campbell (eds), *The Culmination of Capital* (London: Palgrave, 2001).

12. Marx, K., *The Poverty of Philosophy* (New York: International Publishers, 1936), p. 121.

13. Arthur, C., 'Hegel's *Logic* and Marx's *Capital*', in F. Moseley (ed.), *Marx's Method*, p. 86.

14. Marx had already criticized economics in his 1844 manuscripts for failing to attend to the specific social forms and purposes of the capitalist mode of production (Marx, K., *Economic and Philosophic Manuscripts of 1844*, trans. M. Milligan and Dirk J. Struik, in K. Marx and F. Engels, *Karl Marx, Frederick Engels: Collected Works* 3 (New York: International Publishers, 1975), pp. 270–1), and he harps on it for the rest of his life.

15. Marx, K., 'Theses on Feuerbach', in K. Marx and F. Engels, *Karl Marx, Frederick Engels: Collected Works* 5 (New York: International Publishers, 1976), p. 7.

16. Marx, 'Letter to P. V. Annenkov (December, 28, 1846)', in *The Poverty of Philosophy*, p. 181.

17. Marx, 'Letter to P. V. Annenkov (December 28, 1846)', in *The Poverty of Philosophy*, p. 181.

18. Marx and Engels, *German Ideology*, in *Collected Works* 5, p. 53.

19. Marx, *Grundrisse*, pp. 460–1.

20. I shall return to items (ii), (iii) and (iv) in the context of the diachronic aspect of systematic dialectics.

21. See Marx, *Grundrisse*, p. 162.

22. Polanyi, K., *The Great Transformation* (Boston: Beacon, 1944).

23. Shortall, F., *The Incomplete Marx* (Aldershot: Avebury, 1994). On Shortall's relationship to the Uno–Sekine conception of the 'dialectic of capital', see Michael Lebowitz's review of *The Incomplete Marx*, 'Explaining the Closure of Marx', *Historical Materialism*, vol. 3 (Winter, 1998), pp. 171–88. See also the exchange between Shortall and Lebowitz in *Historical Materialism*, vol. 6 (Summer, 2000).

24. Compare Lebowitz's complaint (in his 'Explaining the Closure of Marx') against Shortall that he tends to flip-flop between too much necessity – internally begotten crises will bring the revolution – and too little – the heroic self-organized opposition of the proletariat will bring the revolution.

25. This disjuncture turns up in Chris Arthur's statement 'The systematic approach need not lead to closure; for, critically presented, the logic of the capitalist system can be shown to be caught in a contradiction of positing as fully subsumed under its forms necessary conditions of its existence that exceed its grasp. I hope to show elsewhere that this is true of (a) its internal other, the proletariat; (b) its external other, nature' (Arthur, C., 'Against the Logical-Historical Method: Dialectical Derivation versus Linear Logic', in F. Moseley and

M. Campbell (eds), *New Investigations of Marx's Method* (Atlantic Highlands, NJ: Humanities Press, 1997), p. 37, n. 75). True, the proletariat and nature are posited by capital as 'others', and they are not fully subsumable, but this way of avoiding closure of the 'dialectic of capital' leaves us with abstract negations, whose oppositional force is, so far, left unrelated to disintegrative forces that build with the growth of capitalism. For a contrasting approach, see Postone, M., *Time, Labor, and Social Domination: A Reinterpretation of Marx's Critical Theory* (Cambridge: Cambridge University Press, 1993), where he develops the notion of 'shearing pressures' developing within capitalism.

26. Geert Reuten accurately defines the Hegelian (and Marxian) notion of a 'moment' as follows: 'A moment is an element considered in itself that can be conceptually isolated and analyzed as such but that can have no isolated existence', in 'The Difficult Labour of a Theory of Social Value', in F. Moseley (ed.), *Marx's Method*, p. 92.

27. 'If the life of the subject-matter is now reflected back in the ideas, then it may appear as if we have before us an *a priori* construction' (Marx, *Capital*, vol. I, p. 102).

28. Marx, K., 'Letter to Engels (December 9, 1861)' as cited in Murray, *Marx's Theory of Scientific Knowledge*, p. 109.

29. Marx, *Capital*, vol. I, p. 102.

30. For a more extensive treatment of this conception of Marx's conception of inquiry as phenomenological, see my 'Marx's "Truly Social" Labour Theory of Value', *Historical Materialism*, no. 6 (Summer, 2000).

31. On this structure of mutual presupposition in *Capital*, see Bubner, R., 'Logic and Capital: On the Method of a "Critique of Political Economy"', in *Essays in Hermeneutics and Critical Theory*, trans. E. Mathews (New York: Columbia University Press, 1988); and Arthur, 'Against the Logical-Historical Method: Dialectical Derivation versus Linear Logic'.

32. Marx, *Capital*, vol. I, pp. 102–3.

33. This requirement of Marxian systematic dialectics appears to be incompatible with the more strictly Hegelian requirements as identified and embraced by Geert Reuten: 'All axioms are eschewed. Rather, anything that is required to be assumed, or anything that is posited immediately (such as the starting point), must be grounded. But it should not be grounded merely abstractly (i.e., giving arguments in advance), because this always leads to regress. That which is posited must be ultimately grounded in the argument itself, in concretizing it' (G. Reuten, 'The Difficult Labour', p. 92). I do not think that the sort of presuppositions Marx has in mind can be justified in the way called for here.

34. Against 'the Germans, who are devoid of premises' (p. 41), Marx and Engels write in the *German Ideology*, 'The premises from which we begin are not arbitrary ones, not dogmas, but real premises from which abstraction can only be made in the imagination. They are the real individuals, their activity and the material conditions of their life, but those which they find already existing and those produced by their activity. These premises can thus be verified in a purely empirical way' (p. 31).

35. See Mattick, 'Marx's Dialectic'; and Rosenthal, J., *The Myth of Dialectics* (London: Macmillan, 1998).

36. Smith, T., 'The Relevance of Systematic Dialectics to Marxian Thought: A Reply to Rosenthal', *Historical Materialism*, no. 4 (Summer, 1999), and the exchange that follows in *Historical Materialism*.

37. Mattick, 'Marx's Dialectic', p. 117.
38. Mattick, 'Marx's Dialectic', p. 125.
39. Mattick, 'Marx's Dialectic', p. 129.
40. Marx, *Capital*, vol. I, p. 103.
41. Marx, *Capital*, vol. I, p. 102.
42. Ollman, B., *Dialectical Investigations* (New York: Routledge, 1993).
43. See Murray, P., 'Why Did Marx Write so Little on Method?' *Scientific Knowledge*, ch. 8.
44. Hegel writes, 'it can only be the nature of the content itself which spontaneously develops itself in a scientific manner of knowing', *The Science of Logic*, trans. A. V. Miller (Atlantic Highlands, NJ: Humanities Press, 1969).
45. Marx and Engels, *The German Ideology*, p. 37.
46. Marx, K., 'Letter to Engels (February 1858)', as cited in Murray, *Scientific Knowledge*, p. 110.
47. Murray, *Scientific Knowledge*, p. 113.
48. For a critique of Engels and Meek, see Arthur 'Against the Logical-Historical Method', in Moseley and Campbell, *New Investigations*.
49. On the 'transformation problem', see Mattick, P. Jr, 'Some Aspects of the Value-Price Problem', *Économies et sociétés* (Cahiers de l'ISMEA Series), vol. 15, no. 6–7, pp. 275–81; and the papers by F. Moseley and G. Carchedi in Moseley, *Marx's Method*.
50. Reuten made this remark at the York conference; it is quoted with his permission.
51. For more on the tendency/trend distinction, especially with reference to the 'tendency of the rate of profit to fall', see Reuten, G., 'The Notion of Tendency in Marx's 1894 Law of Profit', in Moseley and Campbell, *New Investigations*.
52. Smith, T., 'Brenner and Crisis Theory: Issues in Systematic and Historical Dialectics', *Historical Materialism*, no. 5 (Winter, 1999), p. 166.
53. Marx, *Grundrisse*, p. 106.
54. 'In capitalist production the tendency for all products to be commodities and all labour to be wage-labour, becomes absolute' (Marx, K., 'Results of the Immediate Production Process', in *Capital*, vol. I, p. 1041).
55. Marx, *Capital*, vol. I, p. 280.
56. Marx, *Grundrisse*, p. 278.
57. And some form of globalization is on the agenda: 'The tendency to create the world market is directly given in the concept of capital itself. Every limit appears as a barrier to be overcome' (Marx, *Grundrisse*, p. 408).
58. Marx, 'Results', p. 1024.
59. Marx, K., *Theories of Surplus-Value*, vol. III, trans. J. Cohen and S. W. Ryazanskaya (Moscow: Progress Publishers, 1971), p. 253. I am indebted to a paper by Tony Smith for calling this quote to my attention.
60. Marx, K., 'Letter of 1877', cited in S. Avineri (ed.), *Karl Marx on Colonialism and Modernization* (Garden City, N. Y.: Doubleday, 1968), p. 5.
61. Marx, 'Letter of 1877', cited in Avineri, *Colonialism*, p. 445.
62. Marx, and Engels, *German Ideology*, p. 42.
63. Marx, *Grundrisse*, pp. 82–3.
64. Marx, and Engels, cited in R. Tucker (ed.), *The Marx–Engels Reader*, 2nd edn (New York: W. W. Norton), p. 151.
65. Marx, K., *Pre-Capitalist Economic Foundations*, trans. Jack Cohen, E. Hobsbawm (ed.) (New York: International Publishers, 1964), p. 83.
66. Marx, cited in Avineri, *Colonialism*, p. 18.

67. Marx, and Engels, in Tucker, *The Marx–Engels Reader*, p. 160.
68. 'Wherever it takes root capitalist production destroys all forms of commodity production which are based either on self-employment of the producers, or merely on the sale of excess product as commodities. Capitalist production first makes the production of commodities general and then, by degrees, transforms all commodity production into capitalist commodity production' (*Capital*, vol. II, quoted in Avineri, *Colonialism*, p. 37).
69. Marx and Engels, *Communist Manifesto*, quoted in Avineri, *Colonialism*, p. 2.
70. Marx, in Avineri, *Colonialism*, p. 13.
71. Marx, *Pre-Capitalist*, p. 83.
72. Marx, *Pre-Capitalist*, p. 84.
73. Marx, *Pre-Capitalist*, p. 84.
74. Marx, *Pre-Capitalist*, p. 85.
75. Marx in Avineri, *Colonialism*, p. 89.
76. Avineri, *Colonialism*, p. 26
77. Marx, *Pre-Capitalist*, p. 85.

10

Marx's Dialectical Method is More than a Mode of Exposition: A Critique of Systematic Dialectics

Bertell Ollman

We live at a time when few people ever use the term 'capitalism', when most don't know what the term means, when an even larger number have no idea of the systemic character of capitalism or how this system works, and hardly anyone grasps the role that economic categories play in contemporary society and in our own efforts to make sense of it all. In this situation, any school of thought that puts capitalism, particularly its systemic character, and capitalist economic categories at the centre of its concern can be forgiven for some of the exaggeration and onesidedness that enters into its work. Such, anyway, is the generally favourable bias I bring to my examination of Systematic Dialectics, whether in its Japanese, North American or European variations. All the criticisms that follow, therefore, however harsh they may appear, need to be viewed in this softening light.

For the purposes of this chapter, 'Systematic Dialectics' refers to a particular interpretation of Marx's dialectical method that a variety of socialist thinkers have come to share. It does not cover all that these scholars have written on Marxism, or even on dialectics, but only their common – albeit, often individually qualified – views on this subject. The most important of these thinkers – judging only from their contributions to Systematic Dialectics – are Tom Sekine, Robert Albritton, Chris Arthur and Tony Smith, and it is chiefly their writings that have provoked these remarks.

The interpretation of Marx offered by Systematic Dialectics can be summed up in three core ideas: (i) that 'Marx's dialectical method' refers exclusively (or almost exclusively) to the strategy Marx used in *presenting* his understanding of capitalist political economy; (ii) that the main, and possibly only, place he uses this strategy is in *Capital*, Volume I; and (iii) that the strategy itself involves constructing a conceptual logic that Marx took over in all its essentials from Hegel.

In this logic, the transition from one concept to the next comes from unravelling a key contradiction that lies in the very meaning of the first concept. The contradiction can only be resolved by introducing a new concept whose meaning fuses the contradictory elements in the previous one. Naturally, not all concepts are equally equipped to play this role, so this strategy also lays down a particular order in which the main categories of capitalist political economy are treated: 'commodity', whose key contradiction is resolved by introducing 'money', whose key contradiction is resolved by introducing 'capital', and so on. In this manner, Marx is said to proceed from the abstract, or simple categories with limited references, to the concrete, or complex categories whose meanings reflect the full richness of capitalist society. Furthermore, the same conceptual logic that enables Marx to reconstruct the essential relations of the capitalist system enables him (if we now look back at where we've come from rather than ahead to where we are going) to supply the necessary presuppositions for each of the categories that comes into his account, and eventually for the capitalist system as a whole. The view seems to be that if each step in exposition can be shown to follow necessarily from the previous one, the complex social interplay that is reflected in the end result will be no less necessary than the conceptual logic with which it was constructed.

Other contributors to this volume, especially the writers just mentioned, will discuss this conceptual logic in more detail. Before passing on to my criticisms, however, I would like to make it clear that I have no doubt about Marx's use of this expositional strategy in *Capital*, Volume I. Nor do I deny its importance for what he wanted to achieve in this work, especially with regard to setting capitalism apart as a relatively autonomous mode of production whose distinctive logic is reflected in the interplay of its main economic categories. But three major questions remain: (i) Is Systematic Dialectics the only strategy of presentation that Marx adopts in *Capital*, Volume I? (ii) What strategies of presentation does Marx use in his other writings? and (most important) (iii) Is it reasonable to restrict Marx's dialectical method to the moment of presentation? What, in other words, is the role of dialectics in helping Marx acquire the distinctive understanding that he expounds in *Capital* and other works?

As regards *Capital*, Volume I, it seems clear to me that Marx had other aims besides presenting the dialectical relations between the main categories of political economy. The short list would have to include – unmasking bourgeois ideology (and ideologists), displaying the roots of capitalist economics in alienated social relations, showing capitalism's origins in primitive accumulation and its potential for evolving into communism, mapping the class struggle, and raising workers' class consciousness. All of these aims required strategies of presentation that have little to do with Hegel's conceptual logic. The result is that *Capital*, Volume I contains whole sections which, according to the proponents of Systematic Dialectics (who place great importance on both the character and order of this work), simply do not belong there.

There is no conceptual necessity, for example, calling for the discussion of labour (as the substance of value) between the discussions of value and exchange-value. Hence, Tom Sekine considers this an error on Marx's part, but Marx thought it important enough to devote ten pages to labour – starting only three pages into the book.[1] Why, too – if *Capital*, Volume I is ordered by a straightforward conceptual logic – does Marx pay so much attention to the expansion of the working day? Where does it fit into this logic? But perhaps the biggest waste of time, Systematic Dialectically speaking, is the 100-plus pages at the end of *Capital* devoted to primitive accumulation. Systematic Dialectics dispenses with the history of capitalism and, for that matter, its eventual replacement by communism, as well as how capitalism has worked in different countries at different stages of its development. The conceptual logic with which it operates has no place for them. But Marx found a place for them in *Capital*, and for other critical discussions of what has happened, is happening and is likely to happen in the real world of capitalism. Their inclusion would seem to come from other strategies of presentation in the service of other aims.

There are still at least two other major features of *Capital*, Volume I that suggest strategic choices other than those acknowledged by Systematic Dialectics. The theory of alienation, for example, which plays such a major role in the *Grundrisse* (1858), the extended essay of self-clarification with which Marx prepared the ground for *Capital* (1867), is barely present in the finished work, and then chiefly in the one-sided version represented by the fetishism of commodities. Yet, labour, whenever it comes into the analysis in *Capital*, is always alienated labour, with all that this implies, and has to be for the equation of labour and value (and hence, too, all forms of value) to hold. This is undoubtedly why Marx introduces labour early in the discussion of value, even before the mention of exchange-value. Omitting a fuller account of the theory of alienation from *Capital*, therefore, does not represent a change of mind – as Althusser and a few others have held – but a change of strategy in expounding his systematic political economy, probably in the interest of making his analysis easier for workers to understand and act upon. A similar aim seems to lie behind the decision to use far less of the vocabulary associated with dialectics than is found in the *Grundrisse*.

In sum, as important as it is, Systematic Dialectics is simply unable to account for many of the strategic decisions that were responsible for both the form and content of *Capital*, Volume I. In making it appear otherwise, Systematic Dialectics has simply fallen victim to a danger that Marx himself recognized when, in finishing his preparations for *Capital*, he noted, 'It will be necessary later ... to correct the idealist manner of the presentation, which makes it seem as if it were merely a matter of conceptual determinations and the dialectic of these concepts.'[2]

Marx's varied strategies of presentation

A second difficulty, as I indicated, with Systematic Dialectics is that it concerns itself exclusively, or – depending on the writer – almost exclusively, with *Capital*, Volume I, while exposition was a problem that called for strategic decisions in all of Marx's writings. Marx's subject matter was so large and complex, and the difficulty of bringing it under control and making his interpretations understandable and convincing so great, that how to present his views was an ongoing worry. In treating the Marxian corpus as a whole, it is important, of course, to distinguish occasional pieces from longer, more deliberate essays, published writings from unpublished ones, works on political economy from works on other subjects, and, to some degree, between writings from different periods. And each of these distinctions marks some corresponding effect on Marx's strategy of exposition.

As our main concern is with Marx's systemic writings in political economy, provisionally we can ignore most of these divisions. Viewing Marx's economic writings as a whole, then, what strikes us most sharply about his exposition are the following: (i) the main effort goes into uncovering and clarifying relationships, the most important parts of which are not immediately apparent; (ii) the work is unfinished, as indicated by Marx's various plans, drafts and notes; (iii) Marx changes his mind several times on where to begin and what to emphasize, as indicated not only by these same plans but also by his different 'false starts' on *Capital* – his *Contribution to a Critique of Political Economy* (1859), the unpublished 'Introduction' to this work, and the *Grundrisse* (1858); and, if we want to go further back, the *Poverty of Philosophy* (1846) and 'Wage Labour and Capital' (1851); Marx's substantial revisions for the French and second German editions of *Capital*, Volume I, together with his plans (cut short by his death) to revise *Capital* once again, offer further evidence against taking any presentation of his ideas as definitive; (iv) each of the main subjects that enter Marx's account is presented as it appears and functions from several different vantage points; (v) each of these subjects is also followed through the different forms it assumes in its movement, both organic/systemic and historical; (vi) every opportunity is taken to project aspects of the communist future from capitalism's unfolding contradictions; (vii) the ways in which capitalism is misunderstood and defended receive as much critical attention as the underlying conditions of capitalism and the practices of capitalists themselves; and (viii) the entire project proceeds through a complex mixture of presenting the conditions and events in the real world of capitalism while analyzing the concepts with which we think about them. It is clear from all this that Marx is neither an empirical social scientist nor a Systematic Dialectician, if these are taken as mutually exclusive designations, but once we understand how he combined the two, there is no difficulty in viewing him as both.

A brief sketch of the features that dominate Marx's exposition throughout his works on political economy is found on those pages of his unpublished 'Introduction' to *Contribution to the Critique of Political Economy* devoted to the complex interaction between production, distribution, exchange and consumption (already referred to in items (i), (iv) and (v) of the above).[3] We learn here that these processes are not only related to each other as necessary preconditions and results, but also that each is an aspect of the others; and – through their internal relations with other neighbouring processes – each is also a version, albeit one-sided, of the whole that contains them all. In presenting the interaction between these processes from the vantage point of each process in turn, Marx makes use of all of these possibilities. Moreover, his flexibility in expanding and contracting the relations before him in this manner is reflected in an elasticity in the meanings of the concepts that are used to refer to them? This creates serious problems for Marx in presenting his views, and for us in grasping the categories with which he does so. Every serious student of Marx has encountered this difficulty, which was given its classic statement by Vilfredo Pareto when he said, 'Marx's words are like bats: one can see in them both birds and mice'.[4] How exactly Marx manipulates the size of the relations he is working with will be explained later. Here, I only want to make clear that this is what he does and to indicate the effect this has on the meanings of his concepts.

Marx once compared his condition to that of the hero in Balzac's *Unknown Masterpiece* who, by painting over and retouching, constantly tried to reproduce on the canvas what he saw in his mind's eye.[5] But, as Paul Lafargue, Marx's son-in-law and the only person to whom he ever dictated any work, noted, Marx was never quite satisfied with his efforts 'to disclose the whole of that world in its manifold and continually varying action and reaction'.[6] Hence all the fresh starts and the frequent revisions, coming on the whole from different vantage points, and organizing the parts in different ways. Viewed in this light, Systematic Dialectics can only be understood as a misguided attempt to reduce Marx's varied strategies of presentation to a single one, albeit one that does play a major role in expounding the systemic nature of the capitalist mode of production in *Capital*, Volume I.

Marx's dialectical method in the broad sense

So far, my criticisms of Systematic Dialectics have dealt with what it has to say about Marx's method of presentation. My third, and far more serious, criticism is that Systematic Dialectics is wrong in restricting Marx's dialectical method to just one of its several interlocking moments, that of presentation. For the thinkers in this school usually make it appear as if Marx 'worked out' his understanding of capitalism in *Capital*, Volume I, rather than 'laid it out' there, and that there is nothing problematical, or unusual, or particularly dialectical in the understanding that Marx brought to writing *Capital*, Volume I. In my view, Marx could never have written a work like *Capital*, Volume I if his own understanding of capitalism, the mode of inquiry used to acquire it and the way of thinking that underlay his inquiry were not already thoroughly dialectical. But this requires that we expand the notion of dialectics beyond the conceptual logic that Marx used to expound some of his views in *Capital*, Volume I.

For me, the problem to which all dialectics – Marxs and everyone elses – is addressed is: how to think adequately about change, all kinds of change and interaction, all kinds of interaction. This assumes, of course, that change and interaction are a big part of what goes on in the world, and that it is very easy to miss, or minimize or distort important parts of it, with grave consequences for our understanding, and even our lives. What's called 'Marxs dialectical method' is his attempt to come to grips with this problem as it affected the subject matter with which he was particularly concerned. Broadly speaking, it is his way of grasping the changes and interactions in capitalism (but also in the larger world) and explaining them, and it includes all that he does in mentally manipulating this reality for purposes of inquiry and exposition.

Marx's dialectical method can be conveniently broken down into six interrelated moments, which also represent stages in its practice. These are: (i) ontology, which has to do with what the world really is, particularly with regard to change and interaction; (ii) epistemology, which deals with how Marx orders his thinking to take adequate account of the changes and interactions that concern him; (iii) inquiry, or the concrete steps Marx takes – based on the mental manipulations undertaken in the previous moment – to learn what he wants to know; (iv) intellectual reconstruction (or self-clarification), which is all that Marx does to put together the results of his research for himself (the *1844 Manuscripts* and the *Grundrisse*, neither of them meant for publication, offer us instances of this little-studied moment); (v) exposition, where, using strategies that take account of how others think as well as what they know, Marx tries to explain his dialectical grasp of the 'facts' to his chosen audience, and to convince them of what he is saying; and (vi) praxis, where, based on whatever clarification has been reached thus far, Marx acts consciously in the world, changing it, testing it and deepening his understanding of it all at the same time.

It is not a matter, clearly, of going through these six moments once and for all, but again and again, as Marx does, since every attempt to grasp and expound dialectical truths and to act upon them improves his ability to organize his thinking dialectically and to inquire further and deeper into the mutually dependent processes to which we also belong. In writing about dialectics, therefore, one must be very careful not to focus on any one moment at the expense of the others. The problem comes not from stressing one moment in dialectics, but rather in neglecting the others (mistaking the part for the whole, a common undialectical error), so that even the moment that is stressed – because of all the interconnections – cannot properly be understood.

Like Systematic Dialectics, my own attempts to explain dialectics have also priviledged one moment – in this case epistemology – over the others, but I have always tried to integrate it with the rest. I chose epistemology because I believe it is pivotal for grasping and putting to work any of the other moments. Epistemology is also an ideal entry point for explaining Marx's overall method, since it requires me to make fewer assumptions than if I had begun elsewhere. This is not the place, of course, to give my interpretation of Marx's epistemology, but I would like to sketch just enough of it to indicate the theoretical basis for my main objections to Systematic Dialectics.

In his only systematic attempt to explain his method, Marx said this method starts from the 'real concrete' (the world as it presents itself to us) and proceeds through the 'process of abstraction' (the activity of breaking this whole down into the mental units in which we think about it) to the 'thought concrete' (the reconstituted and now understood whole present in the mind).[7] It is striking that Marx feels he can summarize all that goes on in his coming to understand anything as the 'process of abstraction'. In my view, this little-studied process is the core feature of Marx's epistemology, with close links not only to the rest of his epistemology but also to all the other moments of his method.

The process of abstraction would not play such a key role in Marx's method if the units in which nature (and therefore society too) is divided were given as such; that is, as particulars with clear and concise boundaries separating them from each other. Operating with a philosophy of internal relations taken over from Hegel – and never criticized by Marx in all his discussions of Hegel – Marx considers reality to be an internally related whole whose aspects can be combined mentally in a variety of ways, and therefore into a multiplicity of different parts. To be sure, where boundaries are drawn is based to some degree on the real similarities and differences found in the world, but equally important in effecting these decisions are the aims, needs and interests of the party doing the abstracting. Furthermore, on this view, any part can be expanded or contracted in conception along axes laid down by its relationship to the whole as called for by one's aim in studying or presenting the part in question.

In a world without absolute borders (unfortunately, not politically, but ontologically speaking), the process of abstraction provides the indispensable first step in getting the thinking process started. The world with which we make contact through our raw sense perceptions is simply unmanageable.

We can think only in parts and about parts of one sort or another. Marx believes, therefore, that everyone abstracts, and that we learn how to do it 'appropriately' – that is, in ways that allow us to function in the culture in which we live – during the process of socialization, and particularly when acquiring a language.

Once the work of theory is done, however, most people come to treat the culturally determined units of thought that result from the process of abstraction as reflecting absolute divisions in the real world. Not Marx. Aware of the role that the process of abstraction plays in his thinking, Marx has much more flexibility in putting it to use. It is not only that the boundaries he draws are invariably different, usually including something more of the processes and interconnections involved than what is conveyed by others' concepts of the same name, but that he alters them frequently to include or exclude other aspects of their constitutive relations. Here is the explanation for how Marx could grasp (and therefore study and present) production, distribution, exchange and consumption as separate processes, or as aspects of each other, or as aspects of a larger whole to which they all belong. It is also this epistemological practice (itself both allowed and required by the ontology of internal relations), which lies behind the elasticity in the meanings of Marx's concepts, that has confounded and annoyed so many serious readers of Marxism (see Pareto's remark on page 177 above).

Three kinds of abstraction

The boundaries Marx draws in the world with his process of abstraction are of three kinds – extension; level of generality; and vantage point – and each of them has important implications for Systematic Dialectics. Marx's abstraction of extension functions in both space and time, setting limits to how *far* a particular unit is extended in the system to which it belongs and, equally, how *long* a period of its evolution is included as part of what it now is. It is Marx's process of abstraction that allows him to view the commodity as an 'abstract' (with but a few of its determinations) at the start of *Capital*, capital as a 'concrete' (with a multiplicity of its determinations) later on, and provisionally to omit – as Systematic Dialectic correctly recognizes – the historical dimensions of the categories he uses in order to focus on their logical character.

With the abstraction of level of generality, the second mode of abstraction he employs, Marx separates out and focuses on the qualities of people, their activities and products that come out of a particular time frame, and provisionally ignores others. Here, the boundary is drawn between degrees of generality on a scale that ranges from the most general to the unique. Everyone and all that affects us and that we affect possess qualities that are part of the human condition (that is, present for the past 100,000 to

200,000 years), part of class society (present for the past 5,000 to 10,000 years), part of capitalism (present for the past 300 to 500 years), part of modern or the current stage of capitalism (present for the past 20 to 50 years), and part of the here and now. These qualities are all 'real' and important, though often for different purposes. They also interpenetrate in a variety of complex ways and are very easy to confuse with one another. In order to study the systemic character of the capitalist mode of production, it was necessary for Marx to abstract society at the level of generality of capitalism and to omit qualities from other levels that would interfere with his view of what is specific to capitalism. In privileging this level of generality, Systematic Dialectics underscores Marx's effort to present modern society as first and foremost a capitalist society, and to bring into focus the interlocking conditions and mechanisms that this involves.

The abstraction of vantage point, Marx's third mode of abstraction, sets up a vantage point or place within a relation from which to view, think about and present its other components, one that highlights certain features and movements just as it minimizes and even misses others. Meanwhile, the sum of their ties, as determined by the abstraction of extension that is used, also becomes a vantage point for making sense out of the larger system to which it belongs. The boundary here is drawn between competing perspectives. By starting *Capital*, Volume I with the commodity, Marx provides himself and his readers with a particular vantage point for viewing and piecing together the complex configuration that follows. On the whole, Systematic Dialectics does a good job in presenting the analysis of capitalism that derives from this vantage point.

All three modes of abstraction – extension, level of generality and vantage point – occur together, and in their interaction order the world that Marx sets out to study, understand and present. Except that the decisions made regarding each mode often vary. Marx's abstractions of extension, for example, can include the social dimension of classes that embody the main economic functions of capitalism as parts of the fuller meaning of categories that appear to point only to the latter. In this way, 'capital' can also refer to the capitalists, and 'wage labour' to the workers. This also allows Marx to analyze the class struggle as an objective/subjective condition within the very relationship of capital to labour, and not as something that gets tacked on later as a result of what the parties involved decide to do.

Similarly, Marx's abstraction of the temporal extension of the relations that come into his analysis often includes important parts of their real history and future potential. Their process of becoming, including stages through which they have gone and whatever seems to lie ahead, are conceived of here as essential aspects of what they are. The point is that Marx's concepts, as reflections of reality, contain history as well as system, but can be abstracted to omit most or all of either in order to bring the other in better focus. Thus the abstractions favoured by Systematic Dialectics are best suited to grasping how the capitalist system works, while those favoured in more traditional Marxist accounts are better suited to analyzing how this system developed, where it breaks down, what kind of society is likely to follow, and the role we have played and may yet play in all this.

Similarly, Marx's abstraction of level of generality does not only focus on capitalism in general, but often on what I have called class society and modern capitalism, and even, occasionally, on the level of the human condition (what is most general), and on that of what is unique (the most specific). The interaction between the dynamics that distinguish capitalism in general (chiefly the production and metamorphosis of value) and what marks modern capitalism plays a particularly important role in the volumes of *Capital*, as it does in structuring both the major problems and the historically specific opportunities for solving them that define our current situation. Restricting Marx's analysis to the level of capitalism in general (as does Systematic Dialectics) or to the level of modern capitalism (as do most non-Marxist economists with their current fix on 'globalization') removes a full half of what we need to know not only to understand the world but also to change it.

As regards abstraction of vantage point, here too Marx shows exemplary flexibility in adopting different vantage points in keeping with what he wants to see, grasp, present or do at different moments of his method. Systematic Dialectics does not stay bound to the vantage point of the commodity, with which Marx begins *Capital*, Volume I, but uses the vantage points of the various economic categories that come into its conceptual logic to present the interlocking character of the capitalist system. However, labour (that is, alienated labour, the activity that Marx considers the substance of value) is never accorded this honour. Consequently, the processes involved in bringing the capitalist market relations privileged by Systematic Dialectics into existence are never brought clearly into view. But, as the American playwright, Amiri Baraka, has wisely pointed out, 'Hunting is not those heads on the wall'; and alienation, exploitation and the reproduction of capital, the ongoing activities that produce capitalist conditions, can never be perceived adequately, let alone understood, from vantage points located in their results.[8] One's grasp of the results also suffers from ignoring the insights that can only come from viewing them from the vantage points of the processes that brought them into being. If, for example, value, as the substance of labour, acquires what workers, through their alienation, lose in producing it, then – it follows – the entire metamorphosis of value traced by Systematic Dialectics tells the 'story' not only of capital but also of labour, or of what happens in capitalism to the workers' alienated life activity.

There are other important vantage points (such as primitive accumulation or the relationship between forces and relations of production) that are rooted in history or on levels of generality other than capitalism overall that Marx uses, and Systematic Dialectics does not and cannot, locked as it is in its conceptual logic on the level of capitalism. Here is the gateway to the past and the future, and the unfolding contradictions that move us from the one to the other that Marx perceives (and presents) and that Systematic Dialectics doesn't. But without a dialectical analysis of the contradictory processes and tendencies found on the level of generality of capitalism overall (but also on the levels of class society and modern capitalism), real world contradictions that are even now pulling contemporary society apart and providing a rich source of evidence for what might follow, the analysis of capitalism offered by Systematic Dialectics appears to promise only more of the same. Without any connection to the degree of determinism Marx uncovers in history, the necessity Systematic Dialectics uncovers in the interplay between the categories of political economy leaves history as it finds it. Its logical necessity functions historically, whether intended or not, as a closed circle. From within the confines of the conceptual logic provided by Systematic Dialectics, it is hard to see how capitalism could ever change, or what one might do (and even with whom one might act) to change it.

Conclusions

In *Capital*, Marx tried to show not only how capitalism works but also why it is a transitory mode of production, what kind of society preceded it, what kind of society is likely to follow it, and how a change of this magnitude can be brought about. And all of this is contained in his dialectical analysis of how capitalism works. One might say that Marx was a unique combination of scientist, critic, visionary and revolutionary, and it is important to grasp how these qualities fed into one another in all his theoretical work. Viewed in this light, Systematic Dialectics can be seen as an effort to reduce Marxism to a science, a science consisting of the manner in which Marx presents his understanding of the capitalist mode of production. But without the critical, visionary and revolutionary dimensions of his thinking, even this science – as I have argued – cannot adequately be understood. Yet it remains the case that a great deal of *Capital* is organized around a conceptual logic. By exaggerating the role this conceptual logic plays in Marx's dialectical method – chiefly by limiting this method to the moment of exposition and to only a few of the many abstractions of extension, level of generality and vantage point that Marx uses in his exposition – Systematic Dialectics (with the partial exception of Tony Smith among the leading figures of this school) has kept many of its critics from recognizing and making use of the extremely valuable contribution it has made to our subject.[9]

Notes and References

1. Sekine, T., *The Dialectic of Capital*, vol. 1 (Tokyo: Toshindo Press, 1986), p. 119.
2. Marx, K., *Grundrisse*, trans. M. Nicolaus (Harmondsworth: Penguin, 1973), p. 151.
3. Marx, K., 'Unpublished Introduction', *Contribution to a Critique of Political Economy*, trans. N. I. Stone (Chicago: Charles Kerr, 1904), pp. 276ff.
4. Pareto, V., *Les Systemes socialistes*, vol. II (Paris: 1902), p. 332.
5. Quoted in Berlin, I., *Karl Marx* (London: Oxford University Press, 1960), p. 3.
6. Lafargue, P., 'Reminiscences of Marx', *Reminiscences of Marx and Engels* (Moscow, n.d.), p. 78.
7. Marx, 'Unpublished Introduction', *Contribution to a Critique*, pp. 293–4.
8. Baraka, A., *Home: Social Essays* (New York: William Morrow, 1966), p. 73.
9. A more detailed account of Marx's process of abstraction can be found in Chapter 2 of my book, *Dialectical Investigations* (New York: Routledge, 1993), while a fuller explanation of his philosophy of internal relations can be found in Chapters 2 and 3 of my book, *Alienation: Marx's Conception of Man in Capitalist Society* (Cambridge University Press, 1976). These chapters and other essays bearing on these subjects will soon be republished in *The Dance of the Dialectic: Steps in Marx's Method* (Champaign Ill.: University of Illinois Press, forthcoming).

11
The Specificity of Dialectical Reason

Stefanos Kourkoulakos

B51

B41

> Philosophizing requires, above all, that each thought should be grasped in its full precision and that nothing should remain vague and indeterminate.[1]

The problem

This chapter begins to address a particular theoretical need, the need for a more thoroughly theoretical and – given a certain level of abstraction – determinate treatise on the nature and structure of dialectical logic or method.[2] The notion of theoretical determinacy must be understood here in the relative sense; that is, as an ongoing contextual (level-of-abstraction-dependent) process, which exists in relation to other approaches or developments in a field of thought.

The degree of relative theoretical determinacy of a given conceptualization or theory has serious ramifications for its cognitive validity status and theoretical usefulness. A theory or conception that remains largely indeterminate on grounds of theoretical clarity, consistency, coherence, comprehensiveness, precision, or any combination thereof, either lacks the qualifications for undergoing basic tests of validity,[3] or passes them very partially, provisionally and even unmeaningfully.

Theoretical (as distinct from social, political or ideological) usefulness denotes the extent to which a conceptualization can be employed fruitfully for the generation of more adequate knowledge. As such, it is linked closely to questions of validity. If validity becomes a casualty of theoretical indeterminacy, the conceptualization or theory in question becomes unusable. The point I am stressing is that a conception, argument or theory that is insufficiently worked out and is, theoretically, markedly more indeterminate than not, is destined to remain cognitively ineffective, a conceptual liability instead of a resource.

Marxism, in all its variants except the analytical, has always had a high regard for dialectical logic. In terms of their theoretical determinacy, however, Marxist approaches to dialectics generally leave a lot to be desired. They are often remarkably unspecific on the subject and although they can be lengthy, typically they limit themselves to little more than making sweeping assertions about the potency of dialectics, accompanied by broad and often trivial generalizations about its aspects or 'laws'. Theoretically concrete and rigorous questions probing in depth into the distinctive elements and structures of dialectics are rarely posed.[4] Dialectics seems to be already known.

Let me offer an observation, which can serve as a familiar and convenient starting point for our discussion. There exists a set of disarmingly simple and plausible core theoretical assumptions concerning dialectics, which is shared to a greater or lesser extent by almost all approaches to Marxism, as diverse as these are. Schematically speaking, this core comprises five closely knit postulates. They are presented below in the form of a lax inferential sequence, in order to illustrate typically how they function and support one another (bearing in mind, of course, that neither all inferences or initial postulates need be valid ones, nor all supports adequate to their task):

(i)   Nothing in the social or conceptual (or even natural) world exists and functions independently or separately from all else. Everything is directly or indirectly interrelated with all, or practically all, others. Everything simultaneously acts or acts upon others and is acted upon by others.

(ii) Interrelation is a process. Every process is a process of change. Everything is in process. Nothing remains unchanged.[5]

The role of these postulates is to furnish the basic ontological groundwork underlying the standard Marxist conceptions of method:

(iii) Dialectics describes (and even exemplifies) the process(es) of this interrelation and change.

(iv) Dialectics is a general method.

(v)   Marxist theory needs and uses just one method, namely dialectics.

The last two postulates are usually unstated, but with the exception of three approaches I know about – the analytical,[6] the Uno–Sekine (more below) and C. J. Arthur's – they are standard features of Marxism.

This set of postulates has remained completely unchallenged. My contention is that it deserves much of the blame for the theoretical indeterminacy characterizing typical Marxist discussions of dialectics. The presence of this set in a given Marxist theory forms a weak link in its explanatory capacity. The central orientation of that theory, be it modernist or postmodernist, does not rectify this weakness.

Let us look at the aforementioned five mutually supporting postulates a little more closely. The first two are trivially true, if overstated, descriptive generalizations. They do not explain anything in, and by, themselves.[7] Their role is to supply the elementary foundations for more concrete theoretical propositions. These concrete propositions, however, cannot be generated out of the first two postulates. They require additional sources. As elementary ontological postulates, they are no different in this respect from the corresponding postulates of other theories. What is different about them is that they are helplessly unspecific. They are thus compatible with a very large range of diverse theoretical problematics. Moreover, they are not particularly useful in the process of knowledge, aside from helping to steer us away from some extremely unreasonable and crude suppositions (such as, everything is self-determining and independent from all else, or things always remain the same). Unquestioning allegiance to them and lack of corrective qualifications can lead to theoretical distortions. If, for example, everything changes all the time, and if that includes our conception of dialectics, we will tend to associate more changes with dialectics than there are to be found.

The remaining postulates are, directly or indirectly, remarkably misleading. The third postulate represents (in part) an ontological claim, in so far as dialectics is a process not confined to the realm of thought, but also occurring in the (primarily extra-discursive) real. This (correct in itself) claim can lead, if unchecked, to two sorts of problems:

(i) *Homogenization (often undetected) of historical diversity*: Like the first two postulates, it does not distinguish (or sufficiently distinguish, depending on the Marxist approach in question) between different kinds and rhythms of change. If dialectics is the one process that exemplifies the basic processes of the world, and if these latter processes are processes of change, then all change shares the same structure which is itself unchanging.

(ii) *Neglect of methodological specifications*: Unless followed by suitable clarifications, this assumption can retard the methodological understanding of dialectics, that is, the extent to which dialectics reflects irreducibly methodological processes, reasoning and strategies. The claim that dialectics constitutes an ontology not only offers no substitute for serious methodological introspection, but also unthoughtfully reverses the cognitive order of things as its very intelligibility depends on the prior clarification of methodological matters. It is the apprehension of dialectics as method that leads to the discovery of homologous structures and processes in the world, not the other way around. Moreover, apart from side-stepping the question of the distinctive properties of dialectics as method, uncritical emphasis on this ontological claim also obscures the question of any unique purpose that the dialectical method may be designed for (beyond the obvious general one of producing knowledge). For, if dialectics is viewed primarily as ontology (that is, a conception of the most fundamental and general structures and processes of the world), it makes no sense for Marxists to pose the question of its purpose. That would amount to asking the question of the purpose of the world, and thus venture directly into prohibited metaphysical – indeed, theological – territory.

The fifth postulate can be seen as the other side, or even the direct consequence, of the fourth, but I listed it separately to highlight the surprising disregard for theoretical conditions (and therefore, limits) as well as the theoretical overconfidence displayed by ever so many Marxist approaches.

The fourth postulate, namely that dialectics is a general method which, by and large, can be employed irrespective of the nature of its subject matter, is one of the most unshakeable tenets of Marxist theory. Those Marxist approaches that are predominantly modernist and traditional do not tire of proclaiming the three so-called general laws of dialectics: the interpenetration and unity of opposites; the transformation of quantity into quality; and (somewhat more out of fashion these days) the negation of the negation. These alleged laws are held to be universally and unconditionally valid.[8] There is hardly a theoretical stance that provokes the wrath of Marxists more than a conception which steps out of line with respect to the so-called interpenetration and unity of opposites law. To deny the interpenetration/unity of opposites law is, for Marxism, nothing less than committing dualism – that is, something wrong under all circumstances.[9] The phenomenon of the effect of perceived or real dualisms upon Marxists must be analyzed one day, for the sake both of the Marxist project(s) in thought and the communist project(s) in politics. A conceptual dualism, usually not clearly defined, is typically treated as something directly inducing strategic paralysis or capitulation to class enemies.[10] We would all benefit from some demystification here: as if all non-united differentiations or oppositions constituted dualism; as if all dualisms were conceptually or politically problematic or of one and the same kind; and as if formal logic did not have plenty of resources to deal with problematic dualisms and had to wait for dialectics.

To assume that any and all differences/opposites are in some way interpenetrating (whatever that means) and united, that any and all changes and interactions are dialectical, and that any and all problems of knowledge can be resolved by employing the same means (that is, dialectics) intends to accomplish too much with one stroke and inevitably ends up oversimplifying and distorting. For, how could one method – any one method – possibly do justice to the complexity of the world? Is it so hard to recognize that the first two of the so-called dialectical laws are strikingly trifling and provide no resources for explanatory theory? And how have we failed collectively for so long to realize that in their abstract generality and indeterminateness these two laws are quite acceptable to formal-logical methods, which raises the question of why bother with dialectics at all?

Standard Marxist approaches (that is, those which share the aforementioned set of five postulates) have exhibited a tendency to cast theory and method in overly prescriptive and programmatic terms (as opposed to postdictive and explanatory). As a result, dialectical logic becomes trivialized, misrecognized and conflated with something other than itself. In particular, standard Marxism has not succeeded in differentiating sufficiently (if at all!) dialectics from formal logic, and has therefore failed to grasp the *differentia specifica* of dialectical logic.

Posing the question of its specificity is only possible on condition that the axiomatization of dialectics and its notion as general method is abandoned. The reach of any method (and in particular, dialectics) is not without limits. Forcing it to transgress those limits, attributing to it qualities it does not possess, or even worse, using it to derive conclusions it is unable to generate and support, can only damage its credibility and undermine its usefulness.[11]

Dialectics can, and must, be distinguished consistently and sufficiently from formal logic and, in fact, constitutes a qualitatively radically distinct method of knowledge, one whose field of applicability is a very restricted, optimal, one. This limitation, far from constituting a liability, is precisely where it derives its strength from. The conception of dialectics I shall expound below offers a clear and consistent resolution to the problems of theoretical determinacy and differentiation from formal logic.

Strategic orientations and resources

In theoretical matters (and not only there) it is fair to give one his/her due. Dialectics represents the crowning achievement of the work of Hegel, not Marx. Dialectics is Hegelian dialectics. Therefore it is primarily to Hegel that we must go for consultation (although by no means only to Hegel), because there we can find the requisite and explicit resources for comprehending dialectics.[12]

I referred previously to two Marxist approaches which do not subscribe to the notion of dialectics as general method. The approaches in question are the Uno–Sekine approach and Chris Arthur's approach. The Uno–Sekine approach,[13] first developed by Kozo Uno in Japan in the 1950s and further elaborated by Tomohiko (Thomas) Sekine in the 1980s, precedes the work of Chris Arthur. Their similarity lies in the fact that they both draw systematically upon Hegelian philosophical resources in their theorization of capitalism, and both claim that dialectics is only appropriate for the study of capitalism, and nothing else, and in only one context: the context of an elaborately constructed high level of abstraction. They differ primarily on how to theorize capitalism at that most abstract level, and on conceptualizing other levels of abstraction for the study of capitalism – a direction in which the Uno–Sekine approach has, so far, made more progress.[14]

The easiest way to introduce the Uno–Sekine approach is perhaps to view it as part of the history of Marxist thought, and relate it to some of the history's key moments. Very early on, Engels[15] reasoned that Hegel's dialectical method was bound up with his philosophical system, and that the said system incorporated unacceptable, theoretically (and politically) compromising idealist positions. He thought, however, that the dialectic could be rescued by transposing it into a different system – a materialist one – without having to undergo any change in its structural properties. Much later, and while sharing Engels' apprehensions of Hegelian philosophy, Althusser[16] showed deeper insight when he argued that this method cannot be separated from its system, that the system in question was implicated in the very properties of its method, and that none of these qualities could survive intact its transposition into another system. The only solution that he could suggest was to change both system and method. In doing so, he reproduced the problems of standard Marxism with respect to dialectics, as discussed above, in another form.

If taking the method out of the system, and if changing method and system together, both end up undermining the rigour of the method, these are not the only options. The Uno–Sekine approach has better served the cause of dialectics by taking in both the method and the system (with some modifications into which I will not enter here). Its innovation, and at the same time its improvement upon Hegel and Marx, was to assign to the transposed method and system their own distinct level of abstraction, instead of placing them at the same level with social and historical analysis.

The conception of dialectics I will present is consistent with, and inspired by, the Uno–Sekine approach. Sekine's pioneering work on Marxist political economy has refined dialectics in theoretical practice, but the Uno–Sekine approach as a whole has not yet raised dialectics to theoretical consciousness, and has not studied it as an object in its own right. It has nonetheless given me invaluable assistance in trying to do just that.

This chapter, in essence, reconstructs Hegel's dialectical logic in a new way. I say 'reconstructs', because Hegel's exposition and treatment of his own achievement are not consistently rigorous, comprehensive, clear and uncontradictory (in the formal-logical sense); hence, these cannot always be taken as they stand. I have not found it possible (or desirable) to remain faithful to Hegel's word at all times. My adherence to, or departure from, Hegel have been guided by my understanding of the fundamental and distinctive principles of dialectics that he elaborated, in so far as these are rationally defensible. Hegel, at times, made exorbitant demands on the dialectic and attempted to justify various sorts of conclusions in its name.

His undertaking was of such immense proportions, however, that even if he had been perfectly clear and faithful to his basic principles, he still would not have succeeded entirely, because he lacked the subject matter that would enable him to do so. Therefore, my 'reconstruction' involves, in part, realignment, supplementation and correction.

If standard Marxist approaches to dialectics have failed to grasp its specificity, an alternative approach must ask alternative sorts of questions and pursue them methodically. I submit that the following partial set of questions takes us straight to the heart of dialectical reason: What sort of purpose is dialectics intended to accomplish? What is the scope of dialectical logic? What kind of strategy does dialectics, as method of knowledge, exemplify? Which subject(s) can be known dialectically? Why does dialectical reasoning take the form of contradictions? Under what conditions are contradictions dialectical ones? What is the relationship between dialectical logic and formal logic? How many poles are involved in a dialectical contradiction, and why? What is the nature and function of the positive pole? What is the nature and function of the negative pole? What is the specificity of dialectical polarity? What is the general mechanism of dialectical synthesis? What are the limitations of dialectical logic?

The conception of dialectics I shall present introduces, re-uses and integrates the following basic categories as fundamental tasks, qualities and conditions of dialectics: *special-purpose method; anti-skepticism; inferential necessity/proof; Absolute; expressive totality; thought-experiment and controls; level of abstraction; seriality; bipolarity; asymmetry*; and, of course, *negation of the negation*.

And last, but not least, my presentation of dialectical logic is not itself dialectical. In what follows, I hope to make it clear why it couldn't be.

A resolution

General remarks

Dialectical logic is a structurally distinctive methodological resource, a specific form of systematic, demonstrative, indeed apodictic, reason. In the broad sense, reason can be defined initially as a principled and ordered process of thought in which irregularities (primarily understood as fallacious inferences and other violations of the rules of formal logic) are eliminated progressively and consistently. The most common forms of reason are the various types of formal logic.

Dialectical logic is different from formal or axiomatic forms of logic. Formal logic encompasses not one, but several methods (various kinds of induction, deduction, retroduction and so on), which may or may not be axiomatic. On the other hand, dialectical logic is a single-member family. The categories 'dialectical logic', 'dialectical method' and 'dialectics' are, therefore, used here interchangeably.

The specificity of dialectics rests upon the following: (a) its purpose; (b) the specificity of its object; (c) its relationship to its object; and, (d) its properties as a mode of derivation of categories and construction of theoretical propositions (properties developed, in part, in an attempt to overcome the restrictions of formal logical methods). Methods are geared, more or less, towards particular sorts of problems and questions. Dialectics is no exception. As part of a larger philosophical project, it constitutes a reasoned response to a definite set of problems within that project.

Purpose: anti-skepticism

Hegel's logical system of categories, particularly as expounded in the *Encyclopaedia Logic*, can be construed as a philosophical research programme.[17] As such, it delimits a conceptual horizon within which it sets problems for itself, designs and utilizes particular means and instruments in order to resolve them, and constructs and defends specific knowledge claims.

Philosophy, and in particular, logic, represents for Hegel the highest form of thinking, thinking which aims to arrive at knowledge in the fullest possible sense. His oft-repeated demand that philosophy be done as science[18] illustrates the importance he attached to demonstrating systematically the necessity of the totality of its propositions. The process of derivation of philosophical categories was to be, at the same time, the standard of proof they had to meet.[19] Logic is, for Hegel, philosophical science *par excellence*.

The conception of philosophy essentially as logic has unmistakable epistemological dimensions.[20] This is crucial. It points directly to what constitutes the central problem of Hegel's philosophical encyclopaedia:[21] epistemological skepticism (as distinct from normative skepticism and general epistemological relativism). By presenting a potentially insurmountable challenge to the truth-status of knowledge claims, skepticism effects a fundamental breach between thought and being. The task of philosophy is to overcome it. This is why philosophy aims at the 'scientific cognition of truth'.[22] The Hegelian conception of truth is cast in very distinctive ontologically rationalist and epistemologically objectivist terms. It is defined as the correspondence of objectivity with the (its) Concept.[23]

The Hegelian philosophical research programme is geared towards constructing the means to defeat, and not merely defend against, epistemological skepticism. It is imbued with an anti-skepticist directive from beginning to end.[24] All the resources at its command are without exception put in the service of this goal. Dialectical logic must be seen as Hegel's original response to the problem of skepticism. It is designed strategically as a special-purpose method in this sense, the modus operandi of a large-scale theoretical enterprise.[25]

Hegel had, primarily, ancient Greek skepticism in mind, which he considered to be superior to – and more formidable than – modern skepticism, such as Hume's.[26] Two modes of ancient skepticism received most of his attention: equipollence and infinite regress.

Equipollence (from the Greek *isosthenia* = equal force on both sides) refers to a general procedure of counter-posing an equally strong antithetical proposition to every claim made, but without holding on to it.[27] Equipollence entails equal justification for opposing sides of an issue. This has serious formal logical ramifications. Equipollence represents, in fact, the strongest possible form that can be taken by contradictions in the formal logical sense.[28] Formal logical contradictions are a major concern of Hegelian philosophy in so far as they provide breeding grounds for epistemological skepticism.

As a mode of skepticism, infinite regression arises when grounds are offered to justify a proposition. The justification of those grounds is, in turn, made possible by appeal to further grounds, and so on, *ad infinitum*.[29] The result of this open-endedness is that no justification may ultimately be established. The cognitive status of any possible knowledge-claim appears to be vulnerable to skepticism.

Hegel was also concerned with a mode of skepticism that the ancients did not deal with: namely, the other side of the process of infinite regression – that is, infinite progression.[30] It constitutes a mode of epistemological skepticism in so far as knowledge cannot be conclusively finalized, either because its object is subject to change or because it is unable to exhaust it. Knowledge that is subjected interminably to supplementation or change is, for Hegel, irredeemably uncertain and helpless.

Hegel had the highest respect for ancient skepticism. He called it 'invincible'. It should be clear that, if there is anything that could be done about the threat of skepticism, it would not be accomplished in a single stroke. The dialectic comes on the scene at this point. It exemplifies a particular arduous process of struggle against skepticism. In that struggle, skepticism must be engaged with repeatedly and overcome progressively until it can no longer arise. Hegel's philosophical project in the realm of logic is to identify, construct and sustain safeguards against both the twofold open-endedness of the process of knowledge (infinite regression and progression) and the threat of the various kinds of equipollence that might emerge in the meantime.

The Hegelian solution is to trap skepticism in a motion in which it has already been engaged and overcome. If circles did not exist, the dialectic would have to invent them. Things for skepticism are not nearly half as complicated. Withstanding the force of the dialectic successfully in a single engagement would suffice seriously to undermine, if not to cripple, the integrity of the whole project.[31]

Ontological preconditions

Of course, it is one thing to devise anti-skepticist strategies and quite another to implement them. If dialectics designates the operative mechanism of a process of thought or knowledge, the question is, what kind of object lends itself to such treatment? What sorts of qualities must it possess in order to be knowable dialectically? And where is such an object to be found?

Hegel distinguishes between two fundamental modalities of existence: the finite and the infinite. They are distinct, but united. The former has definite boundaries in time and space (regardless of whether they are changing or not), beyond which it does not extend. A finite existence only subsists in relationship to other finite existences and is conditioned by its relationships with them. It is this reciprocal conditioning and inter-dependence, this lack of self-sufficiency that accompanies every finite being, that renders its knowledge subject to unending deferrals to the conditioning outside and, hence to skepticism. Only an entity with no temporal or spatial limitations would not be conditioned by another. It would, in fact, have no other to itself and be entirely self-subsisting. There is, for Hegel, one such perfectly self-constituting and self-infinitizing subject to be found in God or the Absolute.

The self-infinitizing and self-determining qualities of this subject supply the dialectic with the requisite resources for its battle with skepticism. In approaching the Absolute, the dialectic must reproduce its qualities in thought. But if the subject *is* the Absolute, there is no vantage point extrinsic to it. Dialectics cannot in some way be applied to it from the outside, because the Absolute has no exterior. The Absolute can be known dialectic-ally only in so far as dialectics represents its own immanent method of self-development. The dialectic is the inner logic of the Absolute, or to put it in another way, the Absolute is the ontological *sine qua non* of differentiating dialectics from all types of formal logic. Remove this precondition and dialectics is engulfed by axiomaticity.

One important ramification of this is that dialectics is tethered indissolubly to a particular ontological formation (a self-determining infinity) and a partic-ular epistemological formation (rationalism in the form of absolute idealism). The connection is binding both ways: dialectics cannot be sustained apart from these philosophical bonds, nor can the particular ontological assump-tions and epistemological principles in question be enforced methodologically by any means other than dialectics. Formal logic, in contrast, lacks content and is inherently indifferent to specific objects, ontologies and epistemologies; hence it is compatible with a large variety of them.

Experimentation

Unless we hold with Hegel that the Absolute as such exists and is fully active in the world, or that the process specifying the Absolute as the concrete-in-thought is, at the same time, the process of its real becoming (for which Marx criticized him), we need to situate the dialectic of the Absolute at a locus where dialectical construction can capture the processes of self-infinitization characteristic of the Absolute without committing to any of the aforementioned compromising assumptions. This locus is provided by a distinct, irreducible and relatively autonomous level of abstraction; a level of high – yet determinate – abstraction. Setting it up requires special methodological resources. Dialectical logic signifies a particular process of concretization in thought that can only occur within appropriate parameters of abstraction and control. The concept of the level of high abstraction, as the locus of the dialectical method, denotes the contours of a thought experiment. The creation of such an experiment lays the ground upon which dialectics can both do justice to its subject and engage with skepticism.

The notion of 'thought experiment' is offered in place of the more commonly used 'model'. Typically, thought experiments are limited experiments. They are, however, similar to experiments and they are routinely used even in the so-called natural scientific disciplines. They vary in quality and significance as much as 'real' experiments do. The main difference between them is that thought experiments involve only conceptual elements and relationships. Just because thought experiments are conducted in thought does not mean that they inevitably pertain to matters of thought alone. A cognitively significant and valid thought experiment can teach us something about the world by exploring a hypothetical situation constructed to access or flush out certain properties or functions of our object of study, even fundamental and deeply-rooted ones.[32]

The Uno–Sekine approach is unique in designing and conducting a full-scale thought experiment to study the dialectic or inner logic of capital – a theory of a purely capitalist society (or capitalist mode of production, to use a more familiar description). It does so by rigorously and progressively synthesizing the dialectical contradiction between value and use-value, which begins with the (capitalistically produced and circulated) commodity and ends (coming full circle to the beginning) with the conversion of capital itself into a commodity (the idea of interest-bearing capital). This thought experiment in the field of Marxist political economy is not the result of some theorist's idiosyncrasy, but is part of a measured investigation warranted by capital's own self-abstracting and self-reifying tendencies in history.

Capital is not an Absolute Subject, but is uniquely and sufficiently Absolute-like to be treated (in part, that is, only at a certain level of high abstraction) in similar fashion. The self-reifying and self-infinitizing qualities of the process of capital accumulation exist only as tendencies of varying intensity and effect in historically concrete capitalist societies. In some fundamental ways, however, they render capital as an Absolute-like process, one that necessarily is incomplete and merely Absolute-like, not in fact Absolute. This attribute sharply differentiates capitalist accumulation – itself a historical process – from any and all other historical processes.[33] It is for this reason that capital lends itself to special methodological treatment. Its self-reifying tendencies have a logic of their own. This makes it possible to design a thought experiment in which they are allowed to consummate themselves and develop to completion, something that is impossible in history. The result is a purely capitalist society constructed on the basis of its own immanent – and dialectical – principles. Capital is treated as Absolute in the context of experimental analysis alone.[34]

To reiterate, experimentation in this instance involves extrapolating the distinguishing tendencies of capital to completion in thought.[35] This cannot be achieved without the establishment of suitable controls. If the motion of value is to appear as what it inherently is, the constraints that use-values place upon it must be regulated. The Uno–Sekine approach uses total reification as a mode of experimentally controlling use-values (including labour-power and land) in order to probe into the deep structure of capitalist accumulation. In the experimental conditions of pure theory, use-values are treated as passive obstacles, in Sekine's apt description. They are not without efficacy, but their efficacy and functions are restricted.

Dialectics emerges as a special form of experimental reason, a *sui generis* method of logically constituting and ordering a self-contained, expressive totality (where each part is *pars totalis*, the whole is reflected in each of its parts, and no part exists outside the whole) or infinity (in the context of a distinct high level of abstraction). The very notion of a level of analysis or abstraction implies methodological limits, in so far as it entails a set of distinctions and relations between at least two levels of abstraction. Where the dialectic is concerned, an appropriate level of high abstraction is constructed to adopt the point of view of the Absolute. The dialectic sees only what the Absolute sees. And the Absolute sees only itself; there is no real Other in its field of vision. There is no room for any other infinite to stand beside the Infinite.

Does any of the above mean that dialectics can dispense with formal logic? Hardly! Formal logic has an indispensable role to play in the practice and intelligibility of dialectics. It oversees the setting up of the thought experiment and takes part in it by providing auxiliary support (illustrations, contrasts, communications) to the process of dialectical argumentation. To approach it from another angle: every claim I have made so far – and will make – about dialectics, is an example of formal logical reasoning. The dialectical and the non-dialectical neither contradict one another, nor is it feasible to synthesize them in some 'higher' unity. More on this later in the chapter.

Formal logic points towards the outside of the dialectical universe (the thought experiment) and poses the question of the inside/outside relationship. The problem of the relationship between formal and dialectical logic revolves around defining the terms of their differences and the conditions of their co-operation.

Necessity

Logical inferences – movements from relative premises to relative conclusions – are fundamental constituents of theoretical conceptions, arguments and systems. As Hegel well understood, turning the tables on epistemological skepticism calls for the making of inferences which are logically necessary and whose necessity can be sustained consistently. There are various kinds and degrees of necessity. It is important to be clear about the kind of necessity involved in dialectical logic.

There can be at least two types of argument of necessity pertaining to impossibility. They are of lesser cognitive significance, as they involve partial and indirect generalities, rather than explanations. One, curiously, claims the necessity of contingency (that is, necessity by default) as it points to the impossibility of necessity because of the unavoidability of contingency. Our knowledge is hardly advanced by pointing out that itself as well as its object are necessarily contingent, merely because they cannot be made necessary! If that were true across the board, and if its implications were to be strictly taken, all notions of cognitive error would be rendered meaningless. The second type refers to necessity understood as the impossibility of undoing an already established reality or fact. This again, even when true, hardly helps. What we would want to know primarily is how the reality or fact in question came to be in the first place.

The kind of necessity with which Hegel is concerned, and whose protocols the dialectic observes, has to do with the process of the formation of an object – the process by means of which, out of a given field of possibilities at a given moment, a possibility emerges as the only necessary one and becomes actualized. As a mode of logical inference, dialectics represents a particular deductive-retrogressive method. Dialectically constructed thought-determinations involve a twofold establishment of grounds or justifications. They are deduced from definite conditions. They are grounded by them and, at the same time, retrogress even into prior ones in order to ground them. The theoretical task of dialectics in its struggle with skepticism is to establish the necessity of the totality of its deductions and retrogressions.

Contradiction

Dialectical thought moves from the abstract to the concrete-in-thought. When left to itself, as it so often is, this proposition is another classic example of the kind of theoretical indeterminacy found in Marxist approaches to dialectics. It is neither particularly helpful, nor does it suffice to differentiate dialectics from formal logic. The question is, from which abstract to which concrete, in what sequence, within what kind of system, and by what means? The answer is far from self-evident. Because, at any given point, in relation to a more abstract determination, there exist multiple more concrete ones and more than one way to reach them.

The novelty of dialectical reasoning is that it accomplishes this movement from the abstract to the concrete through a series of contradictions. The centrality of contradiction for dialectical reason has been well emphasized by Marxism, but the specificity of dialectical contradictions has not been as well understood. Dialectics works by means of contradictions, whereas formal logic works away from them. The key to understanding dialectics involves identifying the ways in which the respective contradictions differ from, and relate to, each other. Greater clarity about the specificity of dialectical polarity and the way in which necessity is established by a process of unfolding contradictions in dialectical reason will help prevent conflations between dialectics and formal logic.

The first thing that ought to be noted about dialectical contradictions is that they only stand in the midst of their own company. A dialectical contradiction cannot appear in the flow of formal logical reasoning (which strives to be contradiction-free). It only arises following a prior dialectical contradiction. A dialectical contradiction represents the condition of existence of the immediately subsequent one, and a synthesized development of the immediately preceding one. Dialectical contradictions can only exist as moments in a series of themselves.

Contradiction denotes a relation of negativity. More specifically, a dialectical contradiction denotes a relation of polar opposition. As an initial approximation we may say that a dialectical contradiction has to do with a very specific relationship of mutual dependency and mutual negation or exclusion between being (self) and non-being (other). The relationship is a dynamic one in the sense that it generates changes in both poles and propels them to move to a new phase of opposition. In that phase, the contradiction between (changed) self and (changed) other is renewed; the poles go through changes again and move into yet another phase, and so on. There is nothing new here – this much can be gathered from any Marxist text.

The second most striking feature of dialectical contradictions is their bipolarity. This rather readily discernible feature of dialectics has been staring at Marxism for a long time, but – for the most part – Marxism has in some way managed to miss it. The implications are unforgiving. There can be tripolar or multipolar formal logical contradictions. For example, X is A, B and C at the same time and in the same respect, where A, B and C are fundamentally different from each other. Dialectical contradictions, on the other hand, can only be bipolar. We will see why. Their bipolarity is not provisional; that is, it is not a strategy of studying a simpler state of affairs involving only two poles before we can proceed to a more complex one. Bipolarity belongs to the essence of dialectics, and as such is a crucial index of difference between dialectical and formal logic.

The basic structure of a dialectical contradiction can be represented schematically in terms of a relation between *A* (being) and *non-A* (non-being or naught), between what stands in the position of the positive pole and what stands in the position of the negative pole. *A* and *non-A* are true simultaneously. How can this be?

A and *non-A* do not make up some unity-in-difference between two different entities. *Non-A* is not something other than *A*. It is not a different entity which, relative to *A*, is simply other, that is, a non-*A*. *Non-A* is not some B, C or X. *Non-A* too is *A*, but in a different (alienated) modality of existence. At every given moment of the dialectical process (and only to the extent that the dialectical character of the process is maintained) *non-A* is turned into an exemplification of *A*, which it resists. *A* is all there is. Dialectical contradictions involve one entity and one entity alone, not two or three. The being of *A* entails the sublation of *non-A*.

It is time to look at the poles of the contradiction more closely. Being (or, the self in the logical sense) stands at the positive pole as that which is to be known. Not just anything, however, can take the place of Being in the dialectical positive pole. It must be a Being which is capable of living up to its Concept; that is, its idealized state in which all its qualities have self-developed to an unlimited – infinitized – state.[36] Being is not undifferentiated and static, but develops. Development carries within it the distinction between potentiality or implicit capacity, and actuality or explicit process. By occupying the positive pole, being lays claim to selfhood.

The negative (non-Being) is not merely an absence, but the primary limiting factor that conditions Being. It is not an unregulated conditioning, however. Non-Being denies or negates Being's claim to selfhood by confronting it with the spectrum of that which it is not – yet. Non-Being reflects the inadequacy of Being as it stands at any given moment *vis-à-vis* its own self (that is, Being's). The function of non-Being, at every given moment, is to mark the distance that Being has yet to cover in order to become fully itself. Non-Being presents an obstacle for Being, one that threatens to confine Being to its present incomplete and partially realized state. At the same time as it presents an obstacle in the path of Being, it outlines concretely the field of potentialities open to it at any given moment.

The contradiction between Being and non-Being is not a formal-logical one, because its terms or poles are, in a fundamental sense, neither alien to each other nor contemporaneous. *Non-A* (non-Being) is non-contemporaneous *A* (Being). It reflects an aspect of *A* that has not been reached immanently (or subsumed) yet by *A*, but must be if *A* is to fulfil its claim to selfhood. In essence, non-Being is an elaborate foil. It exists not for itself, but for Being. Its role is to deny the self-sufficiency of Being, and thus give Being the opportunity to overcome its relative self-insufficiency by endowing itself progressively and immanently with more determinate content, if it is so able.

Being has to struggle to assert its status in the face of the obstacle, or it will perish. Being negates non-Being in so far as it proves capable of reaching deeper within itself and generating determinations that can overcome non-Being without external assistance. The very sustainability of the dialectic hangs in the balance in the unfolding of the contradiction between Being and non-Being. Being must come up with a determination that is just sufficient to overcome the obstacle of non-Being. No more and no less. This is the most basic form of experimental control inherent in dialectical reason. If it generates a determination that is more than merely sufficient, the determination would be without adequate supporting grounds and become vulnerable to the forces of lurking equipollence. Inferential necessity would be forfeited and the dialectic would become unsustainable. If, on the other hand, Being generates a determination that is deficient in terms of overcoming the obstacle it faces, Being would be confined to an incomplete state and lapse into finitude; that is, loss of self. In such a case, the contradiction between Being and non-Being would be transformed into a formal logical one.

There is no parity in the status and function of the two poles making up a dialectical contradiction. Dialectical contradictions are fundamentally asymmetrical, necessarily bipolar and involve just one entity – Being.[37] If the contradiction was, say, tripolar, Being would be faced with two conflicting fields of potentialities at the same time, indeterminacy would ensue and it would be impossible to prevent equipollence. A dialectical contradiction, then, features not two Beings, but two modes of Being in a particular sort of immanent opposition to each other: the infinite or universal mode and the finite mode.[38] Dialectically constructed knowledge is not an open-ended process. The need for closure is absolute. The dialectic must complete the process of becoming. If it is successful, it culminates in becoming that has become – the negation of the negation.

Conclusions

This chapter has touched upon most of the fundamental aspects and qualities of dialectical logic. Dialectics differs from formal logic. However, it stands in no formal contradiction to it (because dialectical contradictions violate no formal-logical principles),[39] nor can their differences be synthesized dialectically and sublated by some other higher form of logic. They perform distinct functions. Dialectical logic is only possible with respect to an Absolute or Absolute-like subject matter, and needs to be supplemented by formal logic for the sake of its own intelligibility and the resolution of knowledge problems that are associated with its subject matter, but fall outside its purview.

The specificity of dialectical reason resides in the necessity of the order and mode of unfolding of (non formal-logical) self-contradictions. That necessity obtains to the extent to which formal logical contradictions can be provoked and disarmed before they can be established firmly. For, once formal logical contradictions are established they cannot be undone by dialectical means, but only by formal-logical ones. Dialectics can be viewed as an essentially non-formal-logical means of thwarting imminent formal-logical contradictions from arising. In so far as it performs its task successfully, the necessity of its claims in the process of argumentation/ theorization is established with relative – yet remarkable – immunity from epistemological skepticism.

Notes and References

1. Hegel, G. W. F., *The Encyclopaedia Logic*, trans. T. F. Geraets, W. A. Suchting and H. S. Harris (Indianapolis: Hackett, 1991) p. 80, add.
2. This chapter is a considerably revised version of a paper presented at the 'Dialectics and Political Economy' workshop, held at York University, Toronto in March 2001. Given the inflexible limitations of space and the scope of the topic, the presentation is substantially more condensed than I would prefer. Some important aspects had to be left out altogether, the most important of which is the spiral–circular sequence of dialectical determinations. I reserve a more extended and in-depth treatment of the specificity of dialectics for a later occasion.
3. The complexities arising from the fact that validity is a highly contentious issue, and that there may be several kinds of validity that are relevant with respect to a given theoretical conception, do not alter what here is fundamental: an invalid conception, argument or theory constitutes a shortcoming, an epistemological obstacle in the strict sense.
4. In making these claims about Marxist approaches to dialectics, I resort to a rather sweeping generalization myself. If such a generalization seems exaggerated, it is only with regard to a handful of exceptions, not the overall picture.
5. An index of the ubiquity of these two postulates is that they feature prominently in approaches that lie on opposite sides of the divide between modernism and postmodernism: Ollman, B., *Dialectical Investigations* (New York: Routledge, 1993), pp. 28, 36; and Resnick, S. and Wolff, R., *Knowledge and Class* (Chicago: University of Chicago Press, 1987), pp. 2–5.
6. Analytical Marxism features both (iv) and (v), but substitutes its own method in place of dialectics.
7. That in itself does not necessarily constitute a problem. But Ollman (*Dialectical Investigations*, pp. 10, 65) goes much further when he asserts confidently that dialectics as such explains nothing and proves nothing! It is hard to imagine a greater abdication of basic methodological duties.
8. Ollman, *Dialectical Investigations*, p. 64, again, is a good example of this.
9. Hegel is allegedly the first perpetrator of this indiscretion. He criticizes dualism, however, not in general but in relation to understanding the distinction between the infinite and the finite, and ultimately, the infinite itself. See *Encyclopaedia Logic*, pp. 81 additions and 95.
10. Marxists are concerned with grounding all knowledge, even its more abstract forms, in history, and drawing out its socio-political implications. Simpler tasks, however, should be mastered first. Leaving aside the enormous epistemological

202 The Specificity of Dialectical Reason

intricacies of such a project (intricacies which are rarely appreciated or confronted), we could start by examining conventional wisdom a little more closely.

11. Marx, to take a well-known example, did not help the credibility of dialectics when he considered his famous argument that the processes of the centralization of capital and the socialization of labour lead inexorably to the abolition of capitalism and the expropriation of the few by the mass of the people, to be dialectically warranted. See Marx, K., *Capital*, vol. I, trans. B. Fowkes (Harmondsworth: Penguin, 1976), pp. 929–30.

12. This is not to say that Hegel's conceptualization of dialectics is unproblematic in each and every respect, or that Marx and some other Marxists have not made important contributions, refinements and improvements (explicitly or potentially) on one aspect of dialectical logic or another. Marx had at least one important advantage over Hegel. He was assisted by a more determinate and more suitable subject matter – capital. Ironically, Hegel complained that the chief limitation of formal logic was its formality, and thought he had offered a method which over-came this defect by supplying its formal features with an appropriately determinate content. Most problems, however, with Hegel's own conception of dialectics stem from exactly the same limitation that he attributed to formal logic: its content by and large failed to remain sufficiently substantive and determinate, or else was too unsuitably determinate (nature and history). These difficulties make Hegel's insights into the nature of dialectical thinking, such as they were, all the more admirable.

13. On the specificity of the Uno–Sekine approach to Marxism, see: Sekine, T., in K. Uno, *Principles of Political Economy*, trans. T. Sekine (Brighton: Harvester Press, 1980), pp. 131–66; Sekine, T., *The Dialectic of Capital*, vol. I (Tokyo: Toshindo, 1986), pp. 2–100; Sekine, T., *An Outline of the Dialectic of Capital*, vol. I (London: Macmillan, 1997), pp. 1–22; Albritton, R., *A Japanese Reconstruction of Marxist Theory* (London: Macmillan, 1986), pp. 9–35 and 177–96; Albritton, R., *A Japanese Approach to Stages of Capitalist Development* (London: Macmillan, 1991), pp. 1–65; Albritton, R., *Dialectics and Deconstruction in Political Economy* (New York: St Martin's Press, 1999), pp. 2–9; and Bell, J., 'Dialectics and Economic Theory', in R. Albritton and T. Sekine (eds), *A Japanese Approach to Political Economy* (New York: St Martin's Press, 1995), pp. 108–16.

14. See Albritton, R., *A Japanese Approach to Stages*; and Albritton, R., 'Did Agrarian Capitalism Exist?', *The Journal of Peasant Studies*, vol. 20, no. 3 (1993).

15. Engels, F., *Ludwig Feuerbach and the End of Classical German Philosophy* (Peking: Foreign Languages Press, 1976), pp. 9–12.

16. Althusser, L., *For Marx*, trans. B. Brewster (London: Verso, 1979), pp. 91–3.

17. No commitment to Lakatosian positions is here implied.

18. Hegel, *Encyclopaedia Logic*, pp. 4, 17.

19. Hegel, *Encyclopaedia Logic*, pp. 1, 7. If only more Marxists had taken notice! How many Marxist works even bother to establish any necessity (of whatever kind and extent) in their arguments, let alone attempt to prove them?

20. It is remarkable how many commentators have missed or neglected the centrality of epistemology in Hegel's philosophy. Hegel's deed and word leave very little room for debate on this issue: 'As if philosophy ... were anything else but the quest for truth' (*Encyclopaedia Logic*, p. 6); and 'Philosophy aims at ... what is unchange-able, eternal, in and for itself: its end is Truth ... Truth is eternal; it does not fall within the sphere of the transient and has no history', *Lectures on the History of Philosophy*, vol. 1 (Lincoln, Nebr.: University of Nebraska Press, 1995), pp. 7–8.

21. Hegel, *Encyclopaedia Logic*, p. 22, additions.

22. Hegel, *Encyclopaedia Logic*, p. 4.

23. Hegel, *Encyclopaedia Logic*, p. 213. There is no space here to address the radical novelty of Hegelian epistemology, which sticks with the correspondence theory of truth and seeks to solidify it, by taking it beyond its empiricist and typical rationalist confines.

24. I shall offer two brief and indirect arguments in support of this contention. Hegel criticized the three so-called attitudes of thought to objectivity (that is, influential approaches of his time) on the grounds of their vulnerability to skepticism (*Encyclopaedia Logic*, pp. 26–78). It follows that in his own approach he would be interested in taking all the necessary precautions to avoid similar shortcomings. Also, he thought that the subject matter of philosophy, as well as theology, was God (*Encyclopaedia Logic*, pp. 1, 12, 19, add.). For him, the full knowledge of God was identical to the self-knowledge of God. Alas, if God's self-knowledge could be liable to epistemological skepticism!

25. Space considerations, again, prevent me from addressing Hegel's crucial notion of dialectics in the narrower and more specialized sense as the second of the three moments of logical reasoning (the other two being the moment of the understanding and the speculative moment). See Hegel, *Encyclopaedia Logic*, p. 81. My discussion only reflects Hegel's broader and more general notion of dialectics as the whole of the process of logical reasoning.

26. Hegel, *Encyclopaedia Logic*, p. 81, add.; *Lectures on the History of Philosophy*, vol. 2, (Lincoln, Nebr.: University of Nebraska Press, 1995), p. 331. As a school of thought, ancient Greek skepticism was founded in opposition to Plato's Academy by Pyrrho of Elis in the fourth century BC. The most important surviving works of ancient skepticism are the writings of Sextus Empiricus, a Greek doctor who lived in the second century AD. Ancient skepticism (from the Greek *skepsis* = thought, inquiry) advocated not doubt or disbelief, but suspension of judgment and continued inquiry. The skeptics were those who continued to seek. They 'called themselves the seekers ... and their philosophy the seeking [*zititiki*] (Sextus quoted by Hegel, *Lectures on the History of Philosophy*, vol. 2, p. 339). The distinctiveness of this attitude is that it advocated seeking not in order to arrive at some knowledge, position or belief of one sort or another (that would amount to dogmatism), but for its own sake. Interminable seeking was thought to help the tranquillity (or better 'untroubledness' from the Greek *ataraxia*) of the soul (Sextus Empiricus, *Outlines of Scepticism* (Cambridge University Press, 2000), p. 5.

27. Sextus Empiricus, *Outlines of Scepticism*, pp. 4–6.

28. Hegel, *Encyclopaedia Logic*, p. 48.

29. Sextus Empiricus, *Outlines of Scepticism*, p. 41.

30. Hegel, *Encyclopaedia Logic*, pp. 60, 94.

31. For the sake of simplicity, this introductory essay views the process of Hegel's struggle against skepticism only in his own absolute terms.

32. Sorensen, R., *Thought Experiments* (New York: Oxford University Press, 1992), pp. 3. 133, 186.

33. Albritton, *Dialectics and Deconstruction*, p. 22.

34. Albritton, *Dialectics and Deconstruction*, p. 79. The Uno–Sekine approach has several advantages over Hegel's with respect to dialectics: it avoids what is problematic in Hegel's system, as it relativizes the Absolute or 'lets it be' only within a certain context, and an experimental one at that; it reaps the benefits of dialectical logic that Hegel worked out, as its substantive-theoretical propositions

at the level of pure theory are constructed and integrated with a sort of necessity without par in political economy; and it restores to dialectics its single most important missing piece, something that belonged to it in the first place: its own custom-made level of abstraction; that is, the set of parameters enabling (rather than disabling) its operationalization and delineating a context of cognitive significance appropriate to it.

35. The notion of extrapolating the tendencies of the historical process of capital accumulation in a distinct level of analysis is a uniquely Unoist idea. For more, see any of the works cited in Note 13 above.
36. Hegel, *Encyclopaedia Logic*, p. 24, add. 2.
37. Any homogeneity that might appear in my treatment of dialectics is only a reflection of the logistical context of initial generalities that this short contribution could not escape. There are indeed significant internal differentiations in the structure of dialectical reason corresponding to Hegel's three Doctrines (Being, Essence and Concept). Nevertheless, the general structure of dialectics, as expounded here, is not affected.
38. Hegel, *Encyclopaedia Logic*, p. 95.
39. Smith, T., *The Logic of Marx's Capital* (Albany, NY: State University of New York Press, 1990) pp. 6, 228, also makes this point clearly.

Index